HIDDEN THREADS

A Christian Critique of Sociological Theory

Russell Heddendorf
and
Matthew Vos

D0898396

University Press of America,® Inc.
Lanham · Boulder · New York · Toronto · Plymouth, UK

Copyright © 2010 by
University Press of America,® Inc.
4501 Forbes Boulevard
Suite 200
Lanham, Maryland 20706
UPA Acquisitions Department (301) 459-3366

Estover Road
Plymouth PL6 7PY
United Kingdom

Library of Congress Control Number: 2009934989
ISBN: 978-0-7618-4901-8 (paperback : alk. paper)
eISBN: 978-0-7618-4902-5

Dedication

The principal author of *Hidden Threads*, Russell Heddendorf, died on December 24, 2008, during the period in which this second edition of the book was being developed. My contribution to this volume is the addition of a new chapter on postmodern theory. The chapter, which began as a sabbatical project, was something that Russ and I worked on together–I wrote, and he in his calm, patient, and nurturing way, advised, critiqued, and inspired me. Working on this project with Russ was a gift to me, and it represents the culmination of years of leaning on him for his wisdom, insight, and deep faith. My life is changed because of his friendship and influence. My faith in Christ is deeper because of the time he took with me. Russ was my teacher, friend, mentor, and spiritual advisor. For me he was a giant, and I doubt I'll ever climb off his shoulders. It is to him and to the Association of Christians Teaching Sociology, which he founded, that I dedicate this volume.

Matthew Vos
Summer 2009

Contents

Preface

Popular Christian social thought is, for the most part, shallow. Perhaps a better word would be simplistic. At a time when modern society staggers with the complexity of social life, Christian social thought remains largely naive and uncomprehending of these complexities. Perhaps this is because such thought has become grist for any miller. In short, many Christian commentators on social issues lack the necessary framework for dealing with these questions.

In contrast, early Christian thought was radical in its approach to social life. Its attitude toward women and servants, for example, was even revolutionary. What provoked this view was Jesus' attitudes toward people. He provided a different conception of the person and encouraged followers to act upon that conception. In the face of such perception, a social scientist would have little advantage over a faithful believer.

But the situation is different today. Most Christians accept current interpretations of problems as valid and then respond to them. This is especially true if those interpretations concur with personal biases they might hold. The problem is that contemporary thought is limited in its understanding of God's revelation. As Christians respond to this thought they, too, develop a form of secularized thought and often support the solutions offered by popular notions. This means that, for most Christians, social thinking has become monological; it perceives only the surface issues and fails to enter into dialogue with the real issues of the day. Carried to an extreme, such thought becomes dogmatic in its failure to perceive reality accurately.

This quality of dialoguing with reality should be a primary objective of Christian social thought. If it were, it would share with sociology the objective of pitting its theories against social reality wherever it may be found. Sociology, of course, is limited by its incomplete perception of the reality of God's work in the world. The best it can do is to respond to the cultural definition of reality as understood at the time. At its worst, sociology may also become dogmatic and defensive when it loses touch with reality. But sociology is committed to its task and relentless in its search for social reality. For this reason, it is not surprising that sociology will, on occasion, unearth the same social principles found in Scripture. These discoveries may be serendipitous as well as worthy of our attention and additional study.

Personally, I find a certain excitement in such discoveries. They are like "hidden threads" in the fabric of social thought—Christian principles for social behavior in agreement with social theory. Believing Scripture provides all that we need to know about social, relations, many Christians often separate the Christian principles for behavior from the sociological and lose the inherent richness and truth found in both sets of axioms. Worse, there will often be an attempt to use Christian principles to justify behavior inconsistent with either set of principles.

Let me quickly add that these statements are not meant to be an indictment of Christians alone. Non-believers also have the inclination to separate their views from others' and set those views against them. Social thinkers, especially, are vulnerable at this point as they seek to claim some exclusive truth for themselves. As the history of social thought makes it clear, all conceptions of social reality are fragile and susceptible to the contradictions of social change. It is a reminder that social thought, as all human constructions, is incomplete and in error.

This is a book about social thought and its development. It also provides a Christian critique of that thought as it exposes some of the "hidden threads" found there. It does not attempt to develop a Christian social theory, although some of the building blocks for such a theory will be offered. It always appreciates the richness of social life and the need to hold in tension those theories attempting to explain it.

Foreword

Countless cords weave sociology and Christianity together. Calling attention to them is the innovative contribution of *Hidden Threads*. It clarifies ways in which Christianity enlightens theoretical orientations of social thought and those in which sociology helps to smash idolatrous illusions of "Christian" stereotypes about society that emerge from the ignorance, prejudice, and other errors of closed minds.

Serendipity

Readers, whether they are Christians, social scientists, neither, or both, will discover that this book evokes serendipity, the experience of finding valuable or agreeable things that were not sought or that one was not aware of seeking. Serendipity, closely related to intuitive insight (*Verstehen*) yet seldom addressed in the social sciences, is a central unlabeled theme of *Hidden Threads*. When Heddendorf was his student, Robert Merton's concepts of latent functions and dysfunctions (unintended or unanticipated consequences of social structures and actions) led to explorations of serendipity.

Serendipity was one source of Heddendorf's realization that *hidden threads* unite sociology and Christianity. His Preface intimates that he had "Aha!" experiences, "Oh, of course! Why didn't I notice that connection before?" Most threads, however, were unearthed through his career-long search for thought patterns, concepts, and theories of sociology that are illustrated by biblical accounts or driven home by scriptural principles. Although he insisted that the Bible is not a sociology textbook, his Preface states, "I always get a personal sense of excitement in the realization that these scriptural principles were given by God long before some modern sociologist came across them in research."

Hidden threads of another type brought Russ and me together half a century ago and sustained our friendship until his death. We met through the American Scientific Affiliation, an association of Christians in the biological, physical, social, and other sciences who are committed to understanding and deciphering the complex relationships between science and Christianity. Russ's 1958-1962 column on Sociology and subsequent articles in its *Journal of the ASA* [now entitled *Perspectives on Science and Christian Faith*] were important antecedents of this book.

Russ also was the founder of ACTS (Association of Christians Teaching Sociology). Its annual meetings helped us uncover and analyze *hidden threads.* At the heart of his thought and career was a consistent focus on values and vices in Christianity. His faith in Christ, active church life, and study of the Bible mellowed his insights. Written near the peak of his career, *Hidden Threads* is a product of careful probing, disciplined thought, meditative reflection, interactive teaching, and lifelong learning. It is neither a sermon nor a hasty collection of lecture notes or speeches, but a work of true scholarship that explores his discoveries from an open and balanced perspective.

Openness: The Virtue of Honesty, Truthfulness, and Integrity

Christians, like others, are tempted to "fudge" any evidence that bears on their faith. Whenever there is an admixture of research findings or interpretations, they tend to accentuate the fragments that throw a positive light on the commitments of their own denomination and ministry, or those of Christianity at large, and to deny, omit, play down, or excuse away those that seem negative.

Social scientists tend to do exactly the same in order to sustain a favored theory or other cause.

In contrast, the scientific, ethical, and Christian principle of being open to any and all evidence that is discovered, along with the simultaneous work of verifying it, is obvious in the work of both Heddendorf and Matthew Vos, who updated this book. They tap the teachings and insights of sociology and Christianity with an awareness of the need each has for the other.

At the heart of Christianity is the belief that the Creator of the universe and humanity is revealed today through two main channels: The universe He created and the written Word (Bible) He inspired. The "eyes of science" focus on the former, while the "eyes of faith" call attention to realities like spirituality that extend far beyond the limits of scientific observation. Unfortunately, far too many sociologists and Christians close their minds by rejecting the wisdom of one or the other of those "eyes." Closed minds that deprive sociology of timeless wisdom found in the Bible significantly weaken it, but they also weaken Christianity by causing believers to act on the basis of falsehoods and distortions of reality. *Hidden Threads* shows how the scriptural and sociological revelations are interrelated in so far as it uses both of these "eyes" to overcome the deficiencies of each source of knowledge.

Sociologists are deceived if they cling to the belief that a defective "Christian" interpretation of people, institutions, or society fairly represents all of Christianity. They are similarly deceived when they judge a scientific discipline by only one or a few of its exemplars, or when they use "card stacking" propaganda techniques to reveal only whatever positively supports their interests while they ignore or cover up negative evidence. *Hidden Threads* advocates integrity, openness, and reconciliation on both sides.

Hidden Threads Enrich Both Christianity and Sociology

The virtue of openness is made evident in *Hidden Threads* by the recognition that every classical theory, not only works like Weber's *Protestant Ethic and the Spirit of Capitalism* but even conflict theory and Marxist critiques—has relationships with Christianity. Instead of ignoring the positive influences of Christianity, filtering them away by invoking determinisms and reductionisms or by playing up only its negative features and consequences, many theories offer a relatively balanced picture of both positive and negative contributions Christianity makes to the well-being of persons and the integration of society.

Sociological views of society, however, tend to be like an ever changing "dialectical teeter-totter" that is never perfectly balanced. As noted in Chapter 6, "Christians should avoid the conceptual seesaws of our culture" because the transcendent problems of society demand the transcendent answers found in the Christian scriptures. The "reconceptualization of human and social needs ... brought him [Jesus] into basic conflict with the world ... [That provides] a model for our understanding today, a model which needs sensitive and informed interpretation." It also needs the correction of deficiencies in the area of biblical hermeneutics that often are a source of conflicts between Christians and sociologists.

Jesus' knew that some of his lessons were understood only by his disciples (Matthew 13:10-17; see Isaiah 6:8-10). That may apply also to recognizing or not recognizing the *hidden threads* that weave sociology and Christianity together. These will be exciting serendipitous discoveries for readers who have only superficial knowledge of the Christian faith and an even greater delight if they have been biased by experiences and observations of only deviant sects or other outliers. The Bible has rich expositions of human nature, perceptive descriptions of interior and exterior forces that influence behavior, and insightful analyses of motivations for conduct.

Finding *hidden threads* also will be a delightful experience for Christians who have grown up under the distortions of either ultra-conservative or ultra-liberal versions of the Christian faith. The former tend to see only negative aspects of higher education and the sciences as they hunt through the Bible to find out-of-context verses that shore up their preconceptions. The latter use the Bible only to ferret out details that support their unique agendas. Both need to recognize that its central focus is the Living Word, Jesus Christ (John 1:1-18).

Once serendipitously encountered examples and consequences of behavior, events, and relationships are explained through scientific theory and research, they no longer are serendipitous. Mysteries revealed are no longer mysterious; a serendipitous discovery by one person may be commonplace knowledge to another. However, the Creator still brings about implausible and seemingly impossible events that human beings label as "coincidental," "accidental," "fortuitous," or "happenstance." Countless *hidden threads* in all domains of science and Christianity await future discoveries.

Summary

Hidden Threads is neither an apologetic for Christianity nor an attack upon it. Its main focus is the contributions Christianity and social thought make to each other. Every theoretical orientation needs the corrective influence of biblical insights, but Christian churches and ministries also need the input of sociology. The interrelationships of sociology and Christian faith thus clarify the virtues and shortcomings of both.

This book with its unique focus upon the diverse serendipitous threads that bind Christianity and sociology together is an outstanding contribution to both sociology and Christianity. It will enrich social theory, generate significant research, encourage meditative reflection, enliven the interactions of Christians with sociologists, and stimulate the mind of every reader.

David O. Moberg
Emeritus Professor of Sociology
Marquette University

Acknowledgements

I am grateful to the many people who contributed time, energy, encouragement, and advice, as Russ and I worked on completing this new edition of *Hidden Threads*. Jack Muller and Toni Chiareli, my colleagues at Covenant College, provided valuable support and insight in numerous ways. Mark Ward, my father, provided helpful theological insight into various features of the postmodern world. David Moberg graciously provided editorial support for the new chapter, as well as encouragement in the ongoing task of embracing the call to Christian sociology. Jeff Morton generously donated the artwork for the book's cover. Deborah Peterson reconstructed and reformatted the original text (for which there was no electronic record!). Jeff Hall helped arrange financial assistance for bringing the book to print. Were Russ here, he would also wish to thank David Ward and Richard Humphrey at the Oxford Graduate School in Dayton, Tennessee, for their interest in Hidden Threads, and their enthusiasm for how a *hidden threads* approach can enhance theological education. We also thank our families, who share the hidden threads of our lives.

Chapter 1

Hidden Threads

Buried in my collection of some four hundred sociological comic strips are two that graphically portray the changing public impression of sociology. The first, taken from the early sixties, shows Archie and his father checking out at a supermarket. At the counter, the clerk, a bespectacled, mousy character, greets Mr. Andrews by name. As they leave the store, Mr. Andrews wonders how the clerk knew his name. Archie's response: "He's my sociology teacher."

Some years later in the late sixties, that same strip portrayed a different impression of the sociologist. The principal is proudly showing the school board members around the high school building when they come to a partly open door. Peeking in, they see a beautiful and sexy young woman sitting on the desk, singing and strumming a guitar. When asked by a board member who she might be, the principal sheepishly replies, "That's our new sociology teacher."

These two popular images of the sociologist, one pedantic and stuffy, the other racy and radical, are shared by many Christians. The first image is not taken seriously largely because of the bewildering scientific jargon and statistics with which it is associated. The other is usually unsettling, provoking considerable suspicion in those who believe that sociologists promote rapid and unpredictable social change. In either case, only a partial and distorted image of sociology is presented.

Radical Ideologue or Social Theorist?

Still, evidence for these caricatures may be found in the history of social theory. For some thinkers, sociology was expressed as ideology to be used for espousing social causes or movements. This is the radical form which, though largely dormant today, may still portray the sociologist as a seductive and threatening revolutionary. This is hardly a fair or accurate picture of most contemporary sociologists.

Other sociologists have relied on theory to describe the world as they conceived of it, with charts and statistics. This is the more benign and contemporary form of social thought greeted by most people with some skepticism. This image also provokes considerable respect in a public that looks on any kind of science with awe. The sociologist may even gain the image of social magician, one who locates the answers to all social problems in a book of incantations. This, too, is neither a fair nor an accurate picture of the modern sociologist.

This book is concerned with the development of those forms of modern social thought accompanying these images. It attempts to bring these images of sociology into focus by showing their limitations as well as their strengths. In spite of the helpful insights into society provided by social thought over the years, this knowledge remains inadequate and faulty. In short, we find the problems of two centuries ago buried among those of more recent origin.

By studying the historical and contemporary forms of social thought, we trust the reader will evaluate his or her own views on society and its problems. Our tendency is often to lock into a mode of thinking and then explain all problems with a view that is overly biased by that thinking. Such an approach usually avoids the facts and clings to the convenience of past answers. The study of social thought enables us to look at these issues more objectively and, hopefully, to act more decisively.

Social Structure and Individual Evil

One mode of thinking blames the *social structures* for problems and advocates human freedom. In this tradition, problems result from accumulated past interests and can only be solved with radical social change. While it is true that institutional misconduct is often at the root of social problems, people who accept this pattern of thought as the standard by which they approach all issues will occasionally err in their perception of the facts. What they fail to see are the evil consequences resulting from the actions of many people who believe they are doing the right thing.

The other mode of thinking is more conservative in its defense of traditional institutions. In its conception of reality, evil is located in the *person,* not in the organization. Problems there are solved when laws are enforced and social stability is maintained. People who think this way, however, tend to overlook the covert power always available to those who want to use it, often for what they consider to be "right" causes. Consequently, they are blind to the social evil found in social structures.

Most of us don't think exclusively in these terms; we're not completely liberal or conservative in our views. The world is too complex, too dynamic for a one-sided view of reality. If we're honest with ourselves, we usually vacillate in our opinions of such matters. We may even come to understand that satisfying answers for our problems do not exist, and without such answers there are no bases for evaluating our views. When this happens, our opinions may become largely subjective and scarcely influenced by objective fact.

Christians differ little from others in such matters. Most fall within traditional patterns of thinking and are often caught up in their personal biases.

Faced with a dilemma, Scripture may be used to justify these biases rather than to question them. And yet Scripture, when taken as a whole and honestly evaluated, is even more likely to cut across traditional biases than to support them.

It could be argued, for example, that the Old Testament generally supports society and its divinely-ordained institutions. Laws are to be enforced as mandated by God. But the prophets also attack the evils in social structures and advocate radical social change. In the New Testament, Jesus favors the person but always with a transcendent view of society. Even though earthly institutions may be corrupt, they are not to be attacked but replaced by the kingdom of God.

The study of social thought shows how scriptural principles are frequently in agreement with social principles. This fact is not apparent as long as traditional views are held. But when these views are broken down into their component parts in the study of social thought, scriptural counterparts come into play. In this way, scriptural principles form an objective basis for evaluating social principles and their application to cultural problems.

My major concern in this book is to pick up these "hidden threads" of Scripture as they are found in social thought. I always get a personal sense of excitement in the realization that these scriptural principles were given by God long before some modern sociologist came across them in research. But if this realization heightens our regard for Scripture, it should do no less for social thought. For the Christian, sociology should provoke more respect than rancor, more sentiment than suspicion.

We need to appreciate the contributions of social thought but not stand in awe of them. And if we are to appreciate them, we need to understand them correctly. Hopefully, we will move in this direction while helping the Christian to understand those points of merger and points of tension between Scripture and sociology which, as hidden threads, assist us to shape our own perception of the world about us.

Chapter 2

The Nature of Theory

People have always tried to understand what is *really* going on about them. Even Adam and Eve, living in the simplest and most satisfying world, tried to know more. The fact that they also tried to control that world for their own benefit reflects the flaw of human sinfulness found in social theory as well. But it is this restless desire to know the truth about the world—to discover social reality, so to speak—which provides the initial and most fundamental impetus for social theory.

Tank McNamara is a comic strip football hero turned TV sports commentator. On one assignment, several youngsters approach *him* and ask for his autograph, commenting, "Gee, Tank, you're a lot bigger than you are in real life." Intruding into the scene, the TV camerawoman says, "You know what those kids mean by 'real life', don't you Tank? Television." Tank's comment: "That's scary!"

In the world of Tank McNamara—the world of the mass media—reality is confused. The experience of television is so common to children that the unfamiliar and unexpected (e.g., Tank McNamara in person) assume heroic proportions. They accept the television image as "real life" and return to their sets to experience it. In modern society, this tendency to reverse reality is a common practice. The mass media, advertising, and technology are only a few of the means by which reality is changed to illusion and illusion becomes reality. And as Tank states, "That's scary!"

In fact, there is something devilish in this reversal of the truth. If this seems to be an extreme statement, return to the Eden experience for an understanding of the way Satan reverses the truth. The awe we experience when truth is stretched by magicians or in circus side shows used to be an uncommon experience and was rarely taken seriously. Today, reality distortion is common, and it doesn't awe us simply because we don't understand it as such. For the Christian, the problem of reality distortion challenges one's personal faith daily. We too easily accept the definitions of reality presented to us—for example, by the media—and often put our faith in them.

Objectivity and Subjectivity

To understand reality distortion in social life, we need to turn to social theory and its attempts to separate what we know from what we *think* we know. Theory considers every social phenomenon in two different ways: as it is in reality, and as it presents itself to someone's mind. The first consideration is the objective aspect and the second is the subjective. But in making this division, the social scientist realizes that such separation is not always valid. In one sense, all human knowledge is subjective since some forms of reality always remain outside human experience. This includes the super-empirical world of the objects of our Christian faith. We simply cannot prove by scientific means the existence of heaven or the origin of the earth. In another sense, the distinction should exist as a reminder that although the two forms of reality are different, they need not be kept separate.

Jesus made a similar distinction in his comments about murder in the Sermon on the Mount (Matt. 5:21-22). If a person kills a neighbor, the crime is an objective act for which the person is punished. But Jesus says that being angry at a person, a subjective act, is also murder and deserves the same punishment. In the first case, an attitude leads to the action it intends. In the second case, the same attitude exists, but without the action. Since the attitude is not experienced by another, it remains part of subjective reality.

Paul anticipated some of these problems in his description of sin in Romans 7. That which we would do, he said, we don't do, and that which we would not do, we do. Stated differently, our best intentions will not necessarily result in the expected outcome. The *attitude* is different and separate from the *action*. Further, because of sin, our best scientific efforts in predicting human behavior are frustrated. This inability is due to the subjective aspect of reality which remains unexpressed in some concrete form. In short, a responsible social scientist must acknowledge sin in these terms and be cautious when making predictions about human behavior. For the Christian, a certain satisfaction should be found in these conclusions.

Since not all social scientists are fully responsible, and even fewer acknowledge sin in any terms, we could conclude that they have a tendency to make casual distinctions about what people do and what they *appear* to do. In fact, this is often the case. But in fairness to the social scientist, this tendency is not always intentional. They often simply fail to make a distinction between *objective* reality and *subjective* reality. The tendency of some is to assume that people will do what they intend to do, and when they have done it, the social scientist assumes it was what they intended to do.

Hard Science and Soft Science

Early theorists started with the belief that the social world was composed of the same "stuff that made up the natural world. Taking their cue from biologists who were making great strides in the advancement of their science, they conceived of social reality in the same terms. Consequently, they omitted the subjective side of reality found in the thinking of people. The result was a truncated view of society and the way people related to each other.

This was the "hard science" approach modeled after the natural and physical sciences. It assumed that if something could not be experienced, it could not be "real." What you saw was what you got. This sort of empirical science seeks to reduce reality to some quantifiable form. The assumption is that anything that can't be measured is probably not worth studying. Such an approach works well in the natural sciences where the human factor is not part of the data. But in the social sciences, it is an assumption that leads to much error.

Social theory was revolutionized about a century ago when it became apparent that human consciousness was an important factor in the study of social reality. Theorists then realized that a particular attitude did not necessarily lead to a particular act. The best they could do was to leave room for error and assume that a particular action *might* follow from a certain attitude. Under such conditions, it would be risky to predict a person's actions unless considerable knowledge existed about a host of personal qualities, such as education and occupation. For that reason, a popular approach to the problem was to ask large numbers of people, who were assumed to be typical representatives, how they would act in certain situations. Even then, predictability was weak because the most important factors that influenced a person's behavior might be overlooked.

This later approach eventually led *to* a "soft science" modeled partially on the assumptions of philosophy. It claims that something could be "real" even if it were not experienced. This is non-empirical science because it accepts the idea that reality might exist outside of human experience. What you can't see really might be! If this is true, then it is futile to try to measure reality, for it is the *quality* of the thing that is important, and not the *quantity*.

Most social science of the "soft" variety accepts the idea that much important data cannot be measured because those data exist only on the level of human attitudes. But it was no accident that some social scientists of a century ago, especially those we will consider in succeeding chapters, recognized that certain data could not be measured because they were found in a superempirical realm, a world of spiritual reality that might be experienced but not measured or tested. They believed this world could have important meaning for human behavior because faith was needed to understand it. In short, what you couldn't see might be important.

Modern social science has often had trouble accepting this soft or qualitative approach to social reality. Good science demands that data be packaged in some measurable form for evaluation by others. A convenient approach to this problem was found in the use of statistics, which made assumptions about the probability of human behavior. If a form of behavior were found to occur in 95 percent of some cases, then it would be accepted as having valid application to society. But such a limitation to science would trouble one stalwart empiricist who claimed: "Senses do not lie, but they do not tell us the truth." Nevertheless, in a world that is assumed to be probabilistic, this approach offered the best hope for an empirical science.

We can illustrate this point with the case of the ichthyologist who wanted to find out how small the fish were in a certain section of the ocean. Using a net with a one-inch mesh, he proceeds to bring into the boat a wide variety of fish, none measuring less than one inch in length. If he were to conclude that no fish less than one inch lived in that section of the ocean, he could very well be wrong. His observations are limited because the net he used for his study was not small enough to catch all of the possible sizes of fish to be found there. In other words, what you see might not be!

The Christian social scientist has no trouble accepting both sources of super-empirical social reality: that found in human consciousness, which is influential on human behavior, and that which is of a spiritual nature and remains outside the empirical world. Some would say that such science is weakened because it must rely on faith. But as we shall see later, the more empirical scientist must also rely on some elements of faith. Indeed, any science is "softened" by the faith it places in certain assumptions which are fundamental to its practice. Besides, we need to remember Jesus' Sermon on the Mount statements concerning the reality of human attitudes and their spiritual meaning.

This is not to say that a Christian must avoid the more empirical forms of social science. There are, however, two kinds of assumptions about empirical science that must be avoided. The first is the belief that if our findings are based on statistical probabilities, it means we live in a probabilistic world. On the contrary, a statistic is merely a device used to compensate for human limitations in a world of absolutes created by God.

The other assumption to avoid is the notion that a behavior becomes normative for humans when it becomes the statistical norm. For instance, the dramatic rise in divorce is no reason to make it a norm for marriages. In the case of the probabilistic and the normative, it is necessary to remember that the world as God has made it is not the world as people experience it.

God's Work and Man's Work

Why should this be the case? Why should humans experience a world different from the one God made? The simplest answer is that the world suffers from sin. Divorce, for example, was not the original principle laid down by God for marriage. It was allowed by God because of human frailty (Matt. 19:8). God's ideal for marriage remains that spouses marry for life. Divorce is only one example in a host of social phenomena that combine God's ideal plan for people with a faulty human experience of that plan. For the sake of convenience, we will use the terms "God's work" and "man's work" to refer to this distinction.[1]

God's work was laid down in creation and can be studied empirically, most often by natural scientists. But God's work can also be seen in social principles given for our benefit in social relationships. These are *absolute norms* provided by God for the structuring and stabilizing of society. Marriage and the Golden Rule are examples of this form of God's work. They are less empirical than physical creation and can be studied most effectively with a soft science approach.

	Man's Work	**God's Work**
Empirical Qualities	Applied science and technology 1	Physical *creation* 2
Non-empirical Qualities	Human attitude and thought 3	Spiritual and social principles 4

Figure 1

Man's work need not always reflect the effects of sin, but it is always a result of human limitations and falls short of God's work. Some of man's work is empirical in nature and is found in technology and the applied sciences. These are objective, measurable forms of man's work and have great usefulness for us. Other forms are more subjective and fall outside of empirical science. The products of human thought and attitudes are also expressions of man's work. The subjective side of man's work includes art as well as social and cultural conventions.

Figure 1 illustrates these various forms of God's work and man's work. Each cell represents an ideal form of reality with the qualities found there. If we are to understand the world correctly, we must recognize the implicit distinctions between the cells and how each might relate to the others. Errors in the study of social reality occur when these qualities and distinctions are blurred.

The first error, which could be called a *type one error,* occurs when the empirical approach to understanding is not used when it should be. In this case, the tendency is to substitute a soft science approach when hard science is called for. For instance, God's work in physical creation (cell 2) may not be subjected to empirical study for fear that findings will conflict with claims found in Genesis. It is assumed instead, that only spiritual principles (cell 4) are to be sought in the study of creation. A possible consequence of a type one error is ideology, a topic to be discussed later in this chapter.

A *type two error* occurs when empirical science is used to make some claim about a reality existing beyond the bounds of empirical study. In this case, the tendency is to use a hard science approach when soft science may be needed. For example, it may be assumed that human technology (cell 1) is the solution for all human problems. Ignoring the place that human attitudes and thought (cell 3) have in those problems, a type 2 error fails to appreciate the importance of a soft approach to science. Consequently, scientism, a topic to be discussed later in this chapter, may result from a type 2 error.

The contents of each cell in figure 1 are not mutually exclusive from the contents of the other cells. There is a necessary overlapping that needs to be understood if reality is to be captured correctly. Marriage, for instance, as given by God (cell 4) is also interpreted by people cell 3). How this is to be done and how marriage is to apply to humans is a crucial problem for the Christian scientist. A *type 3 error* in the study of social reality, then, occurs when we don't understand the dialectic between God's work and man's work. We fail to understand the tension to be maintained between God's intention for some social form of reality and human interpretation of that reality. This problem will be touched upon in subsequent chapters, especially chapters nine and eleven. It is enough now to return to the more obvious answer offered earlier: human sinfulness and finiteness prevent us from fully understanding how to resolve the tensions inherent in the overlap of God's work and man's work.

If there is a principle to be followed by the Christian in social theory, it is this: *we must measure man's work in the social world by a proper understanding of God's work in creation.* To do this, we cannot conceive of reality in the abstract. The problems of marriage and divorce need to be broken down into their component parts and studied. How does God's conception of marital faithfulness compare with society's? How can the concept of love, as described in Scripture, be measured? Indeed, we might even ask whether marriage, in the light of Scripture and society's expectations, is to be the norm for the believer. If we don't approach problems at this level of development, our understanding of their reality and what that should mean for the Christian remains limited.

Thought and Theory

For the purpose of discussion, let's consider the following proposition: "Train a child in the way he should go, and when he is old he will not turn from it" (Prov. 22:6). We could accept this as a theological proposition given by God and rest secure in its promise. But if we take it more personally, we are inclined to see the proposition as a statement of parental responsibility to "train" a child. Since "train" implies parental attitudes and social relationships, social science should provide further understanding of the proposition.

Let's further assume that studies have been made by social scientists concerning the churchgoing habits of a father and his children. Since such habits are a form of training children, we may learn whether there is a correlation between those habits and the churchgoing of the child as an adult. The problem is to understand the conditions under which all forms of churchgoing may or may not occur. Since this is a huge task, we might simply accept the theological answer and interpret "train" as we desire. Such an approach, however, might rest on good theology—depending on the theology we used—but it would be poor social theory.

If we should search the literature and find evidence of a case where children's churchgoing with a father leads to comparable patterns of churchgoing as adults, a generalization could be made only when the important conditions surrounding churchgoing are found to be true for other children as well. Put differently, I will accept the claims of the study for the training of my children when I realize that the fathers and children in the study are in the same situation as myself. When we can state such conditions with a high degree of accuracy, we have confidence that the proposition has been stated correctly and that our claim gains more validity. Apparently, children who do accompany their fathers to church will continue going to church when they are adults.

But that is not to say that the proposition has been completely explained. Is churchgoing what the writer of Proverbs meant when he referred to "train"? Would the promise still hold true even if the child did not accompany the father? Would the same result occur if, in a single-parent family, it was the mother and not the father who took the child to church? In short, we still may not know what kind of training will assure us that the promise will be fulfilled. In the final analysis, theology might still be more satisfying than a theory that raises such questions.

But if the theology is satisfying, that does not mean it will also be effectively applied. It is quite likely that a good scientific study of the relationships suggested by the verse will do more to help us apply the theology. What is meant by a "good scientific study"? For one thing, the quality of the theory is high when a cluster of explanations of related phenomena dealing with the same general proposition is provided. In this case, it might be shown that a mother's churchgoing does not have the same effect on children. It might also be shown that the effect of the father's behavior is stronger on his sons than on his daughters. The development and demonstration of the related propositions above are necessary if the proposition that fathers influence their children's churchgoing is to be strengthened.

This discussion should now allow us to explain the meaning of an *operating definition* a critical element in any good theory. Churchgoing is an operating definition if such a specification of what it refers to can be observed and measured. Is it necessary for a father to take his son to church every Sunday, or would attendance once a month have just as good an effect? Operating definitions allow propositions to be tested because they bring the questions down to the empirical level where they can be observed and measured. In short, if a proposition is to be studied by the use of a particular theory, it must have measurable, operating definitions. Without definitions like these, we return to the vagueness on such questions so often found in theology.

By contrast, the failure to state a clear operating definition as part of a propositional statement leads to social thought which is not empirical because it lacks the testability of theory. Churchgoing is a non-operating definition as long as it remains in the abstract and is devoid of a clearly defined and measurable referent. Social thought, then, is more abstract than theory and often initiates the problems studied by theory. At its worst, social thought leads us into the folklore and mythologies of outmoded notions about social life. At its best, social thought generates crucial problems for science and serves to direct inquiry into proper channels for further study.

In the early years of social theorizing, social thought was dominant. One reason was the lack of an adequate methodology to give an empirical basis to theory. Another reason was the influence of philosophy and theology with their non-empirical approaches to problems. Over the years, non-operating definitions have been dropped because of their sterility or refined as operating definitions and included in contemporary theory. *Family,* for example, has lost much of the meaning it once had as a description of a stable set of kinship relationships. Now it is necessary to speak of a *nuclear* family or a *broken* family to define the family as it is often experienced today. This is not to say that all modern theory has the final answers. Far from it. All we can say is that scientists are more knowledgeable about the social world than they used to be. But since there is always a tentativeness to their findings, social theorists must exert considerable faith in their claims. This exercise of faith, it might be added, is not peculiar to the social sciences, but characterizes the physical and natural sciences as well.

Ideology and Scientism

The case for faith in science was argued well by Thomas Kuhn in his seminal work of some years ago.[2] Kuhn claimed that revolutions occur in science when one paradigm used to describe the nature of the world is replaced by another. Rejecting the common notion that paradigm shifts are the sole result of new discoveries, Kuhn emphasized the importance of cultural values held by scientists themselves.

In short, prevailing paradigms in science depend not only on experimental "truths" but also on the shared beliefs of the scientific community. What scientists believe and how they come to agree on those beliefs form a crucial part of theory formation and our perception of what the world is really like. What should this faith that scientists place in their work mean for the Christian?

First, it supports the notion that *much social science today is based on contemporary values.* Even those demonstrable truths about human relations may be held for reasons which are biased and, perhaps, even in error.

Second, it is also true that *modern social paradigms are often more accurate than earlier ones* that lacked the empirical evidence supporting modern science. Recognizing this fact, it is important that Christians not cling to outmoded ideas concerning the theories and beliefs of modern scientists.

Third, and this point is especially important for the Christian scientist, *there must be sensitive awareness to those scientific claims which have sustained the test of time* simply because they may also agree with biblical principles and manifest God's intentions for his people. "Without such awareness, some of the hidden threads of social reality might be overlooked.

The student may experience considerable satisfaction when the merger of faith and science is seen in these hidden threads. But when such a merger leads to a belief system, it may also become an ideology that defines social reality—explaining, justifying, and even sanctifying the vested interests of some group. In this sense, an ideology is a form of pseudo-science because it only attempts to describe social reality. It might be more accurate, however, to describe an ideology as a distortion of science since it reverses the scientific process. Instead of emphasizing discovery with an accurate description of the social world before testing and explaining, an ideology emphasizes explanation whether it agrees with the discovery or not.

Since we are more concerned with ideologies as distortions of science than as substitutions for it, we should not think that ideologies are traps only for the amateur; scientists are certainly capable of ideological thinking. But before turning to some examples, let me insert several warnings for Christians.

First, the Christian should want to avoid ideological thinking, not only because of its casual disregard for truth but also because of its inherent divisive and hostile quality. Second, the Christian should have such confidence in God's plan that security need not be sought in some social program or theory, especially at the expense of others. Without this security, the believer is ripe for any social movement and the claims it might make.

For these reasons, ideological thinking among Christians is usually symptomatic of some deep-seated spiritual insecurity. This may be seen among

Christians who are fearful of taking a "wrong" position on some social issue, believing it will reflect on their maturity as believers. Their major concern is to justify themselves with explanations that may or may not reflect the facts of the case. Others fear an objective study of these facts, believing it will reveal truths threatening to their faith. What is lacking is an informed view of the nature of science and its capacity to support and even enlighten their faith.

Let us consider how scientists may become ideological even in their best efforts to describe reality accurately. Of the many examples to be found among sociologists, Karl Marx quickly comes to mind. Believing there was a basic conflict between the bourgeois middle class and the proletarian lower class, Marx *assumed* that a revolution leading to an ideal state was inevitable. At a number of points, of course, Marx was clearly wrong, which suggests that he didn't have his facts straight.

Marx's ideological thinking was apparent in a number of ways. First, he ignored the complex nature of the world and assumed it was simpler than it was. Now we know that people are not motivated simply by class membership, as he thought, but by a complex array of subtle factors.

Second, Marx's emphasis on economic determinism attributed the quality of economically-motivated behavior to people who were not so motivated. Third, he was Utopian in his desire to provide a revolutionary program and a better society. Fourth, his definitions were usually of the non-operating type and could not be tested.

Finally, he lacked an adequate method for discovering and testing the facts as he understood them. Instead, he relied on a faith which has become a religion for many. This last point is crucial as a reminder that the line between ideology and religion is very thin indeed.

In his discourse on Mars Hill, Paul refers to the Athenians as "very religious" because they erected a statue "to the unknown God" (Acts 17). In effect, he was saying they were thinking ideologically; they had a vested interest in being theologically complete and chose this recognition of the unknown God's existence as the way to do it.

But Paul is also critical of the Jews in the same terms. In fact, in his practice of the "Jewish religion," he outstripped his peers in his faithfulness to the old traditions (Gal. 1:13-14). Whether correct or not, the traditions were believed to justify the Jews' actions, even to the persecution of Christians. In short, the Jews, like the Greeks, distorted their perception of reality simply because it was convenient for their religious belief system.

Ideological thinking, then, is not limited to the scientist, whether professional or amateur. It may also characterize the sincere believer who earnestly trusts that he or she has a complete grasp on the truth. The Christian who places faith in something or someone other than the God of creation may slip into an ideological trap. Once God is known, there is no reason to put faith in an "unknown God"!

If there is one characteristic that sets off ideology from science, it is its dogmatism. Ideally, science is tentative and skeptical with casual evidence, while ideology is quick to accept evidence as "proof." When science loses this quality of skepticism, it verges on ideology. More specifically, science may slip into the ideology of scientism: the belief that science provides the best means to know the world as it really is. This belief, that science alone can understand truth, reflects the characteristic of science as ideology.

Scientism, of course, is a prominent ideology in modern society simply because we have such a vested interest in science. We want to believe that science has the answers and can solve our problems. The sociologist would say that scientism, as an ideology, is functional for society because it meets these needs and integrates society as well. Increasingly, these needs are expressed in technological terms as we rely on technical means to solve problems that, in an earlier day, we left to the providence of God.

It is this quality of usefulness that ties ideologies so closely to their social settings. Since people are anxious to explain some social problem or justify some response to it, they quickly accept ideologies regardless of the facts of the case. For this reason, ideologies support a host of diverse and otherwise unattractive causes. Several decades ago, for example, romanticism strengthened the idea of romantic love as a basis for marriage. Currently, professionalism may become distorted in its support of the professional image of expertise and infallibility. In any case, people rally to ideologies that seem to "work" and help in the decision-making process of daily living.

Ideological thinking, then, should not be associated only with the bomb-throwing radical. Ideologies are a part of everyday life. In fact, we might just as well speak of conservative ideologies as of revolutionary ideologies. Variations in both occur as adjustments are made to real-life circumstances. No ideology lasts long if it is out of step with its social setting. It has to deal with the needs of the day. Only with sensitivity to society and the ability to shift with the times can an ideology maintain a viable dogmatism which remains its hallmark.

One of the paradoxes of social thought is this fact that ideology is often characterized by compromise. One need only look at Russian communism and its seeming tolerance of churches or the Nazis' acceptance of capitalism to realize the truth of this statement. One might even say there is a hypocritical quality to ideology. Certainly it is not uncommon for the "true believer" to be firm in belief and flabby in practice. For that reason, the Christian is well advised to heed James's warning to avoid double-mindedness (James 1:8).

But it might be preferable to think of ideology in terms of dialectic rather than paradox. Ideology and theory are cut from the same cloth; each tries, in its own way, to present its perception of reality. And this is not all bad. If we return to the work of Kuhn, we discover a dialectical quality in science as one paradigm tests itself against another. Periodically, paradigms will even overlap as they seek acceptance from the scientific community. More often, ideology and theory will eye each other jealously and covet the qualities of the other.

What needs to be stressed now is the realization that this dialectical quality must be openly acknowledged. Unless this is done, we fall into the trap of asserting that polar extremes should exist in a world believed to be dichotomous. We come to believe that some are true scientists while others are ideologists. We also come to believe that we are "true believers" while others (who may disagree only on minor points) are heretics. Since we are usually dogmatic in making such claims, we indulge our own form of ideological thinking. Worse, we fail to see our own sinfulness.

Conclusion

This chapter started with the idea that the mass media distort reality. While this is true, we have come to understand that the distortion of reality is a very common practice in modern society. Consciously and unconsciously, we seldom represent the social world as it is. In a multitude of ways, we distort reality in our everyday lives.

A graphic distortion of reality is seen in the case of My Lai, the Vietnamese village destroyed by a task force of American soldiers in the Vietnam conflict.[3] Portrayed as an example of group evil, the circumstances surrounding the operation baffled the soldiers. Were the villagers hostile? What was the specific purpose of the mission? What should be the conscience of a soldier? In short, how should the soldiers act when the facts of the situation are not clearly known?

Few Christians are called upon to deal with a My Lai in their lifetimes. But all of us, if we are honest in our evaluations of daily life, grope to understand what is going on about us. A critical spiritual element exists here that gains little illumination from social theory. Nevertheless, we need to understand those problems more clearly as theoretical problems too, if for no other reason than we can pray more knowledgably about them. And as we gain understanding, we also perceive our responsibility and how to implement it.

Chapter 3

The European Heritage

The eighteenth century was one of those periods in history well suited for a revolution in social science. Only a century earlier the revolution in physical science had dramatically altered the way scientists looked at the world. For many, this revolution offered a distinct challenge to transfer this same understanding of the physical world to the social world.

Of the underlying social conditions for this revolution, three may be singled out. The first condition was the scientific revolution centered in Newtonian physics. The effect that this had on the thinking of the day was enormous. The French Revolution and the ensuing long period of political and social turmoil was another critical stimulus for the development of new patterns of social thought. French philosophers, especially, wanted a new basis for social order in a modern age. Finally, the attitude toward the religious structure dominating European society since the Middle Ages was completely revised. In addition to the attack on the church, including the crucial question of church-state relations, basic theological beliefs held inviolate for centuries were open to question. Such was the setting for the development of what has come to be known as sociology.

The Enlightenment

It would be a mistake to see this period as the result of mere circumstances. Many of the philosophers of the day sought a revolution not only in the structure of society, but also in the fundamental belief systems. What they were often reacting to was an authoritative religion propped up by its relation to the state—a far cry from many of the ideals of the Middle Ages. In the thinking of most of the philosophers, science had replaced the authority of the church and given credence to the idea of human omniscience.

French philosophers, especially, led the way in challenging society just as the scientist had done a century or so earlier. Paradoxically some of these men, such as Turgot and Condorcet, were caught in a dilemma which scarcely seemed to faze them. Believing in the inevitability of progress, they tried to convert philosophy to a natural science while faced with the ideological bias of philosophy's scorn for objectivity. Science, they believed, would be in the vanguard of social development. The result was often a distortion of social reality as it existed. Facts were ignored as reality was reconstructed to fit the prevailing beliefs of the new class of critical philosophers. Despite their efforts to be scientific, however, these men remained largely ideological.

These "philosophes" were unlike other professionals of the time who were moving toward specialization. The leaders of the Enlightenment were largely generalists, men of letters who held to relativist positions on all issues except freedom, tolerance, reason, and humanity. But if they were dogmatic on these issues—and they were—ambivalence characterized their approaches to other social concerns. They sought to change institutions, seeing this as the only viable means of improving society but also recognizing that anarchy might result. For most, the reasonable solution was to encourage the reign of a philosopher-king, an enlightened ruler who would bring in the age of enlightenment.

Although the philosophes struggled with solutions to the problems as they saw them, they were agreed in their radical view of the causes of evil: man's problems were social and not religious. This view led to a complete revision of the doctrine of sin as it had always been taught. Instead of believing that man was sinful, Rousseau, for example, taught that man in a state of nature is good. Pressed to explain how people could be good in an evil society, he concluded that social man was no longer "natural." Society had caused him to degenerate.

This radical view led to an early form of social determinism, which became the cornerstone of much of modem sociology. It further served to justify the development of social science as a discipline to study social evil as theology had studied spiritual evil. Since the orthodox Christian view had been that man had to resolve the internal spiritual struggle before he could act properly, it was natural for the philosophers to believe that society had to be changed before man could once again become good inwardly. Social sin, in their opinion, always caused individual sin and never the other way around.

At first the philosophers, many of whom were deists, believed in natural law as the basis for science and social living. As one of the early exponents of this thinking, David Hume said, "The science of man is the only foundation for the other sciences [and] the only science of man [is] Human Nature."[1] But Hume never intended that this science should be neutral. Rather, science was to return morality to man as well as stability to society. This would be done by reforming the church with the institution of natural religion and separating it from state control. Yet this humanistic approach to religion and the science of society met with little success. By the latter half of the Enlightenment, the advocates of deism and natural law had become atheists and espoused utility over nature.

Although the philosophers were the ancestors of modern positivism, they were also militant and Utopian in their efforts to bring in a better society. Despite their efforts to develop a method of social research derived from natural science, the tension with ideology was lost as they consistently fell back on claims that became little more than dogma. Social thought remained ambivalent and unstable without the method and conceptual development necessary for a science.

Charles Montesquieu, considered by some to be the best example of a sociologist at this time, represented those few social thinkers who had the right idea about science. "The true is not always probable," he observed in his efforts at objectivity.[2] But though he claimed to draw his principles from facts which were meant to serve values, the results were often inconsistent. In fact, his attempt to draw laws of nature from his observations seldom distinguished clearly between fact and value. Nevertheless, his wide travels and perceptive eye confirmed an early form of the principle of cultural relativism, and he recognized the complexity of society as few had.

Thanks to the popularity of Montesquieu, these new thoughts became influential.

For most, the French Revolution was a fulfillment of enlightened *thinking* and represented a threat rather than a promise. Conservatives like Louis de Bonald and Joseph de Maistre preferred the stability of medieval society and sought a return to its characteristic hierarchical relationships. Others such as Claude Henri Saint-Simon and his disciple Auguste Comte were more influential and opted for a modern society, one in tune with the developing science and industry of the early nineteenth century. They were especially critical of the "negative" philosophy of the philosophes and argued for the affirmative principles of "positive" philosophy.

It would not be stretching a point to see this positive philosophy as an ideology that conceived of freedom as the rational submission to natural laws. Its objective was to counter the critical spirit of the Revolution and the Enlightenment. Further, it conceived of a modern future, one which would unfold as social science applied the principles of physical science to its problems. It was this conception of "social physics" or *sociology* as it came to be known that earned for Comte the title "Father of Sociology," a sobriquet not recognized by all. Nevertheless, the positive method which Comte advocated emphasized observation, experimentation, and comparison, the basic requirements for any science at that time.

It was one thing, however, to *claim* scientific truth in authoritative ways and quite something else to *discover* that truth. The ultimate test for Comte was the establishment of a "positive society," one that gave up the search for absolute causes and relied on a belief in science. He became the "Pope of Humanity," a visionary "torn between the twin demands of order and progress," who tried to cultivate an audience for his ideological views.[3] He was largely unsuccessful in this effort. As for Comte's positive society, it scarcely got off the drawing board.

It was in such a period of paradox that sociology was conceived. It combined religion and science, utopianism and conservatism into one restless and unstable intellectual system. Out of that, Comte believed, would emerge a moral and religious system that could then proceed to direct the political.

The religious system, he postulated, would have to be radically new. It could not support the traditional doctrines and practices of the church. Instead, it would be a religion of humanity, one of moral worth capable of producing unity and love in society. Such a religion was necessary to sanctify and shape the temporal power.

In one sense, Comte's system remains a skeleton without flesh. It provided an effective rationale for the development of sociological thinking and little else of historical consequence. In another sense, it provided a skeleton for American closets in the form of civil religion, that curious counterpart of Christianity which periodically finds its way into our holidays, presidential addresses, and patriotic fervor. It was Rousseau who first coined the phrase *civil religion* in his work *The Social Contract* to describe those elements of religious faith recognized by the state, all other religious opinions being held privately by its citizens. But it was Comte, probably more than any other follower of Enlightenment thought, whose social program sought to use religion as a means to gain the unity of the state and then of the human race.

Marxism as Ideology

In 1843, when Comte was involved in some of his most important work, Karl Marx visited Paris for a two-year period. He sought in that city, known for its intellectual and revolutionary spirit, a haven from the oppressive atmosphere of Germany where, he claimed, "one can only be false to oneself."[4] Specifically, he hoped to find answers for the failure of the French Revolution. Although he was largely unsuccessful in this search, the stay in Paris from 1843 to 1845 set the stage for the rest of his work.

Marx learned that the French had little sense of the role of history in the development of society. History, he claimed, was a record of human conflicts manifesting the transformation and expansion of human nature. Progress resulted from the expansion of human capacities to fulfill, both spiritually and materially, individual needs. In contrast to the French whose positivism limited their notion of society to the present, Marx believed there should be a natural unfolding of human potential for the fullest development of the social order. In short, social conflict was justifiable as a means of bringing in the ideal state.

What we have here is not simply a difference of opinion between Marx and his French contemporaries. Instead, it is a critical difference in the philosophies of science and world views of these two traditions. French social science, as influenced by Comte, emphasized a realism which could be understood completely and effectively with a positive methodology. It was a world of cause and effect, one in which social facts always yielded to the proper application of science.

The Hegelian tradition in which Marx had been immersed was, first, idealistic and, second, dialectical. Hegel's idealism focused on consciousness and the spirit of society as the basis for social change. The sweep of history was largely beyond the influence of individuals whose primary responsibility was to understand their place in the process of change. Cause and effect in this tradition had little meaning because of the dialectic of forces at work in the world. If science was to understand such a world, it would have to be radically different from earlier models.

In effect, each tradition had a different view of reality. For one group of French philosophers of the time, reality was collective and the group was a determining influence on behavior. This environmental determinism required social stability and traditional morality if problems were to be solved. Reality was limited to society conceived largely as a closed system which left little room for historical, or other external, influence. In short, if God was to be at work, he would have to be in society.

In the dominant view of the German tradition, reality was located in social change, especially as it could be understood in the culture of the people. This view conceived of society as an open system, one which was responsive to historical and other external influences that could have a real effect on society. For this reason, traditional scientific methods were inappropriate, and a new "cultural science," which could study the "essence" of social phenomenon, had to be developed. Although the major contributions to this new science were to come from others, Marx laid some important foundations.

Always the individualist, Marx rejected Hegel's idealism while enthusiastically receiving his dialecticism. According to Marx, "Hegel makes man *the man of self-consciousness* instead of making self-consciousness the *self-consciousness of man,* man living in a real objective world determined by that world."[5] Having said that, Marx did not accept the idea that man should be determined by the world. It was a force to be resisted. Unlike the French who would have studied that world devoid of man, Marx recognized the critical dialectic of man involved in his world. Man's consciousness of his place in the world required not that he study it *objectively* but that he understand it *subjectively.* Only then could he fulfill his potential and offer any hope of the collective fulfillment of society.

These two views of reality shape much of the development of social thought even to the present day. For the Christian who has to make a choice, the temptation would be to shy away from the Marxist model and approve the French, especially with its concern for the religious support of the community. But the French model is suspect largely because of its social determinism, empiricism, and low view of religion. To accept the French model, one must recognize society as a closed system with no external influence and be willing to approve of it as a final reality. In short, one must be of the world as well as in it.

The Marxist model; however, seems to offer a distinct option largely because the social world is not a final reality. Consequently, one is to discern between the truth that comes from external sources and the falsehood which is internal and social. That discernment comes only through the dialectic of man's self-conscious resistance to the world's influence. Another way of putting it is to say that man is in the world but not necessarily of it.

To resolve his own struggle with society's influence, Marx argued his own form of dialectical materialism, which focused on dialectical relationships in the material world. But it was this materialism that stamped Marx as an economist, rather than a sociologist. In fact, neither Marx himself nor others at the time considered him to be a sociologist. Most of the early social thinkers approved of the conservative position of the French and rejected his views. This was especially true in America where social science generally accepted the positive conservatism of post-Enlightenment thinking until the renewal of Marxist thought in the mid-twentieth century.[6]

It is this dogmatic view of materialism which gives Marx's work an ideological rather than a theoretical bias. Indeed, German sociologists were inclined to reject Marx because of his materialistic views. Max Weber, the dominant proponent of this tradition, did not believe that modern society could be explained in terms of what seemed to be a single-cause theory offered by Marx. Society was too complex, too dynamic to think that materialism alone could have brought it to pass. Further, he believed history showed that other factors, including religions, influenced social change. Weber would have agreed that nonsocial forces were influential in society, but these were often of a religious, and not solely historical, nature.

In spite of Marx's economic and ideological biases, however, he should not be denied the recognition he deserves for contributions made to sociological theory. Unlike Comte, who added little conceptual value to the field, Marx has enormous importance for contemporary sociology.

First, Marx contributed the concept *of alienation,* the idea that man is separated from reality. Since Marx considered the material world to be the basis for all reality, this meant that man was separated from his work and his products in a capitalist society. Extending this notion, Marx conceived of man as separated from his fellow workers and even his own qualities as a person. Unwittingly, he gives up his power to society and its institutions, which, in turn, subjugate him in his alienated condition. The result is an inversion of reality. Instead of capitalism being a source of wealth, it becomes for Marx the basis for enslaving the worker. Similarly, the state should be seen as man's captor, not his servant.

This position, of course, was a natural result of Marx's humanism. Man was perfectible if allowed to reap the benefits of his labor. Unlike the French who failed in their revolution and sought to perfect their society by other means,

Marx saw revolution as the only means by which man would finally escape his alienation. His view on alienation was also an expression of his atheism. Instead of believing that God made man, Marx claimed the process should be reversed; man made God in his own image and gave his power to the church. Thus, the church, often with the help of the state and industry, controlled the minds of the believers and religion became the opiate of the people.[7]

Marx's second contribution was the concept of *consciousness*, the idea that people differed from animals in their ability to choose among forms of action. In other words, there is a willfulness in people directing their future action and for which they are responsible. Consciousness, however, was not a characteristic of individuals alone. As persons in social classes view life with the same awareness and concern, they developed class consciousness. Social class, then, is deterministic of behavior and forms the distorted perception of society. Such inaccurate awareness is false consciousness, referring to the erroneous notions held by proletariat and bourgeoisie in a capitalist society. In both cases, class members are unaware of the way consciousness is influenced by society and the effect it has on their perception of it.

When people do become aware of the true conditions of their lives, Marx believed the natural result was *conflict,* his third contribution to sociological thought. In simplest terms, this refers to the inevitable revolution against the state, resulting in a communist society. But the idea of conflict is so basic to Marx's thought that it goes beyond the principles of revolutionary activity. Conflict is inherent in the dialectic and the necessary flexibility of subjective thought struggling for an accurate perception of society. Conflict assumes resistance against things as they are, always with the expectation that social change will shape things as they should be. This idea of conflict has become so basic in sociology that it has formed a whole school of social thought.

Finally, Marx influenced developments in the *sociology of knowledge,* a tradition in sociology claiming that consciousness is a social product. While Marx could never claim sole responsibility for this tradition, his work certainly formed one of its major roots. Class consciousness, for example, provides a view of society in agreement with its social context. If social classes should have an incorrect perception of their condition, then they would have a distorted view of reality shaped by their social consciousness.

This brief overview of Marx's work omits many of his other contributions. Some of these have been highly influential in sociology while others have not stood the test of time. But even though Marx is a good example of the rich merger of theory and ideology, we must conclude that his ideology always dominated his work. Despite efforts at objectivity, the powerful bias of his thinking, especially as it applied to the use of revolution, invalidated many of his explanations. As C. Wright Mills, a sympathetic sociologist, has observed, Marx usually asked the right questions but arrived at the wrong answers.

It would be a mistake for Christians, especially, to ignore Marxist thought and the questions it raises. His way of seeing problems as inherent contradictions in society should provide considerable help in understanding the world as it is and guiding us in our efforts to live in it. The sociology of knowledge provides a useful and accurate model in the social construction of reality against which to critique modern society. Ironically, Marx also gives a warning to the Christian against idolatry, for we are, regrettably, idolatrous when we seek to make God in our image. If we fail to perceive this tendency in ourselves, just as we often fail to see our inclination to civil religion, we miss some of the rich lessons social theory has for us.

Social Evolution as Ideology

The publication of *Origin of Species* in 1859 was part of that watershed of evolutionary thinking which dominated thought into the twentieth century. Though not directly influenced by Darwin, Herbert Spencer was the major figure in that revolution to apply evolutionary principles to the social world. A believer that social phenomena are no different from natural phenomena, Spencer had no trouble also believing that social institutions, like plants and animals, adapted to their environments.

Spencer shared with Comte the belief that social laws were as deterministic as natural laws. Without such laws, social order and stability would not be possible. But while Comte wanted to discover how those laws could be used to develop a stable society, Spencer argued that these laws should be allowed to work without human involvement. Only then could evolutionary principles, the dominant force for progress in history, work to the benefit of humanity.

This idea that progress was an uncontrollable scientific law was readily accepted in early Victorian England. It was a time of prosperity, optimism, and empire building. Spencer's work provided much of the justification it needed and offered hope for its future progress. Consequently, it became an ideology well suited for the day.

But Spencer never thought of his work as ideology. He believed evolution described all change from "relatively indefinite, incoherent homogeneity to a state of relatively definite, coherent, heterogeneity."[8] This process, he claimed, explained not only changes occurring in past societies, but also those changes to be expected in the future. At the time, social trends seemed to justify this claim.

Earlier, Comte had espoused this same kind of unilinear theory—that society progressed from the simple to the complex. Spencer came to reject these views, presumably later in life when the increasing complexity of British society brought unilinear theory into question. In its place he developed a multi-linear theory, one that recognized the possibility of stagnation and retrogression in social change. Spencer then argued that it was possible for a social structure to reach a point of equilibrium in the process of adjusting to the environment. With equilibrium, there would be no further change in structure.

Spencer gained considerable flexibility for his prediction with this adaptation of his original theory. But he lost credibility, since it was no longer able to be universally applied as an explanation for change. Without the possibility of predicting whether a structure would progress or regress, the theory lost its scientific basis. Today, most schools of sociology give little credence to environmental determinism of any sort.

That is not to say that Spencer did not make important contributions to sociological theory. He did. But it does suggest that the ideological quality of his work gained greater prominence. Perhaps this was because it provided a definite alternative to the ameliorism of his day. This view held that *individuals* were the cause of social problems which could be removed only with reform of the offender. The hope was that this approach could reform society, thereby avoiding the alternatives offered by Marx and the philosophes before him.

Spencer was diametrically opposed to such a view. He believed people were perfectible if allowed to adjust to the circumstances found in a progressing society. He claimed "for every society, and for each stage in its evolution, there is an appropriate mode of feeling and thinking... no mode of feeling and thinking not adapted to its degree of evolution, and to its surroundings, can be permanently established."[9] It was through society, and society only, that human potential could be realized.

But the person was expected to adjust. This was the basis for "the survival of the fittest," a phrase coined by Spencer before its popularization by Darwin and others. Spencer seemed to carry this philosophy to the extreme when he said, "Fostering the good-for-nothing at the expense of the good, is an extreme cruelty.... There is no greater curse to posterity than that of bequeathing to them an increasing population of imbeciles and idlers and criminals. . . .The whole effort of nature is to get rid of such, to clear the world of them, and make room for better."[10] Clearly, this view did not sit well with those supporting an ameliorative position.

But Spencer's views were well received by those in tune with the progressivism of the times, notably those members of the upper classes who could remain blind to society's problems. For them, evolutionary theory confirmed what they had suspected all along—the lower classes were inferior and deserved no assistance if they were unwilling to help themselves. Consequently, the theory also justified those in power as more "fit" and deserving of society's benefits. In fact, those who pursued their own best interests could do so with a clear conscience.

Running parallel with this idea of the survival of the fittest was Spencer's theory of progress and increased social heterogeneity. Society became so complex, he claimed, that the effects of tampering with unknown causes could not be known. He compared the problem to planishing, the art of smoothing metallic surfaces. Assume for a moment, that an inexperienced person delivered a direct blow to a bump on a metallic plate. The result, he claimed, would be worse as new wrinkles and dents appeared. The necessary approach would be to use indirect blows of differing strengths on the plate. Similarly, the complex problems of society required the same deft, indirect approaches requiring a knowledge which, unfortunately, was not available at that time. The answer, therefore, was simply to leave things alone.

For Spencer, this laissez-faire approach should dominate all policies. The state, especially, was to have only the power necessary to protect individual rights and to guard the nation against outside enemies. All other rights were left to individuals acting in their best interests. In effect, he opposed all social reform and wanted social life to evolve free of any external control. For Spencer, any disregard for human need resulting from such an action was not wrong. Evil, as he saw it, resulted from non-adaptation to the environment, and government intervention supported this evil. Consequently, evolution manifested its own virtue in opposing this evil.

The religious overtones on any ideology should not be overlooked. A necessary dimension of faith is present in every ideology simply because of the absence of scientifically convincing evidence. But it is also true that an ideology contains the seeds of science, and this is no less true for Spencer. His major problem was to explain the development of society in evolutionary terms, for it was only through evolution that society developed its structure. Through a gradual process of growth, differentiation, integration, and equilibration, society became complex and progressed. In this way, evolution becomes a model for explanation and prediction of all subsequent change.

Although Spencer's ideological bias has found little favor through the years, reaction to his theory has always been mixed.[11] Most of the concern has focused on his use of the organic analogy to describe the development of social structures, which he compared to biological organisms. With differentiation, each part of the organism relates to the other parts and makes them possible. As reciprocal aid causes mutual dependence of the parts, each part has difficulty performing the functions of others. Consequently, social institutions result from meeting functional and structural needs of society and are not the result of arbitrary choices.

Some intriguing problems are inherent in this view of social development, most of which we will return to in later chapters. But it is important here to point out that organicism is clearly modeled in 1 Corinthians 12, where Paul compares the church to a body. He does not describe an evolutionary process as Spencer does. Rather, Paul portrays a clear and mutual dependence of believers resulting in the enhancement of both the whole and the parts. Unlike the apostle, who recognized that such an organic functioning was possible only by God's provision, Spencer explained human development in terms of adaptation to social environments. Human personality and qualities were always referred back to social structure. Social thought simply left no room for a supernatural explanation.

Put another way, parts were to be explained in terms of wholes and wholes in terms of parts. This idea led to the notion of *structural functionalism,* one of those pivotal theoretical ideas that turns up again in contemporary sociological thought. As structure develops, each new part acquires needs to be met by another structure. Consequently, new functions develop, especially on the institutional level, to meet these structural needs. Preservation of this structure benefits from a strong conservative bias used to prevent its disequilibration.

Important byproducts of this process of developing structures and functions are personal biases resulting from social affiliations. Spencer singled out educational, patriotic, class, political, and theological biases as problematic for social science. On one hand, biases were necessary if the person were to interact fully in the social group and adapt to it. On the other hand, such biases prevented complete objectivity in study of the social world and weakened social scientific efforts. Personal objectivity could no longer be taken for granted. It would always be in tension with subjective elements, a fact that left its imprint on modern sociology and which we will consider later in this book.

Although Spencer made provision for some destructuring in the evolutionary process, he was not prepared for the problems developing at the end of the century. Government expanded with other institutions to develop new colonial policies, making laissez-faire thinking a thing of the past. Modern society posed challenges that evolution could neither explain nor predict. Observing this, Spencer became increasingly pessimistic and cynical, undoubtedly aware that evolutionary thought would fail to survive in the new century.

Classical Sociology

The residue of evolutionary thinking became apparent in the institutional malaise in Europe at the end of the nineteenth century. It was a time when the emergence of subtle new realities could not be contained by old practices. Calling for a radical departure from past ideas, social thinkers developed a subjective attitude toward the world. Consciousness and non-rational thought became the means by which they hoped to interpret social life in a modern world.

In sociology, this thinking took a unique twist with the introduction of the sacred into theoretical attempts to understand and explain social life. What was different about this perspective was its attempt to use religio-sacred phenomena to interpret ostensibly non-religious phenomena as well as the religious. Indeed, it was sociology alone, among all of the social sciences, that offered such a view. Turning from the rationalist and positivist efforts of the past, it pushed explanation beyond social bounds to include the divine.

Setting the stage for twentieth-century sociology, classical sociological thought revised some simplistic notions of the past. First, it established the realization that sociology was a separate discipline with its own methodology. Gone were the attempts to compare it with the biological sciences or to rely upon their easy assumptions. In their place a new methodology arose as well as a new conception of social reality. In addition, a new view of human nature emerged, one which neither encouraged man's radical efforts to remake society nor accepted his submission to historical forces. Instead, man was acknowledged to be an actor in a meaningful world, someone who initiated action and responded to its influence. Finally, classical sociology developed a realistic view of progress. From the failures of the past it became evident that modern life was neither simple nor responsive to easy change. New social and human resources were needed to go along with this modern conception of social science.

A significant feature of this classical period is the cosmopolitan quality of its giants: Max Weber, Emile Durkheim, and Georg Simmel. Always the outsider, Simmel, a German Jew, represented Kantian philosophy in his taut, brilliant analyses of social life. Thanks to his popularity as a lecturer, Simmel attracted a circle of American scholars who carried his influence to the States. Simmer's countryman, Max Weber, enjoys the reputation of being the most complete sociologist who has ever lived. A German scholar in the grand tradition, he was a systematizer whose work laid the foundation for much of modern sociology. Durkheim, from a long line of French rabbis, broke from this heritage with his agnosticism. More than the others, he represented the founding fathers of sociology while shaping the field into a legitimate academic discipline.

Emile Durkheim

Since Durkheim does perform this key bridging function in the history of social thought, he offers a logical introduction to classical thinking, especially as it attempted to break with the past. For Durkheim, this meant establishing the meaning of *social facts:* that "group of phenomena which may be differentiated from those studied by the other natural sciences."[12] Avoiding a reductionist view of social phenomena, Durkheim emphasized the existence of these social facts as external, and prior, to the individual. They emanated from society or some segment of it and constituted the only proper domain of sociological research. With these views, Durkheim remained faithful to the earlier French attempts to establish an objective basis for social science.

Durkheim also believed that social facts have a coercive power which influences a person, independent of his individual will. Although free to resist social practices, a person experiences strong social pressure to conform. Durkheim's justly famous study of suicide provides an illustration of this principle. Relying on a novel and creative use of statistics, Durkheim showed that interacting persons constituted a social reality separate from their individual consciousnesses. He found that suicide rates increased when cohesion weakened, a condition he referred to as *anomie* or *normlessness.* Anomie suicide, he concluded, was a function of the breakdown of social integration and acted as an index of disintegrating forces in modern society. Despite resistance to much of Durkheim's thought from many contemporary sociologists, the idea of anomie remains an intriguing and profitable concept to study.

Durkheim further argued that the function of any social fact should be sought in its relation to some social end. The explanation of a social phenomenon, he claimed, depends on the cause producing it and the function it fulfills. As an act of deviance, crime, like suicide, has a useful function; it defines an acceptable level of deviance. In fact, Durkheim suggests there should be concern when crime rates drop significantly since it implies some disorder in the social structure.

Durkheim's attempt to explain social life solely in terms of social phenomena led to an organic view of society not unlike Spencer's. Although he rejected Spencer's organic analogy to life systems as well as his individualism and evolutionary dogma, Durkheim was influenced by Spencer's suggestion that social life evolved from one level of development to another. *Mechanical solidarity,* he claimed, existed when individual differences were minimal and unity was the result of common group bonds. This evolves into *organic solidarity* in which division of labor functions to unify individual differences in strong group bonds. In short, unity in a modern, differentiated society occurs when individuals depend upon each other.

However, Durkheim now faced a problem with the origin and functions of religion. He realized that much of the unity found in simple societies came from religion and the norms and values it provided. But with the differentiation of society and the development of organic solidarity, religion lost much of this function. To Durkheim's credit, he realized the importance of religion in a modern society. In his last published work, *The Elementary Forms of the Religious Life,* he concluded that society is the source of all religion, a notion reminiscent of Comte's views on religion. In fact, he believed that worship of the divine is simply worship of the power of society. As an agnostic, he had little interest in developing new forms of modern religion. But he did believe that citizens should encourage civic morality as a form of religious expression capable of improving people both socially and spiritually.

Durkheim presents a challenge for the Christian. Surely his view of religion must be rejected as an expression of civil religion. But he did make a distinction between the sacred and the profane which still has importance for today. The sacred, he claimed, is the essence of religion and includes all those aspects of social reality set aside as divine. The profane includes all the mundane, every-day aspects of life. Since an object is intrinsically neither sacred nor profane, man attributes religious or non-religious meaning to it. Consequently, the individual has the opportunity to maximize the religious meaning in the world.

Implicit in Durkheim's thinking is the necessity to resist social facts and to struggle against their effects. In the same way, it is necessary to resist the secularizing quality of the profane in society and to invest sacred meaning where possible. The Christian, always seeking to separate Caesar's possessions from God's, also struggles with the meaning in the world and his responsibility in it. He is on the edge of the world while trying to avoid conformity to it. We will consider these problems in more detail in the study of social action theory.

Although he does not dwell on the topic of secularization, Durkheim recognizes the problem it creates in society.

> But, if there is one truth that history teaches us beyond doubt, it is that religion tends to embrace a smaller and smaller portion of social life. Originally it pervades everything; everything social is religious; the two words are synonymous. Then, little by little, political, economic, scientific functions free themselves from the religious function, constitute themselves apart and take on a more and more acknowledged temporal character. God, who was at first present in all human relations, progressively withdraws from them; he abandons the world to men and their disputes.[13]

Despite the "God is dead" theology apparent here, Durkheim does single out secularization as a characteristic problem of modern society.

Is there any answer to secularization? Durkheim believes there is and, as always, he finds it in social life. It is the development of organic solidarity with its reliance on division of labor. But the distinction between this model and that found in 1 Corinthians 12 is important. Scripture states that God's work produces harmony in the church by giving unique importance to each individual part (spiritual gifts bestowed by God) for the purpose of gaining the unity of the whole. God is the cause and the effect of social unity. In Durkheim's model, harmony results from the social importance of the individual differences which lead to unity as each depends on the other.

Max Weber

Durkheim clearly omits the place of the individual in social groups. He never clarified the importance of individual consciousness and the place it might have in social dissent. Another classical sociologist, Max Weber, provided a balance to this view. Influenced by German idealism, especially its concern for

human spiritual qualities, Weber's emphasis had several important consequences.

First, he rejected positivism and its efforts to understand the natural bases of
social behavior. He understood that humans were thinking beings guided by
conscious and unconscious motives falling well outside the limits of traditional
scientific inquiry. Ideas, therefore, had real consequences in the development of
history—what people considered to be meaningful usually affected how they
acted. All of Weber's work was directed toward understanding the part played
by ideas in the development of Western history. Consequently, he leap-frogged
over Durkheim and Spencer by suggesting that social phenomena were primarily subjective and not purely natural or social.

The way to study such phenomena, Weber believed, was to understand
them rather than to attempt to predict them. After all, people are unpredictable
and given to irrational behavior. Since that is the case, it is necessary to repro-
duce motives by interpreting the meaning of actions and words. This required
the researcher to understand *(verstehen)* the meaning associated with the action
of an individual or collectivity since no action occurred without subjective
meaning attached to it. Although the method of *verstehen,* the key to Weber's
methodology, is far removed from Durkheim's positivism, it offered another
view of social reality, a view more consistent with modern life.

Taking German Idealism's idea of the infinite nature of the world, Weber
claimed we are prevented from having any accurate and final statement of cau-
sality. Instead, an interrelationship is always present among social factors making it necessary to think multi-causally. From the human point of view, the
world is probabilistic and must be interpreted in that way. Science cannot make
any final statements or predict with any assurance. The best it can hope to do is
to understand the meaning and value attributed to any particular social action
and then to develop causal relations. When this is done, the scientist has a deeper and more complete understanding of human behavior. In short, Weber opted
for a "soft," insightful science to complement a "hard," empirical approach preferred by earlier sociologists.

Weber was quite realistic as well as radical with this view. He realized there
was a tension between social data and the values society used to interpret them.
Rather than denying the tension, he tried to understand how the researcher could
maintain and interpret it. The problem was how to be both objective and subjective at the same time. He concluded that values were necessary for the choice of
problems as well as for the interpretation of the research results. But the research process itself was to be "value-free," a notion implying a scientific ideal
rather than some realistic expression of research practice.

Weber had little trouble speaking in ideal terms. In fact, the *ideal type* is
one of his most important contributions to social science. Since social reality
could never be described accurately, Weber relied on this means to describe and
measure reality. The ideal type was a logical arrangement of empirical facts that

do not appear *in* the real world *in* their logically pure form. The idea of a "value-free sociology," then, became an ideal type of what sociological research should be. But there was always the realization that a value-free approach was impossible. The social researcher was a product of his culture and could not completely separate himself from its values.

The best way to pull together these diverse ideas is to look at Weber's famous study, *The Protestant Ethic and the Spirit of Capitalism,* one of the most controversial and influential works in social science. In contrast to Marx, who believed that materialism and the class struggle were inevitable in all societies, Weber tried to show that Western civilization had a unique development with a religious basis. In short, he reversed the Marxist thesis by arguing that spiritual causes could have material consequences.

Weber suggested that one of the causes of Western capitalism was a new form of ethic based upon the religious convictions of Protestantism in the Reformation. The idea that people had a religious "calling" to fulfill God's will gripped believers at the time and motivated them to break with the traditional notions of the Catholic church. The result was a sense of responsibility that taught the Puritan to pursue wealth as a religious duty.

> The world exists to serve the glorification of God and for that purpose alone. The elected Christian is in the world only to increase this glory of God by fulfilling his commandments to the best of his ability. But God requires social achievement of the Christian because he wills that social life shall be organized according to his commandments, in accordance with that purpose.[14]

It was in this unique merger of the spiritual and social that Weber found a key to the development of Western civilization. *Man was motivated by social and economic objectives but always for some transcendent and ultimate purpose.* It was this spirit which Weber referred to as *inner-worldly asceticism:* "a rationalization toward an irrational mode of life."[15] Stated differently, worldly means could be used to seek non-worldly ends. Weber recognized that this type of asceticism was unstable; motivation could become unbalanced and stress either the rational or the irrational. In Western society, of course, the trend was toward the rational. Weber quotes John Wesley to illustrate the point: "I fear, wherever riches have increased, the essence of religion has decreased in the same proportion. . . . So, although the form of religion remains, the spirit is swiftly vanishing away."[16]

This idea that the spiritual was disappearing from modern life was one of the major characteristics of the process of rationalization. Weber referred to this process as *disenchantment:* the loss of religious elements from social life and their replacement by systematic, predictable elements. This process was inevitable, Weber thought, and bound modern man in an "iron cage." Although this process of rationalization could not be reversed, people had a responsibility to attach subjective meaning to their actions and resist the trend of secularization. Always interested in politics, Weber wrote a famous essay calling upon politicians to resist the bureaucratizing trends in their profession and to work for its original purposes. In a companion piece on science, he encouraged scientists to seek the ultimate meanings of their discipline and to avoid giving themselves completely to its application.

If any hope remained for modern man it was in this willful and subjective use of meaning to resist the trends of modernization. In fact, for Weber, sociology's main purpose was first to interpret social action in terms of its subjective meaning and patterns and then to move to causal explanation of its occurrences. Doing this, Weber isolated two forms of social action which he considered to be revolutionary. One was the *calling,* the religious spirit originally behind the Protestant ethic. The original word used by Weber was *beruf—a* "task set by God"—the same word used by Luther in his translation of the Bible.[17] The other concept was *charisma:* the attribution of special powers to a person enabling *him* to acquire a radical view of the world. As influential as these powers might be for directing a leader and his followers, charisma will eventually be reshaped by rationalizing processes and conform to the trends of modern society.

Weber sees no final solution for the problem of rationalization. Charisma offers a reprieve but eventually succumbs to new forms of routinization, which continue the cyclical pattern of rationalization and irrationalization in history. Despite his perceptive analyses of modernity, Weber never moved beyond the social and psychosocial meaning of religion. He recognized none of the eternal hope claimed by the Christian. Unlike his predecessors, however, he did recognize the revolutionary effect of Christianity on history. If his system did not include the direct intervention of God, it was probably a result of the limitations of science as well as his own agnosticism.

Conclusion

The mood of Western society had altered greatly in the century since Comte began his work. World War I, especially, deepened the pessimism greeting the twentieth century and humbled even men of responsible idealism like Durkheim and Weber. Durkheim immersed himself in public service during the war and died in 1917, shattered by the senselessness of the times. Always struggling with his ideals, Weber died in 1920 after great efforts in the reorganization of Germany.

With that change in mood came a further change in European sociological awareness, one reflecting more clearly the nature of society and the kind of science needed to study it. It was apparent that society was far more complex than originally thought and remained uninfluenced by good causes, even those supported by science. Despite his best efforts and predictions, Western man could not bring in the utopia he hoped for. What was needed was responsibility, not revolution.

It also became apparent that society could not be explained with a unilateral approach to social theory. Ample room was left for new paradigms and empirical evidence. The idea that one all-encompassing theory, whether social evolution or Marxism, could fully describe the world became an antiquated notion. Also relegated to the past was the confidence that had been placed in ideological thinking. In the future, ideological thought would have to stand the test of empirical fact-finding, which now helped to define the field of modern sociology.

Finally, an unwitting acknowledgement of biblical principles had arisen in the explanation of social behavior. Man was not a passive being upon whom social and natural forces worked but rather an actor, a willful being who responded to social choices. Further, principles for organizing society and human relationships were recognized by social thinkers, principles that had first been elicited in Scripture. These principles acknowledged that the strength of organization was found in the reliance members placed upon other members. These principles were some of the hidden threads of social life given by God in his Word for his people, hidden threads that were increasingly exposed by a maturing sociology grappling with the complexities of modern society.

Chapter 4

The American Tradition

In 1907, Edward Alsworth Ross, a pioneer in American sociology, published an influential little book entitled *Sin and Society*. Oliver Wendell Holmes found it to agree with his naturalistic jurisprudence and recommended it to Theodore Roosevelt, who praised its progressive tone. Ross himself considered it to be the most influential work of his long career. It also represented a curious benchmark in a century of American social thought.

Ross's intention was simple; it was to encourage rationality, not morality, in the attitude of people toward others. He rejected the public's contentment with "the surface look of things" and argued that a new perspective was needed as society progressed. Ross contended that modern sin results from the interdependence of people who learn to take advantage of others. Modern sin is also impersonal and more likely to be found in corporate structures than in dark alleys. According to Ross, "the sinful heart is ever the same, but sin changes its quality as society develops."[1]

Ross's thesis is striking for a number of reasons. First, sin, even in this nominal form, is recognized as a factor in human behavior. It is a form of social sin that influences individual sinfulness toward others. Note, too, that the solution is rationality, not morality. Good sociology, then as now, required understanding the meaning of society, not its morality.

Finally, Ross brings society and the person into tension. He recognizes the evolution of society but calls for personal responsibility to reverse its ill effects. Modern society produced new forms of impersonal sins, which public opinion only served to reinforce. The answer to modern sinfulness, Ross believed, was to be found in the enlightenment of the individual and the rationalization of public opinion.

The problem that Ross struggled with was not new in American sociology. For fifty years, naturalistic explanations of the origins and future of society had relied on evolutionary theories. These ideas developed into *Social Darwinism,* the ideology that dominated American social thought in the last half of the nineteenth century. Over against that thought, others had stressed human behavior and explained it in terms of individual consciousness or will. Known as *voluntaristic nominalism,* these ideas assumed that "the structure of all social groups is the consequence of the aggregate of its separate, component individuals and that social phenomena ultimately derive from the motivations of these knowing, feeling, and willing individuals."[2] Ross's work shows how difficult it was to separate these two views of social reality and to move social thought into the twentieth century.

The Pioneers

It is generally agreed that American sociology was born in the post-Civil War period. Social thought at that time responded to the urbanization and industrialization of the nation and the resulting problems. With a frontier and agrarian mentality, the early sociologists, most of whom had roots in the Midwest, sought to understand and influence the new forces of social change. They brought to these problems a diversified zeal for social reform and moral improvement. Intellectually, they relied heavily on the contributions of the European social thinkers of the day.

Although these pioneers also shared a strong religious tradition, its impact on their work was not orthodox. As Hinkle and Hinkle state, "their reformism was a secular version of the Christian concern with salvation and redemption and was a direct outgrowth of religious antecedents in their personal lives."[3] In addition to William Graham Sumner and Albion Small, two of the most influential early American sociologists, at least six others had theological training and had spent some time in the Protestant ministry. Two others, Lester Frank Ward and Franklin Giddings, came from families which included ministers. Since Edward Alsworth Ross had been an orphan brought up in a strong, orthodox Presbyterian family in Iowa, this left Charles Horton Cooley as the only important pioneer without some significant Christian influence in his background.

These six men, Sumner (b. 1840), Ward (b. 1841), Small (b. 1854), Giddings (b. 1855), Cooley (b. 1864), and Ross (b. 1866) are looked upon as the founders of American sociology. Each, in his own way, did much to establish the theoretical foundations and academic integrity of the field. Each was committed to a value-free approach and none, with the possible exception of Small, supported socialism. Each also had to come to grips with the dominant influence that Herbert Spencer had on American social thought at the time. As Cooley has said, "Nearly all of us who took up sociology between 1870, say, and 1890, did so at the instigation of Spencer."[4]

Although Cooley had little enthusiasm for Spencer, this was not true for Sumner, who became the leading advocate in America of Spencer's work. Evolutionary thought had been in vogue in America since the Civil War, largely because of the ready answers it provided for a host of problems in an industrialized society. But social evolution became more popular than it was in England partly because of the prevailing conservative mood in politics and eco-

nomics and partly because of the influence Sumner had upon several generations of Yale students. The result was Social Darwinism, an ideology which
elevated Spencer's views into gospel and dispersed them throughout the halls of
power.

It would not be extreme to say that Social Darwinism was revolutionary in
its effect upon nineteenth-century world views. Hofstadter describes it as a "se-
cularist philosophy... under which economic activity was considered to be above
all a field for the development and encouragement of personal character."[5] Certainly this revolutionary quality can be seen in the following statement of John
D. Rockefeller, Sr.: "The growth of a large business is merely a survival of the
fittest. . . . This is not an evil tendency in business. It is merely the working-out
of a law of nature and a law of God."[6] Listen also to Andrew Carnegie, one of
the most enthusiastic supporters of Spencer: "I remember that light came as in a
flood and all was clear. Not only had I got rid of theology and the supernatural,
but I had found the truth of evolution."[7] And so died the Protestant Ethic. Social
evolutionary thought had killed it in those who exemplified it best.

Although Social Darwinism made its greatest impact on the business world,
it was first accepted into American universities because it offered an alternative
to traditional religious views. The prevailing emphasis was on science, and English science was considered preeminent. But Darwinism's influence quickly
spread to the church as the clergy gained support from men of science. By 1870,
Social Darwinism had made significant inroads into the more conservative, as
well as liberal, church groups. Even Henry Ward Beecher referred to himself as
"a cordial Christian evolutionist" who acknowledged Spencer as his intellectual
foster father.[8]

In spite of its conservative foundations, Social Darwinism was progressive
in its tone and objectives. It relied on a realistic and calculating rationalism in
social relations, and it sought to revolutionize Western society. Benjamin Kidd,
a leading evolutionist of the day, put it this way:

> That the moral law is the unchanging law of progress in human society is the
> lesson which appears to be written over all things. No school of theology has
> ever sought to enforce this teaching with the directness and emphasis which it
> appears that evolutionary science will in the future be justified in doing. In the
> silent and strenuous rivalry in which every section of the race is of necessity
> continually engaged, permanent success appears to be invariably associated
> with the ethical and moral conditions favorable to the maintenance of a high
> standard of social efficiency and with those conditions only.[9]

It is ironic that at the time this was written Weber was lamenting the loss of our
Western religious tradition and its replacement by the kind of rational thought
advocated by Kidd.

William Graham Sumner's Social Darwinism

It was possible to see Social Darwinism as a logical extension of the Protestant Ethic. Sumner certainly saw the successful businessman as a fulfillment of the Protestant ideal, someone who was "fit" to survive in the struggle for existence. In those days one could readily argue by analogy from examples in the animal world simply because the social sciences lacked the basis for supplying contrary conclusions. Believing that competition was a law of nature, Sumner argued that the production of capital was the greatest step forward in this struggle. Since heredity was necessary for the continuation of natural selection, progress was possible only when superiority could be transferred to future generations through such means.

According to Sumner, the American ideals of equality and natural rights were negated by social evolution. For him, the Enlightenment idea that men were equal in a state of nature was clearly false. Rights were given by laws resulting from the evolutionary process. Since poverty was a part of the struggle for existence, it could be abolished only by successful competition in the struggle. This meant that economic virtues determined moral progress which, in turn, determined human progress. Poverty, like all evils, could be done away with in several generations with proper parental training of children. In short, people could rationally and willfully influence, if not determine, their future as well as that of society.

Despite the ideological tone of Sumner's thought, he was a respectable theorist. To his credit, he lacked the determinism of Spencer, who saw society gripped by the intransigency of the evolutionary process. According to Sumner, in order for man to survive, he had to respond to social laws as he responded to physical laws. Since good science required an explanation of those social laws, in 1906 Sumner wrote his magnum opus, *Folkways,* a study of moral progress and probably the best work in a specialized field of sociology at that time. His objective was to show that all institutions can be traced back to the customs from which they evolved. Starting with the simple observation that people meet their needs by trial and error, he concluded that "men begin with acts, not thoughts."[10] These acts are the folkways which become mores when they acquire some moral sanction.

The test of Sumner's theory is whether it describes reality. If we omit Christian standards from the test, Sumner seems to provide a good case: people do tend to act before they think, and these actions do seem to crystallize into institutions with their accompanying definitions of morality. But if we apply Christian standards, we find Sumner's work deficient. We know that for an action to be in agreement with God's will it must come from a transformed mind (Rom. 12:2). If it doesn't, sin will multiply and produce the kind of social sinfulness Ross was so bitterly opposed to.

Nor can the Christian accept the notion that all institutions evolve from human action, as true as that might be for some institutions. If that were the case, God could not have ordained marriage and the family, for example, and the Ten Commandments could not exist. Indeed, in Sumner's thought, if the mores are contrary to religion, then religion must be changed to agree with the mores. To put it more succinctly, religion is always subservient to the mores and never operates outside their authority.

In fairness to Sumner, the blend of ideology and theory in his work was typical of early social thinkers who had difficulty separating "what is" from "what should be." This distinction was blurred in nineteenth-century American social thought largely because of the increasing secularization of society. Sumner was correct to describe the mores of his day as more influential than religion, although he erred in believing it was a necessary pattern. Weber, remember, thought otherwise. Despite his bias, Sumner made enduring contributions to the field. The concepts *in-group, out-group,* and *ethnocentrism,* for example, continue to be useful. More importantly, he provided necessary evidence for the principle of cultural relativity, one of the building blocks of modern social science.

Albion Small and Lester Frank Ward:
The Basic Assumptions of Early American Sociology

As influential as Sumner was, the social thought of the time cannot be judged by his work alone. In the same year that *Folkways* was written, Albion Small, another pioneering sociologist, wrote an article laying out four assumptions characteristic of early American sociology. These were (1) the importance of natural laws as an influence in social life, (2) the idea of progress in the development of society, (3) the use of sociology for melioristic intervention in society, and (4) the importance of individual behavior as influential in society.[11] Together these ideas offered an alternative view of society and man's place in it, a view which had more durability and support over the years.

While Sumner's view of natural law was more popular with the laity of his day, it was Lester Frank Ward's view which gained more acceptance from his colleagues. Although accepting general evolutionary principles, and thus to a degree, Small's first assumption, Ward gave more importance to human involvement in the process of natural law. Human achievement, Ward believed, was the proper subject matter of sociology and was needed for social progress. Since society was not a natural object, sociology could not be compared to the physical sciences. Instead, it shared common roots in natural law with psychology and should study the person before it studied society.

Ward rejected the evolutionary principle of survival of the fittest, arguing that mental activity compensated for other human frailties and was necessary for human progress. Pooling human resources led to the formation of institutions,

especially governmental agencies necessary for the stimulation of social improvement. Although Ward broke radically with Sumner's laissez-faire policies,
he spoke to a sensitive issue in traditional thought: the theological question of
freewill or predestination. Since Ward rejected any religious basis for social
progress, he never intended to raise the issue in a religious context. Rather, he
perceived the intellectual tension residing in these doctrines and shifted it to
social thought. Man was not completely free to do as he would because of the
limitations imposed by evolving social phenomena. Neither was he helpless to
shape social change. Social progress came when the individual and the social
were merged in accordance with principles of natural law.

The idea of social progress, the second of Small's basic assumptions, was
shared by most of the early sociologists. It was a congenial notion at the time,
one which merged evolutionary theory with basic Christian hope in the future. It
also did much to explain urbanization and industrialization, which were recognized as the bases for new levels of progress. Ward, who referred to himself as
"an apostle of human progress," saw the development of education and individual intellectual abilities as key elements in human progress.[12] According to
Ward, the mind and the use of rational means were the forces behind social
change.

A concern for social reform, the third basic assumption of early American
sociology, divided many of the pioneers. Always distrusting the intentions of
government, Sumner was reluctant to give it responsibility for social reform.
Evolution could work best within the context of natural law when government
didn't interfere in the problems of the lower class or other needy groups. Ward,
however, took a populist position and believed that government could, without
bias, express the popular will. In fact, if the general welfare were to be sustained, government would have to take a more aggressive role in meeting the
needs of its citizens.

Believing that sociology's main responsibility was to improve human relations, Edward Alsworth Ross argued that social reform was necessary to attain
this purpose. As the most widely traveled of the pioneers, Ross had observed
that only government could take the direct action necessary to deal with such
problems. Left alone, they would form the seed-bed for revolt and the social
instability that followed. Social progress, Ross believed, was not to be found in
any laissez-faire thinking.

Finally, the assumption of individualism carried with it the idea that society
was not more than the sum of its parts, as Comte and his followers had believed.
Highly influenced by Ward, most of the pioneers sought to understand the human drives and interests which, they believed, shaped society and its component
parts. Even though the explanatory framework offered by natural law remained,
the search for individual motives became an obsession of early American social

thinkers. For most, this meant that individual forces somehow produced group processes and social structures. This idea—that persons are the source of all that is understood as society—became the basis for the developing voluntaristic thinking in American sociology.

This mélange of social thought was too complex, too unstable to remain for long. Some overriding goal or principle was needed to shape the social paradigm and focus it toward the twentieth century. Evolutionary thought continued to have an impact, but it lacked the flexibility to adjust to emerging needs. Besides, it had been imported from England at a time when American society felt less confident about its future. What was needed now was an indigenous social thought, one which expressed American ideals in a new way and could gain the support of the people.

The Social Gospel

The claim that the Social Gospel was a reconstitution of Puritanism is probably not far from the truth.[13] Although it integrated the various post-Civil War humanitarian interests, the Social Gospel should not be seen as a traditional religious attempt to relate the ways of God to man. It would be more accurate to see it as "a vindication of the ways of society to man."[14]

It has also been suggested that theological Christianity was weakened by earlier social thinking and the church was powerless to cope with the problems it faced in the early twentieth century.[15] Consequently, the Social Gospel emerged as a new and unorthodox expression of Christianity, one which was to be "equal to the task of *saving* modern civilization, and of harmonizing its warring interests, classes, nations, and races."[16] The idea was to shape individual motives to overcome social problems with the influence of proper social values, an ideal far removed from the aspirations of social evolution.

Another view of the Social Gospel saw it as a reaction against earlier social thought. On the one hand, it was a progressive force, protesting against the evils of industrialism and individualism produced by evolutionary thinking. On the other hand, it was also a conservative force, reluctant to support the protests of unions and the hostility of the poor. Most advocates of the Social Gospel supported the middle-road approach it offered and believed that pursuit of the Social Gospel was the only way to walk between these competing ideologies. As Washington Gladden, a leader in the movement claimed, "We may go far beyond Mr. Spencer's limits and yet stop a great way this side of socialism."[17]

If the times called for a synthesis of thought, the Social I Gospel was optimistic in its ability to meet the need. Liberal theologians saw in Spencer's organic conception of society an opportunity to replace individual salvation with "social salvation." Orthodox notions of individual depravity were no longer needed. It was now possible to change society by transforming individual character, a notion congenial to evolutionary thinking and the individualism of the day. The objective, of course, was the establishment of an earthly kingdom of God, a Utopian notion well suited to evolutionary dogma. The intended result was a new religion which could put "religion in the service of human evolution, and [set] up a religion of humanity without destroying the religious attitude toward nature and the ultimate reality which lies behind nature."[18]

It is not surprising that another leading social theorist of the day, Charles Ellwood, describes this new religion as "positive Christianity" and agrees with Comte that "one may conceive a positivism with a God."[19] Here was the same kind of merger of science and religion that energized the founding of sociology. By itself, it was thought, Christianity was unable to cope with the problem of modernity. It needed the authority, as well as the method, of scientific thinking. As Ellwood claimed, "Christianity, as soon as it has become transfused with the spirit and transformed by the method of modern science, will bring about the Millennium."[20]

The movement failed in its effort to develop scientific respectability even though it established an American Institute of Christian Sociology at Chautauqua, New York, in 1893.[21] The purpose of this short-lived endeavor was "'to study in common how to apply the principles of Christianity to the social and economic difficulties of the present time 'and to present the kingdom of Christ as 'the complete ideal of human society to be realized on earth!'"[22] Such a goal, of course, could not be accomplished. Its intent was Utopian in objective and radical in method. Consequently, this sort of Christian sociology was unrealistic and as out of step with the scientific thinking of that day as it was with religious orthodoxy.

In other terms, the Social Gospel was an ideology intended to meet the needs of its advocates. It relied on sociology for its ideological support, not its scientific content. As an ideology, the movement ignored the reality of sin as defined in Scripture and provided a definition to support its own purposes. Walter Rauschenbusch, the guiding light of the movement, described individual sin as "selfishness" and claimed that corporate sin "is transmitted socially through custom."[23] He also redefined the atonement in terms of social solidarity, since Jesus had died for the public sins of all those who represented the totality of human evil.[24] As in all ideologies, truth is distorted to serve the purpose of the movement.

To refer to the Social Gospel as a movement might be overstating the point. Instead of a strong organizational base coordinated by a unified leadership, activities were directed by a loose network of persons each working in different progressive contexts. Even individual views differed enough to produce tensions among many of the supporters. The drift to socialism encouraged by Rauschenbusch and others was too much for many in the church who saw an anti-

Christian bias in the humanistic programs of socialism. While it would be impossible to state when the death knell sounded, there's no doubt that World War I destroyed much of the optimism of the day and left the Social Gospel in wreckage.

Paradoxically, the demise of the Social Gospel was linked with a new effort to establish the scientific integrity of sociology. In 1892, the University of Chicago was founded with the financial support and blessing of John D. Rockefeller. A Baptist, Rockefeller had been encouraged to use his wealth to develop a university where Christian learning would provide moral training for leaders of a modern society. The possibility that this endeavor might be inconsistent with his strong evolutionary bias apparently was not considered by Rockefeller.

The person asked to form the first department of sociology in this new university was Albion Small, a son of a Baptist minister who leaned toward Christian socialism. Small had been committed to the Social Gospel, spoke at Chautauqua in its cause, and wrote in its behalf. Given the opportunity to make sociology a formal academic discipline, he naturally merged it with his liberal Christian beliefs. His credo at Chicago was, "In the apparent conflict between self-interest and the collective welfare, the religious motive exerts a most powerful influence in securing social or altruistic conduct."[26] Most of the faculty at Chicago shared this view, even when not committed to the Social Gospel.

Small's statement on the use of religious motives is insightful. First, Christian faith was useful for stimulating moral behavior. It was a means for the attainment of some wider social purpose and for the resolution of social problems. Second, religion provided a mediating influence between the good of society and individual need. It was recognized that people apparently need some religious faith to resolve the tension between these two conflicting interests.

Small's views would have been considered a "Christian sociology" at the time, the kind of social thinking sought by Ellwood and others. It was an attempt to merge sociology and the Christian faith in the interest of a cause. The objective was to produce a new society in agreement with biblical values and consistent with sociological principles. As an ideology, the Social Gospel tried to *construct* reality, not *describe* it. What it overlooked were the realities of human sinfulness and the complex social forces influencing its behavior.

This idea of a Christian sociology is, at best, a precarious notion. An instability existed between the empirical goals of science and the claims of faith in science that could not be easily resolved. Even though a softer form of science might tolerate the kinds of values found in religion, a subjective bias remained that nudged it toward an ideology. It was this bias of faith *in* science that needed to be balanced by an objective view of the world as God intended it and not reinforced by a Utopian program for social change.

The American Renaissance

The twenty-five year period from the founding of sociology as an academic discipline at Chicago to the end of World War I was a time of transition. The enthusiasm of many to Christianize society in a single generation gradually died out. Hope was now placed in education and the possibility of creating a new science of social behavior. Repudiating social evolutionary thinking, the new brand of social thinker conceived of mankind as responsive to social as well as environmental factors. Man was, in short, a social as well as a human being.

In one sense, this view was a rejection of the influence of Spencer and Comte. Members of the Chicago faculty, including Small, studied in Germany and brought with them a fresh approach which gradually replaced traditional social thought. In another sense, it was a synthesis of Spencer's struggle for survival with its response to environmental change, and Comte's concern for natural law and the development of a moral social order. The result was a flood of studies that laid the basis for an exceptionally rich development in American social thought.

There was a freshness to this approach that stemmed from a desire to observe groups in their natural settings. Chicago sociologists studied all forms of environments, from hobo havens to elite neighborhoods and from juvenile gangs to ethnic communities. Their intent was to understand these settings and the effect they had on people. They were also realistic in estimating the impact they might have on the problems found in those settings. While lacking the optimism of their predecessors, they also understood their human limitations and lived under no illusions of the changes they could make.

Without false pretenses, these sociologists saw society in a different light. For them, society had none of the absolute, concrete quality given to it by social reformers. It was not an organism left over from Enlightenment thinking to be healed when something went wrong. Instead, society was recognized as a loosely integrated and complex set of relationships among motivated persons who acted consciously, intentionally, and voluntarily to attain some objective. To understand this kind of society required a new kind of science, one which avoided easy solutions because it posed new problems.

A major shift in thought occurred here, a caution bred by years of failure in efforts to renew society. The attempt was to avoid absolutism in favor of relativism. With greater scientific care, sociologists avoided the dogmatic claim in favor of the careful description of the problems dogging society. Another result was a concern for human relationships as the basic building blocks of society. People, with their needs and desires, had to be understood if problems were to be solved. Evaluating the work of Chicago sociologists of the day, it is probably correct to say that they were more successful in understanding problems than in solving them. If they were less involved in attempting to solve problems than some of their predecessors had been, it was because they stressed the scientist's responsibility to remain detached and objective in the study of them.

At first glance, Christians would justifiably be dismayed at this shift. Chicago sociologists relativized problems and solutions in new and insightful ways. Although many came from orthodox Christian backgrounds, they developed a thoroughly; secular and pragmatic view of human behavior. But they also did a service by focusing on people and their problems, for that is a proper New Testament concern. Jesus never adopted an earthly and social kingdom of God as envisioned in the Social Gospel and earlier social thought. He was always concerned with the spiritual and human needs of people. Because the Chicago sociologists failed to understand spiritual needs, their contributions were limited and faulty. But their understanding of other human needs did much to correct earlier notions and even agreed with many biblical principles.

The agenda at Chicago was clear and surprisingly forthright; it was to explain the behavior of people in specific social situations. This was not a new concern in American sociology, for it had surfaced periodically in the social psychological work of Ross, Ward, and others. What was new was the aggressive and prominent part it now played in social thought. Certain basic assumptions about people and how they behaved had always been recognized in the voluntaristic tradition. Now these assumptions began to shape theory in new ways.[26]

A fundamental assumption of the Chicago school was the importance of *personality*. They believed a person's consciousness and will influenced individual action as well as the behavior of others. Personality was not to be explained, as it had been in the past, by heredity or simple response to external stimuli. Behaviorism was vigorously rejected because it denied the importance of thought and imagination in human action. Instead, man's ability to construct and communicate symbols was deemed crucial since it allowed man to image an action before actually performing it.

Attempting to correct earlier assumptions, the Chicago sociologists unfortunately went too far. In their minds, environmental factors were the dominant influences on human action. Even human personality was usually seen as nothing more than a social product. Robert Park, a leader of the Chicago school, believed with others that social interaction allowed a person to live in the minds of others as well as in his own imagination. One finds little to suggest the spiritual or innate human qualities of the personality. Thus, it may be concluded that people derive their human qualities from their involvement in social situations and nothing else.

Even though problematic for Christians, this view does affirm the unique qualities of human personality. It also asserts the importance of individual responsibility in the use of thought. People possess an enormous capacity for creativity in their ability to make symbols. And when this creative ability is employed, one gains a unique understanding of human and social problems.

The exercise of human will led to another basic assumption: *man's end-seeking behavior*. Despite the influence of social determinism, people are goal-oriented, often in creative and unpredictable ways. With their ability to enter into the minds of others, people may seek unfamiliar goals or even create new ends for themselves. This is not to say that ends are random. According to sociologists, they are shaped by social forces about us. The important thing is that people believe there is freedom in choosing among ends.

Although sociologists share with Christians the belief in freedom of choice, their belief in social determinism is often substituted for the belief in God's sovereign influence over human lives. Consequently, they ignore the importance of obedience and the need to seek those ends God deems best for them. Instead, man wants those social ends supported by the influential group at the moment. The choice of any other end may produce deviance but never sin, which falls outside the assumptions of this social thought.

The idea *that people rationally sought the means to attain their ends* was a third assumption of the Chicago school. It was assumed an actor, before taking action, could understand a relationship between an end and the means used in obtaining it. By anticipating this relationship, the actor knew what to expect and, perhaps, even how to control events for gaining the end. Consequently, the actor need not stand outside the relationship; he may become part of it and even attempt to gain the end by direct intervention.

This kind of rational thinking in which man believes he understands the best means to his best ends is common today. It may lead to distorted notions of human influence and ignore God's intervention in human affairs. It may also distort notions of the nature of human personality as others become simply objects of means to the attainment of some end. Even the actor may be objectified as he becomes a means to his own end.

Such a concern for means is not foreign to the Christian. On numerous occasions, Jesus refers to the proper means to be taken for the achievement of some end: for example, the "narrow way" and the "straight gate." The difference is that the means are not always phrased in social terms; they may fall outside the common and everyday experience of the actor. Encouraged to seek such means, the Christian is moved outside the orbit of social influence and given a choice to be influenced by God.

A fourth assumption the Chicago sociologists made was an acknowledgement that *mental reflection is a necessary basis for any choices a person makes.* Since the attainment of an end is problematic, rational thought is needed to choose the most reasonable means to the end. Once chosen, the means must also be justified before the action can be taken; the person must have some confidence that the action will be successful. If the action is successful or if others follow the same pattern, the choice may then become routine for similar future situations. In short, the choice becomes a rule or norm, but only after logical thought has led to the solution of a problem.

This idea that thought should precede action reverses Sumner's dictum for the establishment of norms: act, then think. People do not choose norms because they maximize the chances for survival but because they have the ability and need to anticipate moral choices in the future. Unlike animals, which learn only from past experiences, people can influence preferred future experiences. Although this assumption, that rules are the result of choice and not change, implies a higher view of humanity, it falls short of the Christian view that norms are chosen because they reflect God's moral essence. The last assumption has to do with *rules* and the fact that they *influence behavior*. Chicago sociologists were quite pragmatic in their view of rules, seeing them as the basis for choosing certain means and ends for the solution of a problem. In general, the rule formed the best response to a certain social situation. In this sense, rules are relative to the situation and form the basis for the moral response within the situation.

In contrast, traditional views of morality had assumed a natural basis for rules. Compliance and morality were not relative to circumstances but were intrinsic to human nature. Most previous social thinking accepted this notion and the ready-made morality it implied. It assumed that people naturally sought the "good" and followed the rules for attaining it.

Neither of these traditions is fully acceptable at face value to the Christian. There is an innate quality to rules suggested by the moral conscience of humans. Regardless of the social setting, rules are absolute because they were ordained by God and established in creation. Sin exists because of this fact and defines human fallibility in terms of disobedience to God, not a lack of judgment in choosing rules.

What is striking and pervasive in the work of the Chicago sociologists is how their treatment of reality differs from earlier American social thought. Much of this view comes from German idealism and its strong influence on Albion Small, Robert Park, George Herbert Mead, and William I. Thomas, all leaders in the Chicago program. Instead of seeing reality as emanating from nature and imposed on people, they conceived of reality as shaped by humans. Reality was formed in the human consciousness because nothing could exist unless it had first existed in the consciousness. The world was not separate from the self but merely a manifestation of personal experience. Reality was never completed but was always in the process of being formed by the person.

The Thomas Dictum

This view was epitomized by W. I. Thomas in a statement so trenchant and influential that it has come to be known as the Thomas dictum. Concerned with social disorganization, he stated, "If men define situations as real, they are real in their consequences."[27] Thomas's problem was how to explain social disorganization and its consequences. He concluded that people organize their lives differently because they are unique and have different needs. As a result, social disorganization is a real and on-going problem that produces additional real problems. In this sense, the human thought process forms reality and must be considered before any action is taken in social issues.

Thomas did not attribute social problems to individual differences alone. He recognized that problems also resulted when social rules broke down. Since social disorganization is found in all societies at all times, there is nothing inherently evil in it. Society is always changing and social disorganization is merely symptomatic of social strains inhibiting the accomplishment of human desires and needs. But, Thomas would say, it is also true that there is nothing inherently moral in social organization. A "good" society does not necessarily make "good" people and vice versa.

This kind of social thought is a radical departure from the past. It is the kind of thinking that was bound to shred any remaining hopes of the Social Gospel. It also left little room for the development of ideological thinking. While the Christian has obvious problems with such a relativistic view of the world, it is also true that this conception of reality goes a long way toward explaining the effects of sin on people and society. When people make choices that ignore God's plans, those choices cause real problems.

The consciousness of modern man is so influenced by this kind of thought that one finds traces of it all about us. A notable contribution of Robert Park was the *marginal man,* a concept developed more fully by his student, Everett Stonequist. Modern man, Park claimed, is characterized by social maladjustment preventing him from satisfactory adjustment to any social group. Consequently, he finds himself on the margin of each. This is the marginal man, a personality type arising from group conflict and change who becomes a stranger in the world. Although living intimately in the world, he can be critical of it because of his detachment from it.[28]

It is also intriguing to consider the Christian as a marginal man simply because of being "in the world" and yet "not of it."

The believer recognizes this marginality when he or she is not completely assimilated into society. This is especially apparent when the person realizes, as a member of a subordinate group, that he or she has a different role in society. Here the person's consciousness is altered as he becomes a critic of the dominant group and thinks perceptively of its inconsistencies. Adjustment is necessary and found in the faith that produces a new meaning for the need to live in a world and to be in tension with it.

The Two Traditions

To this point in the development of American sociology, social thought stemmed from, or was a response to, Comte and Spencer. In particular, sociologists struggled with Spencer's question, "What is a society?"[29] They differed in their definitions of social reality while still sharing many of the same assumptions. Each thinker, however, roughly represented one of two traditions that can be traced back to the founding of sociology and beyond.[30]

The one tradition claims that society has a reality separate from the person; the person is more object than subject and is shaped by society. Society produces data which accurately describe how people are influenced. If people are to be understood correctly, they must be observed by empirical means. This is the tradition of Comte and Durkheim which led to naturalism and evolutionary thought. It was the tradition that tended to dominate Western thought until modern times.

The other tradition conceives of society as composed of interacting persons who, as social beings, make society what it is. In this case, society has no existence apart from people whose reality is expressed in their actions. Here, a human is not an *object* but a *subject* who acts in a willful manner. This is the tradition of Marx, Weber, and the German idealists who further influenced the tradition of Chicago sociology.

But as stated earlier, neither tradition is completely acceptable to the Christian, or perhaps it would be more accurate to say that neither accurately represents the human relationship to God and his creation. Since we are created by God, we are objects in the world he has created and governs by his divine will. In this sense, the reality of the world is prior to humans and must be understood if their actions are to be interpreted correctly. But since people are also made in the image of God and endowed with personality, they are different from the rest of creation. A person is subject as well as object and, in sinfulness, makes a world for himself or herself. There is a reality that belongs to that person alone, and to understand society, it is necessary to understand how social reality is constructed with it.

In the first tradition, that of the positivism of Comte, Durkheim, and modern empirical methodology, the tendency is to reduce all aspects of society to measurement in the hope of defining and predicting social reality. The temptation is to strive for technical control over all social phenomena, a control which may lead to the Utopian thinking so prevalent in social evolution. In this process, the scientist need not be involved with others since there is little of importance to know about them personally. He doesn't have to interact with people or see things from their points of view. Consequently, it is a tradition which may be less humane and responsive to human need. If this tradition seems less problematic, if only because it is better suited for the study of social stability than social strain.

The other tradition of German idealism is less empirical simply because the reality it studies is less observable. This tradition relies on interpretation, not measurement, and requires the scientist to become involved in his data. Since people are the source of all valid data, they are to be understood as subjects, not objects. This means that the scientist must enter into a reciprocal relationship with people and interpret their actions before they act. This was the characteristic practice of Chicago sociologists who poked into very distant and unlikely corners of the city. Since the scientist must attempt to see things from the individual's perspective, he draws close to people and understands their needs and problems. But, with a humanistic bias, there is a tendency to overlook human fallibility and elevate man to an undeserved place of importance. In this tradition, we often find an easy acceptance of relativism and an ignorance of truth outside the world dominated by man.

Neither of these two traditions is complete or satisfactory by itself; the problems of each are partially compensated for by the other. For this reason, the sociologist may best understand reality when both traditions are combined in careful support of each other. Although the Christian may use both traditions to gain a valid and useful understanding of the world, one must always be suspicious of the final interpretation. The two traditions are limited in their attempts to describe social reality and must be supplemented by uniquely Christian assumptions of man and society.

At this point we should examine two of these assumptions. First, since the world, as created by God, extends beyond man's comprehension, *the ultimate nature of the world must be accepted as a limiting condition of social scientific knowledge.* This means that some explanations of social behavior will always exist outside of human understanding. In some cases, people are motivated by goals which cannot be explained in social terms and in other cases people experience inexplicable problems. In any case, the element of faith necessary in any social explanation requires an ultimate, and not simply an empirical, understanding of reality.

The first tradition, the more empirical of the two, has a legitimate concern for scientific credibility and often recognizes this principle of ultimacy undergirding faith. Many sociologists who recognized these empirical limitations but, in their unbelief, could not accept the necessity of ultimacy, opted for a subjective approach and contributed to the second tradition. This, of course, was only a partial answer. By stressing human willfulness, the subjective approach improved understanding of personally motivated behavior but without any basis for predicting it. In short, these thinkers are satisfied in understanding why something happened even when they are unable to explain why it did.

The other assumption is this: *Since people are always constructing a world to their own liking, their sinfulness is a rejection of God's plan for the world and limits understanding of human behavior.* Since Romans 7 tells us that people don't always do what they know they should do, we know they will always have a choice between two options: what they *should* do and what they *want* to do. Without the principle of human sinfulness, we may assume that people will always do what they say they will do. Sociologists recognize this problem in freedom of choice and approach it in either of two ways. The first approach is more empirical and encourages the study of large groupings of people with findings stated in probabilistic terms. Unsatisfied with the statistical solution, other sociologists accept the non-scientific nature of human behavior and shift their attention to *products* of human behavior. The result is they accept what can't be predicted and study it.

Advocates of the second tradition, being more humanistic, tend to be more interested in what people do rather than why they do it. For this reason, they are more accepting of diverse forms of human behavior and do not judge them. But without the necessity of sinfulness in social thought, there is no basis for disobedience or of a moral dilemma. In the final analysis, even inexplicable forms of human behavior may be acceptable.

Modern social thought rarely acknowledges these limitations on its claims to scientific and moral validity. Recognizing these limitations, a Christian view of social reality requires the acceptance of the principles of ultimacy and human sinfulness as boundaries for its study. When these boundaries are defined and applied in specific cases, we understand the limitations of our claims to scientific and moral validity. Hopefully, we also improve the integrity of social thought.

Conclusion

The development of social thought is not measured by the "Eurekas!" of inspired observation. It is only in the slow and accumulated interchange of failures and successes that social thought matures. As nineteenth-century America gave way to the twentieth, this process was dominated by three major trends: the secularization of thought, the shift from a study of society to people, and a concern for theory instead of ideology. These trends have changed little in the past fifty years.

The curious mixture of Puritan theology and Enlightenment philosophy that opened the nineteenth century was too idealistic to continue into modern times. Its moral tone was unrealistic in its hopes for the future and couldn't stand the test of an emerging industrial society. Where Christian expectations were expressed, they often lacked a basis in scriptural principles and usually supported the cultural thinking of the time. Sociologists couldn't make a clear distinction between the way people *should* act and the way they *did* act. Consequently, questions of religious meaning were left behind as the demands of scientific respectability required a concern for empirical data among sociologists.

This period was also characterized by a new conception of social reality.

The old notion of a monolithic society gave way to one composed of an intricate web of relationships among people, private institutions, and governments. Understanding this web was necessary for social science and required a respect for the part people played in it. It was also apparent that this web could be torn when subjected to adversarial relationships as typified by social evolution and the Social Gospel.

Finally, the search for an alternative to early ideological thinking produced a greater respect for, and understanding of, social theory. Instead of building a Utopian society—and nothing has been said of the string of Utopian communities that adorned the country in the last century—the concern was to understand human consciousness and will. For the Christian, there could be a lesson here: a Christian mind is a desirable, and perhaps even necessary, alternative to a Christian society. This seems to be the New Testament model which encourages believers to five as though social circumstances were different; if a racist society cannot be changed, live as though it were a society of equals. In any case, Christian thinking doesn't succumb to the easy assumptions of society. It rejects those assumptions that are mere illusions, develops a unique theory about society, and supports a lifestyle appropriate to it.

Chapter 5

Functionalism

Every social thinker, consciously or unconsciously, must make some basic assumptions about the social world. These constitute a sense of social reality— something to be measured, if one is a scientist, or to have faith in, if one is a believer. If taken seriously, these assumptions form the basis for a scientific theory or a religious faith. A scientist who also holds to some faith would study social reality in terms of that faith as well as in terms of some theory.

Three basic questions are pivotal. Do I stress the reality of structures or persons? Do I explain in terms of consequences *or* causes? Do I look for stability or a change? The history of social thought shows that answers to those questions form a theoretical system and particular attitudes about social reality.

Functionalism has been one of the most enduring yet complex of those systems. Simply *put, functionalism studies social phenomena in terms of their consequences for the larger system of which they are a part.* The functionalist, for example, would ask what a family does for society in the same way that a biologist would ask what a heart does for the body. Faced with the three basic questions above, the functionalist would most likely stress structures rather than persons, consequences instead of causes, and stability before change. Those choices are usually not arbitrary. Traditionally, they result from the social conditions that produced them.

The Background

The roots of functionalism can easily be traced back to the origins of sociology itself. Remember that sociology arose during a time when French society was in turmoil and social philosophers sought the basis for a stable social order. They concluded that achievement of a harmonious society depended on agreement over moral questions, commitment to similar ideals, submission of individual desires to the good of the whole, and a strong religious basis. Although explicitly and vigorously supported at the time, these ideals became more implicit in modern times.[1]

Comte did much to support functionalism with his organic analogy. This conception of the social world as a complex whole not unlike the human body claimed that each part contributed to the survival of the whole. Initially, the question was how various social units contributed to the survival of society. But it became apparent that this was a futile task; the complexity of society prevented the tracing of definable causes and consequences. In modern times, functional analyses of smaller social units have been more fruitful.

The problem was the absence of some notion of the "good" or "normal" society. Without some objective measure of normality, consequences could not be evaluated. Unless it was possible to describe a preferred society by objective standards, one could not state whether a family, for example, was contributing to its own survival. Comte's values preferred a stable society, one in which there is enough equilibrium to return the society to normality in times of stress. In time, these preferences for normality and stability led to the idea that functionalism was more ideology than theory.

Durkheim did much to continue Comte's initial contributions to functionalism. In his first important work, *The Division of Labor in Society*, he found that division of labor was functional because it contributed to the organic strengths of society. Suicide was an aberration in society and a symptom of societal decay. Thus, suicide exemplified the dysfunction of weak social ties. In his final study of primitive people, he suggested that religion performed a major function for societies by providing rituals that, in turn, produced a "collective conscience" external to individuals and unifying them with common symbolic meaning. In short, religion was both the cause and the effect of social unity.

This confounding of functional and causal analysis has been a methodological problem dogging functionalism ever since Durkheim's study of religion. Another questionable aspect of Durkheim's work is the society he studied. Pursuing the idea that religion is universal and performs the same functions in all societies, Durkheim studied the Arunta, among the most primitive people in the world at the time. He assumed that it would be easier to study religion in such a simple society instead of a modern, complex one. Nevertheless, Durkheim developed a tradition of scientific rigor, which continued to characterize functionalist thinking.

The emphasis on empiricism found in most functionalism derived from the presumed reality of social phenomena. According to Durkheim, this reality had its own characteristics which could not be duplicated elsewhere. It influenced a person quite apart from any individual will. This was the world of social facts, a world of good and evil open to scientific investigation.

Although Durkheim stressed the reality of the group over that of the individual, Spencer, whose work had considerable influence on Durkheim, held these two in close balance. While Spencer's evolutionary thought emphasized the person, it was his organismic thinking that led to functionalism. Three principles, especially, characterized this development:

1. Society is a *system*. It is a coherent whole of connected parts.

2. This system can only be understood in terms of the operation of specific structures, each of which has a function for maintaining the social whole.

3. Systems have needs that must be met if they are to survive. Therefore the function of a structure must be determined by the discovery of the needs that it meets.[2]

This statement of principles had a wide influence on the future of functionalism. The problem of discovering needs has continued to produce considerable debate and has rarely been satisfied. For one thing, defining needs implies a subjectivity which may be inconsistent with the objectivity required by the empirical approach. Also, there is a teleological difficulty in the problem of needs that is not readily solved.

Spencer's linkage of structures with functions was the key to the development of structural functionalism, a branch of the functionalist school. It was in Europe, however, that the interests in structuralism flourished while evolutionary theories dominated American thought. In France, especially, structuralists had been highly influential in modern thought and explained human groups as abstractions from their specific content. Structuralists may conceive of persons as biological organisms without social or psychological characteristics. In short, in radical forms of structuralism, people lack consciousness or a mind for thinking.

As with most schools of thought, however, wide differences of opinion exist among structuralists. Claude Levi-Strauss, a prominent French structuralist, believes neither in God nor in man. He believes humanism has failed because it has not understood man in all his contexts. He also believes that order exists not only on the level of social systems but also on a universal level to be found in all societies. According to Levi-Strauss, a pattern of thought may be ingrained in all people making them intellectually equal and desirous of organizing the world in a meaningful way and in agreement with this hidden order.

Spencer's approach to structuralism was less esoteric. Changes in structure, he claimed, produce changes in functions. Since the total social unity depends on these functions being met, its survival is threatened if adjustment is not made to the changing structure. For example, as a structure, the family performs notable functions for society. One of these is the production of children who mature and contribute to society as citizens, consumers, producers, etc. If the family produces few children, society could be adversely affected by this decrease in population in a variety of ways. It is also possible that society might benefit in some ways from such a decrease. It is at this point that the definition of needs is crucial; a definition cannot be stated in general terms but must refer to the needs of specific structures.

Curiously, neither Spencer nor Durkheim had much initial influence on the development of functionalism in America. Only Spencer's evolutionary theory had been of interest to Americans, and Durkheim remained unknown until the late 1930s. Indeed, much of the stimulus for American functionalism came from the desire to provide an alternative to social evolution. It was the interest of anthropologists and missionaries in primitive societies that sparked the rise of functionalism in anthropology, then later in modern sociological circles.

A. R. Radcliffe-Brown and Bronislaw Malinowski, two British anthropologists, were especially influenced by Durkheim's work on religion. They were also aware of the problems in evolutionary thinking and sought an alternative theoretical explanation for the ethnographic data they had accumulated. In contrast to evolutionists who claimed that cultural items could be explained only in terms of their survival, Radcliffe-Brown and Malinowski argued that cultural traits were part of a complete living society, an organism that had to be understood in terms of its related parts.

Two aspects of Radcliffe-Brown's work deserve comment here. First, he asserted, with Durkheim, that *social relations produce social systems*—unique, natural systems unlike any other system. Radcliffe-Brown believed that those systems were influenced by certain universal conditions and that social science could study universal laws by asserting those conditions.[3] Second, *structures can be observed in the interaction of people* who, in their social relations, contribute to the fulfillment of needs. As long as such relations are rewarding, they endure and form structures that are functional.

Like Radcliffe-Brown, Malinowski was intent on avoiding evolutionism by studying societies in the present, not the historical past. He, too, stressed the gratification of biological needs and not merely the survival of society as important for the formation of culture. Believing that gratification of needs was more functional for the group than for the person, he sought to understand what those functions were. He concluded that gratification built social institutions and became more important than the individual for the survival of society.

Since institutions resulted from the gratification of individual needs, Malinowski suggested that universal needs produced universal institutions. Some institutions would be found in all societies simply because all people had certain *common* needs. Specifically, Malinowski gave four such institutional needs: economics, education, social control, and political organization. But Malinowski didn't focus on the question of social integration alone as Durkheim and Radcliffe-Brown had done. He recognized that changes would occur if I an institution didn't perform a specific function. If, for example, the family produced children who weren't-good citizens, society would change. The question that has never been satisfactorily answered is whether society would be worse or only different with such change.

This last point is crucial. It suggests a difference between *descriptions* of institutional change and *explanations* of it. Descriptions of social phenomena don't carry the value judgments implicit in explanations. Unlike other functionalists,

Malinowski didn't assume that he was explaining with his functional analyses. Nor did he generalize from primitive to modern societies, as Durkheim had done. He merely tried to describe simple cultures accurately. In so doing, he did much to reverse the influence of more than fifty years of evolutionary thinking.

The Theory

The anthropological legacy in functionalism provided two notable contributions. First, the tradition of fieldwork provided a rich source of data for analysis. This tradition gave functionalism a uniquely non-philosophical foundation and paved the way for a heritage of classic field studies in sociology. Second, the development of the culture concept emerged as the major social medium by which human needs are met. When commonly understood as *shared meaning,* culture adds an important positive dimension to human relations: people were not the competitive animals portrayed by evolutionism. Although functionalism is primarily concerned with social systems, it makes basic assumptions about people as social beings who fulfill certain social regularities. There is a consistency in human behavior which functionalism is prepared to observe and, wherever possible, to explain. As these regularities become more predictable, they form the social structure and contribute to the social system. When behavior is unpredictable, it is because of deviance which is inconsistent with the shared meaning. But even if deviancy is not functional for that system, it might be functional for another system. In short, deviance could be both functional and nonfunctional at the same time but in a different sense.

To illustrate the working of *functional analysis*—the term preferred to *structural-functionalism*—we can use the example of the incest taboo.[4] The incest taboo is particularly interesting because it is a universal social structure that operates against certain biological needs of family members. Functional analysis first states the part of the system—the incest taboo—to be explained. Then it identifies how it preserves some other part of the system from disruptions. Since the family is organized about cultural expectations, each member has certain shared responsibilities and opportunities, sexual intercourse being reserved for the husband and wife. Finally, the source of the potential disruption must be identified. In this case, it would be the sexual rivalry developing among siblings and, most notably, between father and daughter. Such rivalries would weaken the family structure and the stability it needs to function.

It is safe to assume that the family is one system that should survive. It is a universal institution that contributes important functions to society. That is why the incest taboo functions despite family members' sexual desires; the family is more important than the person. But functionalists do not assume that all structures are functional. Some structures make unimportant or even harmful contributions to a particular system. It is only when we understand the contributions they make to another system that we can explain their continued existence.

A case in point is Robert Merton's well-known analysis of political machines.[5] Merton notes that the dispersal of power in our political systems is not always efficient. Too often the system benefits from leadership that coordinates and consolidates that power. The political boss performs this function in a culturally predictable and even acceptable way in some political precincts. In these precincts, "politics is transformed into personal ties" by political leaders befriending the people and even meeting their physical needs by offering them jobs, educational opportunities, etc. Unlike the welfare worker, the precinct worker offers favors to the poor with no bureaucratic strings attached. For some, politics—directly or indirectly—also offers the opportunity for vertical mobility and the improvement of class ranking. In return, it is assumed that votes will favor the political machine and the party it represents. Without these functions, power would be randomly distributed and the political process would be unpredictable and even chaotic.

As one of the most prominent functional theorists, Merton did much to correct the inherent weaknesses of anthropological functionalism.[6] Three postulates, especially, had been open to criticism. The postulate of *functional unity* held that social systems necessarily showed degrees of integration among their parts. The problem, according to Merton, was that researchers could assume unity and then find the conditions to prove it. Systemic unity, he concluded, should be a finding of research, not an assumption for initiating it. Second, the postulate of *universal functionalism* claimed that if a structure existed in a system, then the system must have positive functions for it. Again, Merton claimed that any positive functions had to be tested before they could be assumed to exist. Finally, *the postulate of indispensability* held that systems have functional needs that have to be met if the system is to survive. Merton argued that, since social systems are uniquely different from each other, functional needs should be empirically established for each system. Durkheim, for example, was clearly wrong to generalize his findings on primitive religion to a modern society.

How does one avoid these three traps of functional analysis? Merton's concern for empirical rigor is one answer. But he also provides another, one in keeping with the idea that people are conscious, willful beings. It cannot be assumed, Merton claims that persons are always conscious of making the best choices in what they do. Persons also unconsciously choose actions that may be harmful to them simply because they don't understand the relationship of the action to its consequences. The compulsive smoker who continues the habit knowing the effects on health is conscious of the meaning of the practice. But some persons may smoke without knowledge of the meaning of their action. Consequently, the *meaning* of any situation for actors must be described before a functional analysis may be completed.

Merton's work recognized the importance of the person in functional analysis and the limitations of his willful behavior. There are always "unanticipated consequences of purposive social action" in any structure: intentional actions that don't always produce the expected results. A famous paradigm developed by Merton sensitizes the researcher to look for *latent functions,* those that are unintended and unrecognized, as well as the *manifest functions,* those that are intended and recognized.[7] In addition, it is important to note the dysfunctions of structures that have adverse effects as well as the functions that contribute to the solution of structural problems.

What Merton proposes in his paradigm is a complete analysis of social structures to understand the balance among manifest and latent functions and dysfunctions. To illustrate the point, Merton refers to Thorstein Veblen's pattern of conspicuous consumption.[8] The idea that people buy expensive items because they are superior in quality is naive according to Veblen. This idea describes a manifest function that doesn't explain all of the consumer's behavior. When we realize that costly products may be bought *because* they are expensive and provide social status, functional analysis has discerned the latent function pattern of conspicuous consumption. In effect, conspicuous consumption is recognized as a potentially dominant motivating factor, suggesting that economic behavior may have important social meaning for many persons.

In one of the most elegant and classic statements in the field, Merton proposed that social structure, not basic drives, may be more important for the production of human motivation. Suggesting that behavior is a response to a relationship between culturally-defined goals and socially-structured means for obtaining those goals, he described five different behavior patterns. Cultural goals were gained in two of the patterns and rejected in the other two. In the fifth pattern, labeled *rebellion,* there is a "rejection of prevailing values and substitution of new values."[9] From this pattern, very different and even unpredictable social structures could result.

An example of how changing values could lead to a new social structure is offered *in* Merton's famous dissertation on religion and science.[10] In this treatise, he writes that Puritanism provided major support for the development of science in seventeenth-century England. Rejecting traditional scientific values in favor of empiricism, the Puritans introduced new values by merging their religious convictions, with utilitarian interests. The result of this union was a new scientific environment viewed by many as the beginning of modern science.

It was this early interest in science that shaped Merton's work and resulted in his recognition as "the father of the sociology of science." Since science was to remain the vehicle for many of his functional inquiries, he never developed a systematic theory of functionalism. This task was left to his mentor, Talcott Parsons, who is recognized as the more prominent and influential functionalist. Consequently, Parsons is also the object of most of the criticism directed at functionalism.

There is some irony in the fact that Merton, the student, published his major work in functionalism before Parsons, the teacher. Merton dealt with the problems raised by Malinowski before World War II and then moved on to other issues. Parsons, however, made his reputation with the publication of *The Structure of Social Action* in 1937 by introducing important European social thinkers to American sociologists. It was only while dealing with questions raised in that book that he became aware of the importance of functionalism and published his seminal and controversial work, *The Social System,* in 1951.

Initially, Parsons was concerned with the individual choices made by people in acting. His original assumption seemed to have been that people have considerable freedom in decision making. They are rational in their attempts to adjust to social conditions and manage to gain the objectives they seek. But it soon became apparent to Parsons that people do not exist in isolation *from,* each other. They interact in social systems, which modify their expectations and limit their rational behavior. In short, people are more conforming than creative in their decision making. Beginning with these assumptions, Parsons set out to develop a conceptual scheme that would explain this process of conformity. The enormously complex system that resulted has received much justifiable criticism on at least two major counts. The first is the fragility of the conceptual scheme which remains untestable and out of touch with reality. As one critic notes, it is "a structure that is all scaffolding and no building."[11] The other criticism centers on the actor as one who is always controlled by the system and not a contributor to it. For Parsons, people are passive recipients of social influence who do little to shape the world about them. In Parsons's thought, the integrity of the social system always takes priority over individual freedom of expression.

Initially, Parsons conceived of three separate but integrated action systems: the *cultural,* the *social,* and the *personality.* Later he added a fourth, the *behavioral* or *organic* system. Together these systems formed a network drawing people together and giving meaning to their action. Of these, Parsons considered the cultural system to be the most important. In fact, on one occasion, he referred to himself as a "cultural determinist." Culture consists of various symbols, ideas, and values that work together to control people. Parsons gives emphasis to moral standards he considers "to represent the superordinate integrative techniques of a system of action."[12]

Actually, Parsons's theory isn't so easily summarized. Parsons goes to great lengths to develop a conceptual scheme known as the *pattern variables* to describe the dilemmas faced by people in decision making. For example, they have to choose between their private and collective interests in order to understand any situation with unambiguous meaning. Presumably, the choice will be a moral one and contribute to the integration of society. But Parsons doesn't clearly state how such decisions may be made or what happens if they aren't. He merely asserts that the equilibrium of the system is maintained as decisions are made.

But Parsons's prior interest is always directed toward the social system and the maintenance of its order. He believes the problems of modern society resulted from its breakdown and would produce, in Thomas Hobbes's words, "a war of all against all." Believing that some of the answers could be found in functionalism, he proceeded to make the following assumptions about social systems:

1. Systems have the property of order and interdependence of parts.
2. Systems tend toward self-maintaining order, or equilibrium.
3. The systems may be static or involved in an ordered process of change.
4. The nature of one part of the system has an impact on the form that the other parts could take.
5. Systems maintain boundaries with their environments.
6. Allocation and integration are two fundamental processes necessary for a given state of equilibrium of a system.
7. Systems tend toward self-maintenance involving the maintenance of boundaries and of the relationships of parts to the whole, control of environmental variations, and control of tendencies to change the system from within.[13]

Reviewing these qualities, one is struck by the similarity the social system bears to an organism. As a former biology major, Parsons quickly saw similarities between living and non-living systems. Consequently, he noted four requirements that all action systems had to meet. Known as the AGIL requisites, they are *adaptation* (the need to adjust to the external environment), *goal attainment* (the need to meet goals established by the system), *integration* (the need to maintain internal harmony in the system), and *latency* (the need to maintain and renew the motivational and cultural patterns of the system). Meeting these four basic needs, Parsons believed, would allow any system to survive.

But what would happen to the system over time? This was a question Parsons could not answer with a static model of a system. Consequently, he developed an evolutionary scheme reminiscent of Spencer's work. The irony here is that Parsons had explicitly intended to move away from evolutionary thinking. Nevertheless, he developed three broad stages of evolutionary development through which societies move. The result is a positive model of social change, one that assumes society will increasingly adapt to its environment. Although Parsons had none of Spencer's ideological tone, his optimistic model of social change strengthened the conservative tone of his work.

With Parsons's death in 1979, much of the influence for functional thinking died as well. Since then, however, some attempts to revive Parson's legacy, if not his theory, have appeared on the sociological scene. Termed *neofunctionalism,* this movement seeks to develop revisions of the earlier work while using some of the basic assumptions. The concern of neofunctionalism is to renew the ideas of normative structures that undergird all of Parsons's work. Its proponents believe that the relativism characterizing social thought in the past few decades has led to the erosion of social structures and social thinking itself. In short, neofunctionalism attempts to challenge much current sociological theory.

In one sense, these are not issues of immediate concern for the Christian. They scarcely seem to relate to the biblical principles undergirding our social thought. But in another sense, the issues are so fundamental in the assumptions they make about people and how they organize themselves, that they cannot be separated from Christian assumptions. For this reason, we turn to a critique of functionalism and the meaning it should have for the Christian.

A Christian Critique

Functionalist thinking, like any system of thought, is not limited to the initiated. All of us decide whether we will use some functionalist assumptions in the day-to-day decisions we make. But since we usually make these decisions on very pragmatic grounds, we rarely understand the implications. Seldom do we ask, "What kind of assumptions are supported when we advocate structural equilibrium? Should we look for latent dysfunctions in organizations?" These are questions hidden in the more immediate decisions made in daily life.

So many issues appear in functionalism that discussion will be limited to four concepts: *culture, universalism, structure,* and *ideology.* It is important to note that functionalism does not exist in a theoretical vacuum; it is both a response to preceding systems of thought and a stimulus for new patterns of thinking. Occasionally, functionalism or any system of thought needs to be evaluated in terms of these historical; contexts as well as the context of Christian values.

Culture

It is the tendency to think in contexts that represents functional analysis so well, especially as it was influenced by Durkheim, who always thought contextually. For Durkheim, culture was *conscience collective,* a common faith providing a moral order for society. A clear distinction between the collective conscience and religion was never made since both functioned to produce in persons a moral obligation to conform to society's expectations.

Parsons developed culture in terms of three components: (1) systems of ideas or beliefs, (2) systems of expressive symbols, and (3) systems of value-orientation. As these parts of a cultural system stabilize, a cultural tradition develops and provides a normative orientation. Like Durkheim, Parsons allows for considerable overlap of culture and religion since both deal with "problems of meaning" in the world. In short, culture and religion may perform the same function in society.

Can Christians accept this idea that culture and religion overlap, or should they see a tension between the two? First, we must remember that much earlier social thinking was atomistic and therefore devoid of any normative consensus. Action was individualistically oriented and competitive. Some functionalists attempted to correct that trend with their own views of functionalism. Modern thinking has returned to much of this self-orientation, and traditional norms are vacuous. Advocates of current values often find the cultural orientation of functionalism to be restrictive and unduly moralistic. But others find functionalism to provide the moral and normative tone needed by society.

Christians could approve or disapprove of functionalist thought. The question is how functionalism compares with a Christian view of culture, and here it suffers. In his classic work, *Christ and Culture,* H. Richard Niebuhr refers to culture as "reality *sui generis*"—the artificial secondary environment—the same term used by Durkheim to refer to the social facts to be studied by sociology. He describes it as the "social heritage... which the New Testament writers frequently had in mind when they spoke of the world."[14] In this attempt to develop a Christian view of culture, then, it can be seen as a corrupted order in need of redemption, not as an order inevitably reducing corruption. "The problem of culture is therefore the problem of its conversion."[15]

In another and more incisive analysis, Henry R. Van Til claims: "Culture, then, may be either godless or godly, depending on the spirit which animates it."[16] Culture is nothing more than a human enterprise if it is animated by nothing more than the human spirit. In turn, we are shaped by culture and directed toward the values it supports. As sinful beings, people also can corrupt culture and are responsible for such actions. But they are also made in the image of God and worship him. In faith, human religious expression can rise above culture and integrate it. In Tillich's succinct words, "Religion is the substance of culture and culture the form of religion."[17]

The blind spot in much functionalist thought is the inability to see that man shapes cultures with his sinful nature as well as being shaped by them. But since he is made in the image of God, he can also influence and direct culture in ways that honor him. Many families today manifest human sinfulness in their brokenness. But others are a fulfillment of God's intention for the family. It is this creative capacity of people in their cultural responsibilities that is so much a part of the Christian view of culture that cannot be understood by functionalism.

A Christian may have three differing attitudes toward culture. *Conformity to culture* is called for when it is in agreement with God's commandments. In this case, culture is a manifestation of God's work in history. But when it is a purely human enterprise, representing worldly standards, *culture is to be resisted.* This is a case of the Christian being "in the world" but "not of it." Finally, there are times when the Christian should seek to *transform culture* by bringing it into line with God's commandments. The personal decision to change, resist, or conform to culture cannot be taken lightly or relegated to the group. It is always a crucial Christian responsibility defined individually or within the group that will wither without a clear understanding of the cultural issues involved.

A Christian, then, can have a high view of culture as seen by God or a low view as seen by man. The temptation is to take a high view and assume that it is the only acceptable view possible. The idea that culture is ordained by God and cannot be relative to different societies can lead to a form of Christian absolutism characterized by legalism and precise standards of objective behavior.[18] To put this view in perspective, we must remember that Sumner made a notable contribution to social science by advocating cultural relativism. Since he argued that the mores made anything right, his cultural relativism can lead to ethical relativism and the denial of any universal ideal. Indeed, some might justify ethical relativism by holding to a high view of cultural relativism.

On the other hand, cultural relativism must be respected simply because it may meet human needs in an integrated system. Modern missionary anthropologists bemoan the actions of early missionaries who, with a "high" view of culture, prohibited polygamy, nudity, and smoking in native cultures. They recognize that customs perform important functions and are to be protected. If this can't be done, then some *functional substitute,* an important functionalist concept, should be provided to meet the need when some custom is removed. In short, a "low" view of culture might be necessary when organic principles of culture are at stake.

Functionalists tend to fall somewhere between these two views of culture. They certainly tried to correct the ethical relativism implicit in evolutionary thinking, even suggesting that universal ethical principles exist. Their view of culture never took the low form found in Sumner's work. But without an awareness of God's work in creation and his control over it, they could not share the Christian's high view of culture. Consequently, functionalists, in an attempt to raise their view of culture, occasionally moved toward Durkheim's view of identifying religion with society. The functionalist view sometimes teases the Christian with its attractiveness, but it cannot be accepted because of its inherent distortion of the Christian faith.

Universalism

Functionalists have been leaders in the quest for cultural universals, those cultural uniformities found in all cultures in about the same form. This is not to say they reject relativism. Modern social scientific data indisputably show that societies differ in the way they meet everyday needs. But the idea that some needs are universal and require universal cultural patterns found in all societies is so intriguing to the functionalist that considerable work has been done on the problem.

In its most general form, universalism suggests that "a consensus of all mankind" exists. This is the notion that some things will be found by all people to be right, real, or attractive simply because they *are* right, real, or attractive. In this sense, cultural universals are responses to inescapable realities expressed in institutionalized forms. Why such a consensus should exist or where these realities might come from are not easily seen as empirical questions open to proper scientific inquiry.

Structuralists like Levi-Strauss suggest that if order exists in the natural world—as found in atoms or planetary orbits—then order must also be found in the human brain. It is this order that is stamped on human beings and uniformly directs all their work in cultural activities. Once the unconscious structure underlying institutions and customs is understood, it may be used to interpret accurately other institutions and customs. In addition, it is the comprehension of this hidden and often mystical structure that brings meaning to an otherwise random and meaningless social world.

The most common functionalist approach to the problem of universalism is to suggest that all humans have similar physiological and psychological needs. In response, societies organize in similar ways to meet these needs: families are established, incest taboos instituted, and religions formed. Since the range of variation among ways to meet these needs is strictly delimited, universal cultural patterns of response result. Ralph Linton, an American anthropologist in the functionalist tradition, even suggested that certain ethical principles existed. Among these principles, he suggests, those that benefit the society are usually granted primary importance.[19]

The existence of cultural universals raises an intriguing question: If universal principles are known and are found to be effective in meeting human needs, why would any other cultural pattern be chosen? Why would some cultures practice polygamy instead of monogamy or others share property instead of having private property? In short, why do cultural relatives exist?

An answer could be the one given in Romans 1: people understand God's truth but reject it in favor of their own form of wisdom. Ethical relativism could simply be a manifestation of man's sinful nature. But could it also be true that God has ordained some relative cultural patterns? God authorized the Israelites to wage war against their enemies. God also evidently encouraged polygamy in some cases (2 Sam. 12:8) and allowed for the sharing of personal property in others (Acts 2:45). Apparently, God has allowed for relative forms of behavior within the absolute forms he requires.

Both Christians and non-Christians seem to agree that cultural relatives and universals may exist together. But they may differ on two points: the reasons for their combined existence, and the content of relative values compared to universal values. Functionalists have difficulty with universalism simply because of the scientific problems involved in describing them and explaining their origins. Without empirical evidence, the argument remains unsettled for the functionalist. Christians, however, may err by referring too quickly to the final authority of God's revelation without considering the available scientific evidence.

Conceptually, the problem has been addressed with reference to the *supercultural:* all "that which is truly beyond culture—for God himself, his nature, attributes and character."[20] What limits the trans-cultural is in the domain of the culturally relative, namely, anything limited to specific times or places. God certainly expressed himself in such ways in his dealings with Old Testament Israel. But he also provides for cultural patterns that transcend the limits of culture and apply to all people in all times. These would include the pattern of marriage in his admonition for couples to leave, cleave, and be of one flesh (Gen. 2:24).

Functionalists take a high view of cultural universals, but not high enough.

The high Christian view of universals is based on the doctrine of creation and the ordination of values for man's common good. This is a proper view, but when held at the expense of a view of cultural relatives, it takes on a meaning that was not intended. Thus, a problem occurs when Christians attempt to raise cultural relatives to the level of universals. This is known as *ethnocentrism* and occurs whenever Christians impose their cultural standards upon others outside that culture. It is the kind of problem God taught Peter about when he sent the vision of animals that Peter considered unclean (Acts 10:9-16). It is just as important to locate cultural relatives on their level and keep them there as it is to locate cultural universals on their level and keep them there. A high view of cultural universals requires this distinction and not merely the assertion that those universals exist.

If there is one thing to be learned from this discussion, it is this: *we cannot assume our judgments on cultural matters are correct simply because we are Christians.* We are also cultural beings and carry that bias with us as well. The first bias encourages good insight into cultural universals, but the second assists in understanding cultural relatives. Each has to be respected for the contribution it makes to the interpretation of cultural matters.

If another lesson is wanted, it would be this: *a balance must be maintained between a high and a low view of cultural reality.* When Christian absolutism denies the reality of cultural relativism, it gives an improper emphasis to cultural universals. Similarly, ethical relativism denies the reality of universals when it gives exclusive attention to cultural relatives. The reality of culture must hold both views in tension, and this cannot be done by empirical means alone. There must be acceptance of the super-cultural basis of culture and a recognition of God as transcendent over all reality.

Structure

All functionalists hold a high view of social structure. Most see organizations as relatively determinate, boundary-maintaining systems in which parts are interdependent to preserve one another and the total character of the system. On the institutional level, a normative system of values guides members' expectations and patterns of interaction. All structures are predisposed to reward conformity and punish deviance.

Christians tend to support these views largely because many of our institutions are rooted in forms of the Christian faith. But rarely do we ask whether the roots are consistent with biblical principles or whether institutions bear the kind of fruit desired today. Christians should take a high view of *institutions* because many are extensions of cultural universals ordained by God. But we should also remember that the New Testament offers little defense for education, the family, or government simply because they were worldly structures at the time. Jesus' primary concern is always for individuals and their relationships with each other. Meaning, in the New Testament, is more clearly found on the human level than on the structural.

Christians, however, can be supportive of the organic principle in functionalism because it is a model offered by Paul for the church (1 Cor. 12). Persons are to fit into the "body" because of the church's importance and because of God's directive will (12:24). But it is also true that people are highly esteemed for the contribution they make to the body (12:22-23). In the final analysis, however, each person has meaning only because of the part played in the body. By implication, the person has no meaning apart from his or her social meaning as part of the body.

Note, too, that equilibrium is implicit in this passage. God has "combined the members of the body" so there would be no division (12:24). But the concern is as much for good interpersonal relations—"that its parts should have equal concern for each other" (12:25)—as it is for stabilizing the structure. Also, all of these matters are less important than the love for others, which maximizes human understanding and potential. In short, structural equilibrium is not an end in itself but a means to a God-controlled end.

It is because the meaning of social structure is defined in God's terms that the Christian view is set aside from the functionalist. For example, functionalists recognize the openness of social structures, but always within boundaries. Organizations are open to environmental influence, but never at the expense of group identity. The early church faced a similar question when it asked, Should the church be limited to Jews or opened to Gentiles? The answer was determined by the fact that the church was no mere human institution. The perception that "God is no respecter of persons" provided a new image of the church that lowered old ethnic boundaries.

Functionalism is also limited by its ignorance of the problem of sin. While it does assume that organizations and institutions are good and people conform to them with the best intentions, analyses of failure to comply are not phrased in terms of human willfulness. In the tradition of Durkheim, it also assumes a certain autonomy of institutions, that they have a reality separate from the interaction of their members. Christians also recognize an autonomous quality in institutions; they were instituted by God and directed by his laws (Col. 1:16).

But some of these institutions are referred to as *principalities and powers* in Scripture and recognized as the work of fallen angels (Eph. 6:11-12). Even though Christ triumphed over the principalities and powers, the effect of evil remains in institutions (Col. 2:15). In short, institutions, in theory, are "good," but in practice, there is an "evil" component.[21]

Despite this evil aspect, Christians are to be submissive to civil authorities (Rom. 13:1). Since God has appointed officials "for the good purposes of public order and well-being" (Rom. 13:7, Phillips), equilibrium in the social system may be divinely ordained. We know, too, that the Roman institution of slavery was to be respected by servants who were doing the will of God (Eph. 6:5-6).

But it is also true that some institutions, when not used as God intended, need to be changed. Jesus, for example, indicated that the institution of the Sabbath "was made for man, not man for the Sabbath" (Mark 2:27). There is, therefore, nothing inherently good or bad in institutions. They are to be evaluated only in terms of their conformity to God's standards.

The idea that functionalism supports a uniformly positive view of social structures requiring human compliance is largely a stereotype based on Parsons's work. Other functionalists support the idea that structures have to be evaluated on their own merits, a position not unlike that found in Scripture. At the other end of the scale, there is even support in functionalism for individual deviance used to promote radical social change. Jesus' rejection of the Sabbath law, for example, is defensible in functionalist terms. The Sabbath was designed to meet a human need, but Jesus, as a functional substitute produced a more perfect resolution of that need. A relationship gained the importance formerly held by the institution.

If we were to single out one point of difference between most modern forms of sociology and the Christian faith, it is this transcending quality that allows Christianity to redefine the meaning of social phenomena. In the same way that Jesus becomes a substitution for human sin, he also replaces the law and claims the obedience formerly given to it. But the law is also designed to show us our human limitations and bring us to Christ (Gal. 3:23-24). In the spirit of Durkheim, who argued that laws are necessary to show us what crime is, the law is not meant to be kept but to be broken so that we might understand the transcendent meaning of the law of Christ.

Sociology cannot reconceptualize social phenomena in this transcendent way. Since there is no absolute basis for it, sociology can only reconceptualize on the social level. It does allow for the redefinition of social meaning, often in terms of the functions and dysfunctions that are performed. A family or community, for example, whether Christian or not, can be analyzed in terms of principles found in sociology and Scripture. Changes in their forms can be described in the same way simply because sociology and Scripture speak to the same shifting human and social problems. But there is always the transcendent potential in the Christian form which sets it apart from other social structures. At this point, the Christian faith becomes non-empirical and unpredictable. It fails the tests of science—as it should on this level.

Ideology

Whenever a transcendent quality is present the danger of ideology looms. Claims of truth may take on a life of their own when they cannot be tested or believed in. This is as true of sociological claims as it is true of the Christian faith. And even though functionalism clings *to* its rich tradition of scientific rigor, it is vulnerable to an ideological bias.

Even in the early stages of modern functionalist thought, Merton recognized the vulnerability of functionalism on this score.[22] In response to charges that functional analysis was ideologically conservative, he argued that this was possible in two ways: if it fell into the postulate traps described earlier and if it was used by groups for non-scientific reasons. In other words, some social component may serve ideological purposes when one claims, without empirical basis, that it is functional for that group.

Parsons was also vulnerable on the question of ideology simply because his theoretical system was difficult to test. Without solid empirical data, the tendency was to rationalize belief in the necessity of individual conformity to a system and reject any contradictory ideas. As expected, Parsons was considered an ideological conservative, a charge he vigorously, and probably justifiably, denied.

This charge that functionalism has a conservative bias began with its inception in the Enlightenment. Durkheim, however, was the one who provided the most important link between conservatism and functionalism, largely because of his claim that society was a unique reality with its own characteristics that could not be found elsewhere. This was the world of social facts open to scientific study and understanding. As long as such scientific validation was possible, ideology was unlikely. But without some empirical basis for social facts, the ideological threat was real indeed.

What was the nature of this threat? First, Durkheim espoused the idea that man was essentially a social being, one whose humanity was derived from society. Second, he believed that moral action in modern society was gained by sacrificing one's self for the social good. Since such sacrifice was not inherent in people, Durkheim believed there must be some common basis for the development of moral obligation. Religion, he concluded, was rooted in society and supplied the motivation necessary for moral behavior.

Here we have a key to ideological thinking: the blurring of the social and the transcendent. Durkheim considered religion to be functional because it encouraged individual support of those group actions believed to be sacred and worthy of unique respect. In his earlier work, Durkheim had logically and empirically defended the importance of the organic principles underlying his theory. But it was in his study of religion as an institution that he emphasized the importance of transcendent values, rooted in society, for helping people to deal with their existential predicaments.

This quest for a moral basis for contemporary society led y Durkheim to outline the elements of a civil religion. With the disappearance of traditional religion, people now had to turn to society as a functional substitute for it. Here was found the civic morality which made people the moral beings they had to be. Society had a transcendent quality as it transformed people into social beings willing to sacrifice their individual desires for the common good. In short, society had the qualities and influence of the divine.

Despite his conclusions, however, Durkheim accurately portrayed the human condition. Rejecting the evolutionary idea that people were biological beings who merely gratified their biological needs to survive, he rightly claimed that human desires were unlimited. Unless these were held in check by societal control, a breakdown in social order would occur. This was the state of nor-maless-ness (anomie), which Durkheim described as characteristic of modern society. Since anomie was likely whenever any crisis *of an* economic or political nature occurred, religion was functional as a bulwark against such rapid and negative social changes.

The Christian can quickly recognize the truth of Durkheim's claims concerning the human condition. For that reason, there is always the possibility that his solution will also be accepted—to locate morality on the social level and to seek social stability. Some even have the desire to see religion as a safeguard against social crises and their destructive consequences. Religion, for them, may only function for its social utility, as described by Durkheim, and make no claims on their submission to an omnipotent God.

So, while the Christian may give some support to Durkheim's diagnosis of the problem, the solution must be rejected as an ideological form of civil religion. Unless the demarcation between the social and the transcendental is clearly defined, we put our faith in the former and try to test the latter. Jesus warned his disciples of this problem when he told them to render unto Caesar the things that are Caesar's and unto God the things that are God's (Matt. 22:21).

The fact that we continue to be attracted to forms of civil religion suggests the truth of the functional analysis of religion. Ideologically, we are committed to forms of economic, political, and social expression and support them with Christian values and symbols. The tendency is as apparent in the practice of apartheid in South Africa as it is in the liberation theology of Latin America. And, more often than not, the truth of the gospel is distorted while it is used to rationalize and defend a particular social program.

Conclusion

Some would claim it is the functionalist that best fits the stereotype of stuffiness and pedantry portrayed in the Archie comic strip mentioned in Chapter 1. In their thinking, Talcott Parsons would most clearly represent this image and give it substance. Consequently, these critics do not take functionalism seriously and dismiss it as a form of *abstracted empiricism,* a term used by C. Wright Mills, a major critic of Parsons and the functionalist school.[23] For them, functionalism is only one attempt to explain what holds a social structure together.

Their point is well taken. Any scientific theory represents a choice among the forms of social reality. Other theories may provide a completely different and, perhaps, even more accurate picture of the real world. On these grounds, Christian assumptions maybe included among those theories and used either to test their validity or to present new definitions of reality.

But it would be a mistake to dismiss functionalism too lightly, especially when we remember that it developed as a response to the assumptions made by social evolution. Functionalism has provided a higher view of society and man than that offered by evolution. Where this view agrees with Christian assumptions, one finds the hidden threads of theory located also in Scripture. It must also be remembered, however, that functionalism is always limited and distorted by its erroneous perceptions of God and his transcendent place in creation.

Chapter 6

Conflict Theory

A homely definition of a sociologist describes someone who goes to a football game, becomes a part of the crowd, and then watches the crowd instead of the game.[1] This is a proper, albeit irreverent, definition. The sociologist's attention is caught *by an* immediate situation demanding explanation. Often such realities are ignored by the crowd, forcing the sociologist into a minority role. In such cases, the sociologist may properly be a curious and critical outsider.

This is the image of the sociologist as a radical critic of the majority view. In the sixties, when such a view was chic, the sociologist could be portrayed as the alluring woman in the Archie comic strip. More often, this radical position threatens us because of its opposition to society and the majority view. Christians, too, may share a radical position whenever they are drawn to a critical evaluation of society.

The sociologist, as viewed by the functionalist, is something of a priest who wants to support traditions and social harmony. The radical view presented in conflict theory describes the sociologist as a prophet, someone who calls for change and repentance for past social sins. This role especially fits modern conflict theorists who gained an audience by denouncing functionalists to the public. They were outsiders in the sociological camp as well as in society. On some occasions, their criticism was well-placed and needed. At other times, their condemnations were ideological messages from false gods.

The Background

One of those false gods was Karl Marx. Despite his many accurate insights, Marx erred in some of his views of reality and man. His ideological commitment to these views justified, in his thinking, world-wide revolution. Conflict was used not merely as a description of the world as it is but as a means for the world to become what he felt it was becoming as a result of the dialectic.

But philosophers had recognized the existence of conflict in society long before Marx. The fragility of organic models of society could not hide the inevitable inter-human conflict beneath the surface. When Durkheim observed conflict, he defined it as pathological and tried to correct it. Christians tend to accept this model, assume conflict is the inevitable result of sin, and seek to eliminate it.

Other philosophers saw conflict as normal or, as in the case of Marx, even inherent. Thomas Hobbes, for example, described the human condition as a struggle for survival. The desire for power was common to all and motivated every act. The state evolved merely to prevent social conflict. To do this, it required final authority and the subordination of all social bodies, even the church. For Hobbes, conflict was the problem and order, the solution.

A similar but more pragmatic approach to conflict was taken by Niccolo Machiavelli, who also accepted power as necessary for the maintenance of social order. Since people are good only when constrained, the prince was advised to use force in direct and indirect ways to keep a secure political order. For Machiavelli, conflict with opposing powers could be the necessary means to a stable society.

Although conflict theorists differ in their interpretations of conflict's role in society, they usually agree on two principles. First, social reality is located on the individual level as well as on the organizational. In either case, conflict results from some attempt to resolve a problem or produce a change. Second, there are as many forces working for conflict as there are stabilizing factors in society. Some of these forces are blatantly hostile and revolutionary while others are merely symptomatic of social change. What the theorist saw among these forms of conflict was usually what he got.

What Marx saw was *economic man,* the laborer who could be free only when his human powers were developed to the fullest. Society's responsibility was to provide the material basis necessary for people to maximize this human potential and individuality. Unless people could be liberated from the material and spiritual constraints of society, they could not develop their individual uniqueness. This was a high view of man that could be maintained only with the omission of God as a higher authority.

A materialist as well as a humanist, Marx believed that the scarcity of property would lead to conflict over the distribution of those limited resources. As persons became aware of their collective interests, legitimate power would be questioned as the powerless found new sources of power to oppose the dominant group. The more polarized the powerless, the more violent the conflict would become. In this view, conflict becomes the major source of change in the social system. As the conflict increases in violence, the changes in the system also become more radical.

Everywhere Marx looked, he saw the need for conflict. Radical change was needed because power was located in institutions and not with people. It was found in the capitalist class and not among the workers. The reason for this distortion was human alienation; man's natural rights had been projected outside of people and reified or personified in institutions. "The powers and capacities attributed to the gods were in fact man's own powers and capacities; the divine law was nothing but the law of man's own nature."[2]

Alienation, as a fundamental quality of humans in a capitalist society, became a series of enslaving relationships experienced by people in institutions. For this reason, conflict could not be abstract. The institutional base had to be substantially overturned if power were to be returned to the people. Unless this tangible struggle was constant, social and human qualities could not be fully realized. It is only through such conflict that human potential could be maximized and people could become the persons they were meant to be.

At the bottom of this thinking was the Hegelian dialectic. But unlike Hegel, who conceived of a dialectic of ideas revealed in the material world, Marx thought of the dialectic in terms of the material. He believed that changing the material would change the ideal and vice versa. And since the dialectic was part of the historical process, conflict in the present would have tangible and positive effects on the future. In short, conflict would bring in utopia.

Marx believed that conflict had to take the form of revolution if society were to be overturned and a new social order established. In his vision of history, revolutions were an expression of historical necessity because they performed necessary functions. When the conditions for revolutions appeared, they would occur. Marx did not believe that revolutions *had to be* violent although their inevitability suggested they *would be* violent.

Marx saw revolution as a political act because it functioned to revolutionize civil society. But since capitalist society is a manifestation of alienation and human degradation, revolution was needed to negate this inhumanity. What revolution would accomplish was "a *restoration* of the human world and of human relationships to *man* himself."[3] As a complete and restored human being, the person also becomes a complete social and moral being in a Utopian state.

There is no question that Marx's doctrine was, for him, a religion. Here we see revolution as the basis for conversion and salvation. Conflict is part of the mystical sweep of history that destroyed the old in preparation for the new. But people could not leave it at that. "Men do not build themselves a new world out of the fruits of the earth... but out of the historical accomplishments of their declining civilization. They must, in the course of their development, begin by themselves *producing* the material conditions of a new society."[4]

No sociologist since Marx has had a comparable utopian vision. For this reason, if for no other, he wears the mantle of a prophet, not a sociologist. Some of Marx's contemporaries, thinkers like the Englishman Walter Bagehot or the Pole Ludwig Gumplowicz, were suspicious of any theory promoting the progress of humanity. They saw the masses as dominant over the person, a condition leading to war and continuous social struggle. This kind of pessimism was more typical of the non-evolutionary theories of the day and certainly portrayed the unfolding of history more accurately.

All of these theories were on a grand scale and typical of the macro-level thinking of the day. But one sociologist who always worked on the micro-level developed a view of conflict that remains important today. This was Georg Simmel, the contemporary of Durkheim and Weber who had such a strong influence on the leaders of the Chicago School. Never ideological and always concerned with the intricacies of hum an relationships, Simmel saw conflict in a different light. It was a normal process in society and posed no necessary threat to it. As part of social life, conflict was an everyday fact that people needed to understand, not to exploit.

Although Marx and Simmel both considered conflict to be inevitable, Simmel stressed its integrative, not its divisive, qualities. Unlike Marx, whose theory is limited to society and its economy, Simmers theory applies to a host of diverse group situations. Conflict, for Simmel, did not necessarily lead to significant social change. Instead, it was part of the normal process that shifted between conflict and cooperation. Conflict simply acted as a stimulus for the group to resolve its problems, and little else.

Since Simmel's theory of conflict is based on his wider views of social relationships, it would be best to summarize those briefly here:

1. Individuals are both inside and outside of society. As Simmel put it, social individuals must recognize that a society is "a structure which consists of beings who stand inside and outside of it at the same time."

2. Individuals are both objects and subjects within a network of communicative interaction.

3. Individuals have an impulse to be self-fulfilling or to be self-compensating; that is, they seek an integrated self-concept. Similarly, society itself tends to gravitate toward the means to its own integration. However, the integrity of the individual and the integrity of society are often in opposition.[6]

These ideas are of special interest for the Christian. People share some of society's interests and oppose others. The result is mixed personal motivation allowing people to see both sides of reality at the same time. Some aspects of society are worthy of support while others need to be condemned. As subjects, they oppose society's views when in conflict with their own. As objects, they come to understand the effects of their actions and support some of society's interests. In effect, people may simultaneously be inside and outside of society.

Here we have a model for the Christian as someone who may be both "in the world" and yet "not of it." Simmers theory allows this model because he isn't committed to the functionalist standard of socialization. People may conform to social standards at one level and reject them at another. This view in no way mitigates the reality of the person or society. Each fulfills its own identity in different and somewhat complementary ways.

Simmel was always interested in the interaction of people and rarely concerned with individual behavior. Conflict, in his thinking, was not caused by a single person or group. It was always a product of group efforts to deal with problems. Since groups experienced the same kinds of problems, conflict did not vary greatly from one group to another. One might find the same kind of conflict in a church or labor union and deal with it in the same way. In other words, the same form could be expressed with very different contents.

In Simmel's thought, forms of domination and subordination led to conflict. Unlike Marx, who limited his perception of power to the class struggle and the inevitability of revolution, Simmel saw conflict in any form of super-ordination-sub-ordination relationship. Slavery in Rome, for example, could be compared to its counterpart in America. It could also be compared to the slavery of a person to a thing, such as an idol or some principle. Even a "conflict of duties," found when a person is the "servant of two masters," illustrates two forms of conflict—one an internal conflict based on conscience, and the other an external conflict with the master.[6] In such a conflict situation, choices have to be made, suggesting there is freedom as well as dominion in some forms of conflict.

With typical brilliance, Simmel analyzed the shifting, complex patterns of an array of relationships, each one moving in and out of forms of conflict. But the dominant theme to which Simmel always returned was this: "Conflict is thus designed to resolve divergent dualisms; it is a way of achieving some loud of unity."[7] If we see conflict only in an isolated relationship, it may appear negative and damaging. It is when we see that relationship in a larger context, one including other distant and even obscure relationships, that the negative and dualistic elements of conflict may appear to be positive. It is then that conflict may even be functional.

Like Marx, Simmel is a humanist. At one point he states, "Man's most valuable object is man, directly and indirectly."[8] People depend on others for their own self-actualization simply because the person and society are both cut from the same fabric. According to Simmel, "the basic struggle between society and the individual is integral to the general form of individual life. It does not derive from any single, anti-social/ individualized interest."[9] Even self-consciousness did not precede human action but "arises as human impulses are fulfilled and as subjects act on external objects that are *separate* from self."[10]

Unlike Marx, Simmel is not a utopian. He had no vision of conflict producing a society with completely harmonious relationships among its elements. For Simmel, incompatibility between people and society would always exist and produce further conflict. In modern society, especially, people cannot be completely absorbed by the group. They have an autonomous quality that needs to be nourished if they are to maintain themselves. Life, for Simmel, meant that persons could not be completely integrated into society, communist or otherwise.

The Theory

This idea of a utopian society was raised by a leading conflict theorist in a provocative essay critical of Talcott Parsons's work.[11] Ralf Dahrendorf compared functional theory to Utopian thought, especially in its ability to maintain existing structures. Dahrendorf's case has merit, although he also could have acknowledged the utopian qualities of a classless state. If functionalism advocates utopia in the present, Marxism seeks it in the future. The idea that two competing theories might be utopian in objective is intriguing because it suggests that both might also share other common ground.

It was this critique of functionalism that gave modern conflict theory a legitimacy it had lacked in the past. When the major critics, C. Wright Mills and Irving Louis Horowitz, called for a "new social science" opposed to the bureaucratic use to which functionalism was put, they found a responsive audience.[12] This critique included an implicit humanism intent on asserting the freedom of the person within the constrictions of an increasingly complex society. It was critical of the new spirit of human engineering found in modern social science. But it also probed the possibility of another form of social reality, *one* which could coexist with the utopian model perceived in functionalism.

Dahrendorf claimed that such coexistence was possible simply because both theories were complements of each other. He saw the need both of an integrative and a coercive theory of society. The first would realize the need in society for ongoing equilibrium through certain recurrent processes; the second would recognize that a social structure is held together by the force and constraint of constant social change. In theory, both models appear to be mutually exclusive of each other. But both theories are needed to deal with the sociological problems to be explained only with the use of one or the other approach. Dahrendorf explains: "For sociological analysis, society is Janus-headed, and its two faces are equivalent aspects of the same reality."[13]

Intriguing questions for the church emerge here simply because it has not always held to one or the other model. Jesus, for example, was opposed to the Jewish leaders but taught in the temple and resisted radical change in its structure (Luke 19:47; Mark 1:44). Martin Luther offers at least as clear an example of a personal struggle to work within the ecclesiastical structure while opposing it (at least for a time). Currently, religious leaders can also accept this inherent ambiguity as a necessary, if agonizing, fact of church life. Consensus theory cannot be limited to the church and coercion theory to society. A realistic view of the church and the world suggests a more complex model of reality.

With this dualistic view of society, it should come as no surprise that Darendorf s theory has been referred to as *dialectical conflict theory*.[14] Institutionalization is a cyclical or dialectical process producing a shifting pattern of social stability and conflict. As one group gains authority, another group resists it with opposing interests seeking to gain comparable but superior power. Conflict is dialectical since the resolution of one conflict pattern creates an opposing set of interests producing another basis for conflict and so on. The result is social change, often unobserved and uncontrolled as society moves into new forms of social structure.

A key notion in Dahrendorf s work is the belief that *authority is always found in positions and not in persons*. This means that a person in authority in one social setting is not necessarily in authority in another setting. In fact, authority may be reversed among persons. A person who experiences dominance over another in one group may be subservient to that same person in a different group. Nor is authority constant. It is constantly shifting among people whose interests and the means for meeting those interests are changing. Clearly this view of conflict is quite different from Marxist theory with its conflict limited to two economic interest groups.

Since modern conflict theory originated as a critique of functionalist theorists in the decade or so after the publication of their early works, it is not surprising that it appears as an inversion of functionalism. Both theories are wholistic in their concern for the interrelationship among the parts of society. Both theories have an evolutionary bias in their perception that society is improving. Finally, both theories are basically equilibrium theories, one wanting to maintain social stability and the other seeking to establish it in the future.[16]

A recent conflict theorist, Randall Collins, offers a more personal view of conflict in everyday life. He sees conflict originating among all those self-interested persons who try to maximize their interests as they see them. Collins also perceives people as non-rational beings who respond to emotional appeals to satisfy their interests. Since persons have varying resources, some are better able to resist such appeals. The poor, for example, are more vulnerable than the wealthy to the "get rich quick" schemes of state lotteries. When inequality occurs, those with more resources are likely to exploit those with fewer. But unlike Marx, who saw such a struggle as a relentless march toward revolution, Collins recognizes that such exploitation could be unintentional and even unconscious. In short, people do not always see how their own behavior may adversely affect others.

Dahrendorf and Collins are not committed Marxist theorists, especially when compared with others who are more ideologically in support of Marx. Some theorists choose not to drop Marxist terminology and continue to work from the assumptions of class consciousness and Hegelian dialectics. Others, in a more critical tone, merely seek to change society for the benefit of individuals. All, however, show an increasingly humanistic bias in their emphasis on the importance of the personal over the social.

We return to one conflict theory buried in this potpourri of social thought that demands further attention: the work of Georg Simmel, especially as it has been consolidated by the noted American sociologist, Lewis Coser. Like Dahrendorf, Coser saw the roots of functionalism and conflict theory as intertwined. But going beyond Dahrendorf, he systematically showed the positive functions of conflict for the maintenance of social systems. Because his theory stresses the positive functions of conflict for the group and not the person, it is referred to as *conflict functionalist theory.*

Coser takes Simmel's thesis that "conflict is a form of socialization" as the beginning point of his own theory.[16] This means that conflict is not merely a pathological expression of functionalism. Instead, it is an integral part of any social system that Parsons and others overlooked. But in his critique of functionalism, Coser is no Marxist. He demonstrates that no group can be completely harmonious since groups require disharmony as well as harmony. All systems have certain needs that can be met only through conflict.

Take, for example, the need to bind a group into an identifiable unit. Coser shows, with Simmel's help, that conflict establishes the identity of a group and maintains its boundaries in a surrounding social world. This is done when the hostility of one group toward another builds in a group-binding quality of high morale and group identity. Since boundary-maintenance is a prime need of social systems in Parsons' theory, conflict or competition with another group may be an essential requirement of any social system.

Enough biblical principles fit this conflict theory to suggest that it contains more of those hidden threads to be found in Scripture. In John 15:18-20, for example, Jesus implies that conflict with the world helps to define the group. The disciples gain an identity as Jesus' followers when the world hates them as it hated him. Conflict provides a boundary for the group, that they might not be "of the world" while being "in the world." But elsewhere, group conflict is deemed harmful for the spread of the gospel, and groups are encouraged to merge. This was the case in the early church when its boundaries were being defined. The old barriers were broken as Gentiles were allowed in (Acts 13ff.). Conflict did occur among the leaders of the church, but it was not of the functional type that helped to define the group.

Since no activity in society compares with spreading the gospel, we cannot always fit sociological models with biblical principles. But that is not to say that these models are irrelevant for the church and believers. Christ and others manifest sociological principles on enough occasions to certify that the principles are exemplary for Christians as well as non-believers. The problem comes in trying to understand when group goals or actions represent the transcendent will of God and when they merely represent some group or individual needs.

Coser considers this problem in his discussion of ideology and conflict.[17] Referring to Simmel's work, Coser states that when objectification of conflict moves a goal away from personal and subjective levels to a collective level, conflict becomes more intense. This is especially true when persons struggle as representatives of groups with which they identify. Depersonalization occurs as the distinction between individual and group values is blurred. The conflict is then raised to an ideological level and the intensity may even lead to violence.

Christians are not immune to such situations. Demonstrations against social evils may require them to share the group's values, with the likely escalation of conflict. The alternative is to personalize the situation and deal with it in terms of personal conscience instead of group consciousness. Believers need to look hard at group actions to decide whether they are consistent with God's purposes. Marx would have preferred to depersonalize the conflict and raise the level of intensity. His purposes were always accomplished in the fervor of group activism. To resist that trend, the Christian must take the issue personally, even to the point of withdrawing from a group of Christians that sees issues only in terms of its own needs.

The problem revealed here is that the Christian's loyalty is not solely to the group. If it were, the issue could be depersonalized, phrased in terms of group needs, and the conflict joined with a clear conscience. Nor can the problem be understood simply in personal terms and dismissed with the exercise of personal conscience. If the Christian's loyalty is to Christ alone, then one of the following positions must be taken: (1) sociological principles cannot be applied to a transcendent situation, (2) loyalty to Christ must be understood either in terms of personal conscience or group consciousness, or (3) sociological principles must be understood in terms of the unique transcendent meaning they have in certain cases. If this final choice is the most intriguing, it is also the most challenging to implement.

Coser might provide a key for the Christian's analysis of conflict when he stresses the importance of consensus. Most dialectical conflict theorists like Dahrendorf believe that causes of conflict come *from,* contradictions or conflicts of interest. Since this approach stresses human interests, people choose conflict when they believe those interests are not being met. Coser, however, believes that people are not aware of their personal conflicts of interest until after they no longer see the system as legitimate. In other words, their lack of support for the system causes them to develop a conflict of interest with it. It is the loss of consensus with the system that legitimates conflict, not the existence of conflicting self-interests.

This is a principle the Christian may work with when deciding to support a group in a conflict situation. If the group's position on some issue seems legitimate on scriptural grounds, and the person can share the group consensus on the issue, then he or she could support the group in its position. But if consensus cannot be given to the group's position, that is, if the group's position on the issue is unclear, then it is likely a decision will be made on the basis of personal conflict of interest alone. The Christian's loyalty, then, is not to Christ or to the group, but only to self.

Coser's theory elaborates a number of propositions concerning various aspects of conflict. To follow these in any detail would lead us astray. Instead, it is important to emphasize two points already made. First, *conflict and equilibrium are reciprocal parts of the same complex reality.* One cannot be supported to the exclusion of the other. Further, *there is nothing deterministic about conflict or equilibrium theories.* Unlike Marx, who saw conflict as part of the historical process, the Christian is responsible for an analysis of and involvement in conflict. There must be an interpretation of the place conflict holds in the immediate situation as well as in the ultimate place assigned to it by God.

A Christian Critique

Sociology involves a study of social contexts. Early thinkers believed that these were simple, involving a person in no more than one context at a time. Marx, for example, believed that social class was the determining social context for human behavior. This apparent error overlooked the fact that we are influenced by a multitude of overlapping and often conflicting social contexts. Since we cannot be in agreement with all of these at the same time, dissensus is inevitable in some.

Christians, too, think in terms of social contexts, but with this difference: there is a transcendent context known only to the believer. For this reason, the Christian's thought pattern ought to differ from that of the non-believer. The compelling need is to be in agreement with that transcendent context and to conform to God's will as one best understands it. That means the Christian can prioritize responsibility, fully aware that conflict in some social roles will also be inevitable. But when these roles are put in a proper order, conflict becomes tolerable as well as comprehensible.

Oversocialization

A popular critique of functionalism argued that it advocated an oversocialized view of man.[18] Today, many still believe that problems are solved by socializing people and integrating them into groups. If people can only internalize social norms and be motivated to fit in with their peers, the argument goes, then social order will be maintained free of social problems.

Dennis Wrong believes that sociology should be concerned with social problems but not by avoiding an open encounter with them. Over-socialization, he claimed, simply had people accept their problems as normal. But when Wrong speaks of social problems, he is not thinking only of those found in modern society. He is more concerned with universal social questions inherent in the very nature of all human societies, questions of concern for the Christian as well.

Another way of stating Wrong's case is to suggest that his interest extends beyond the context of time. The problems found in all societies are not responsive to sociological solutions, least of all socialization and integration. Nor is human nature limited to the one-dimensional quality found in modern society. It is too broad and complex for such containment. A proper view of mankind, Wrong argues, understands those human factors resisting socialization and gives them expression. These are both psychological and biological factors and allow man to be a *social* animal if not a completely *socialized* animal. As important as the social act is in human experience, the subjective influences of emotions and fantasies are no less important. Even biological factors should not be overlooked, for these are the common human ingredients shared by all social animals. Without them, humans are nothing more than abstractions of their real selves.

It is no accident that Wrong wrote his article when he did in 1961. He was in the vanguard of those social critics who opened the way for the protests of the sixties and the attacks on depersonalization in our bureaucratic society. His conceptualization of the problem of over-socialization was both timely and insightful. Having done that, he offered no solutions. He was not part of that emerging Marxist core that advocated revolution, and his best efforts feebly returned the problem to the biological and psychological levels.

Wrong is correct to claim that sociology needs to explain the universal human problems found in all societies. He is also right in believing that these problems can never be "solved."

For this reason, his criticism of functionalism is justified: it may give us a false sense of security that science can solve the human and social problems of mankind. Where he comes up short is in his diagnosis. He cannot understand the transcendent, spiritual nature of the problem which moves the questions out of a social context and into the eternal.

The Christian can approve of a great deal of Wrong's critique. We can see the hidden threads that are there. Surely we can share his indictments of over-socialization and over-integration. If we are to resist the world, we cannot place both feet firmly in it. Nor can we seek to improve our social image if we are first to conform to the image of God. We can even approve of his criticism of those theorists who see no further than a social context. But as a humanist, his understanding of the human condition is inadequate. He fails to appreciate, or even recognize, the insistent spiritual needs of humans.

In fairness to Wrong, he was caught by an abiding problem in social thought. When thinkers saw the sterility in historicism and naturalism, they turned to social explanations. When these social context theories falter in their explanation of the human condition, where does one turn? Wrong took a logical step and turned to the human level for answers. The fact that little help was found suggests that the reality sought by Wrong is not to be found there. Failing to deal with the spiritual problem, he joined other theorists who attack the theories of the day in the hope that a proper balance will be found. When theory is perched on such a seesaw of futility, it will always vacillate in its incompleteness.

Christians can benefit from the failures of social theorizing by noting that little is gained by attacking the social thinkers of the day. This approach merely returns the criticism to the social context and forces Christians to battle their opponents in the secular arena. Even when success is gained, it is likely to be in those problem areas found only in a particular social context. It is unlikely that any progress will be made on those questions of human and social need that transcend all social contexts, the questions that Wrong correctly describes as "inherent in the very existence of human societies."[19] To deal with these questions, Christians should avoid the conceptual seesaws of our culture. Unfortunately, there is a hiatus in this area of hermeneutics that usually forces us back to a critique of contemporary social thought and little else. These are transcendent problems that demand the transcendent answers to be found in Scripture. Jesus offered a conflict model in his reconceptualization of human and social needs. He preached a new kingdom and redefined the meaning of poverty, work, authority, and all those social meanings taken for granted by most Christians today. This was a radical act which brought him into basic conflict with the world. It also provided a model for our understanding today, a model which needs sensitive and informed interpretation.

Disequilibrium

Wrong suggests that over-integration supports "the view that man is essentially motivated by the desire to achieve a positive image of self by winning acceptance or status in the eyes of others."[20] Since this view is linked with over-socialization, if not derived from it, the implication is that we learn to seek status in the eyes of others. Consequently, we need to conform to the group's expectations simply because they represent the fountain of the status we seek. Anything that threatens the group indirectly threatens us and jeopardizes the status we desire. Thus, we support the group and avoid disturbing its delicate equilibrium.

As noted earlier, Christians are inclined to support the equilibrium model because they believe it is right to maintain the social order as described by Scripture. What is not understood is that support of the group may also imply self-pride and personal status-seeking. For this reason, support of the status quo is not always the preferred option for the Christian. There are times when the organization is to be resisted even to the point of causing tension and disequilibrium.

The problem, again, is one of context. Any society that is evil clearly demands resistance from the Christian. But the perception of that evil is not always apparent to the Christian. The point is well-illustrated in the following description of the Christian church under Hitler:

> Christianity had become confused with such a package of cultural factors that it was no longer distinguishable on its own. Christianity was German culture. Christianity was middle-class morality. Christianity was respect for authority. Christianity was for law and order. Christianity represented an established class in its opposition to turmoil from the left. It was on this basis that so many Christians mistook the Nazi movement for a religious renewal.[21]

Over-integration, apparently, may blind us to the true nature of a group.

The reality of some groups, however, is indisputable. The family and church groups, for example, would command our support because of their clear identity in a Christian context. There would seem to be less reason for resistance or conflict with such groups. In this case, over-integration would appear to be more functional than dysfunctional.

Jesus offers us another viewpoint on this matter with his comments on a disciple's proper relationship with his family (Matt. 10:34-37; 12:46-50). The family may be a burden if it keeps a believer from establishing wider relationships. Christians may have to leave the family for the purpose of spreading the gospel even, if it produces family conflict. Further, when Peter expressed his concern for Jesus' welfare, he was chastised because he looked "at things from man's point of view and not from God's" (Matt. 16:23). Apparently the question is not group unity or conflict but whether we see things from man's point of view or from God's.

A principle seems to be at work here, the principle of the transcendent context. When we look at things from man's point of view, we are on the level of social contexts which offer many conflicting opportunities. One is to enhance one's self-image by conforming to group expectations. But this goal is in tension with the Christian value of humility. The problem is resolved by seeing things from God's point of view and resisting conformity to group expectations.

The principle of transcendent context prioritizes our options and resolves our social conflicts by giving priority to God's point of view on a problem. You may remember that Simmel made a similar observation when he said that conflict achieves unity by resolving conflicting dualisms. Without a transcendent view of reality, Simmel relied on conflict for dealing with the problem of "conflicting duties." A transcendent view gives the Christian a basis for decision making, one that legitimates conflict and resolves personal dilemmas.

Wrong put his finger on important problems for the Christian in his criticism of over-socialization and over-integration. We are trapped into relying on
them for solving everyday problems, even those we may find in Christian
groups. Since over-socialization and over-integration lead the believer back into
worldly thinking, they are to be resisted. The transcendency principle gives the
Christian a better option than over-socialization and over-integration because it
legitimates actions that, by worldly standards, are unacceptable. How else can
we explain why people leave their families to go to the mission field? Strong
families may simply be a barrier for spreading the gospel. If so, then conflict and
disequilibrium may be functional requisites for doing God's work.

Counterculture

People who prefer the equilibrium model and social stability should have no
problem accepting Coser's idea of functional conflict. This is a limited conflict
theory without the implication of radical social change. By definition, it solves
problems and often moves a system to a better level of efficiency. It is this kind
of conflict that we readily accept from Jesus.

But we know, too, that Jesus' view of conflict extended beyond that theory.
His followers were to be so different from both the nominally religious and the
non-religious that they would constitute a completely different value system
standing in opposition to the world. This was to be the kingdom of God as believers lived out Jesus' commandment with a telling effect on the world. It was
conflict on the macro level, shaped by the transcendent context and revolutionary in effect.

John Stott has called this kind of conflict a *Christian counterculture* and
finds its manifesto in the Sermon on the Mount.[22] There is in the Christian, he
claims, the same sense of alienation and protest that activated youth in the sixties. Christians, too, seek a cultural alternative to the trivialities and illusions of
modern society. In the Sermon on the Mount, Jesus offers his followers a radical
model that is totally different from the world in outlook and behavior.

The idea of a counter-culture, of course, had been popularized by Theodore
Roszak in 1969.[23] Attempting to explain the revolutionary atmosphere in that
decade, he argued that youthful idealism was counter to the obsessive technological tenor of the times. When these idealistic values came into conflict with
dominant values over issues of peace, civil rights, and freedom of expression, a
revolutionary spirit of thinking and behaving developed to resist and even
change the dominant culture. Attempts to stifle the counter-culture only led to
continued agitation and conflict.

The timeliness of Roszak's book was a key factor in its popularity. It spoke
to the times and the youth who lived in them. But a decade before, a sociologist
had written a paper on the concept of *contraculture* to explain a variety of con-

flict situations.[24] As a technical paper, it neither sought nor gained the popularity of Roszak's book. Nevertheless, J. Milton Yinger's article provides a far more appropriate conflict model for the Christian than Roszak's humanistic treatment of the topic.

Yinger argues that in a pluralistic society, some groups will develop a series of values that are counter to society's. These values differ so greatly that they set the group apart from society rather than integrating the group into it. But even though the conflict of value systems is crucial, there is a sense in which the contraculture, on the surface, appears to be thoroughly cultural. In short, both the culture and the contraculture may share some elements in common.

To be more precise, Yinger claims that a contraculture exists

> wherever the normative system of a group contains, as a primary element, a theme of conflict with the values of the total society, where personality variables are directly involved in the development and maintenance of the group's values, and wherever its norms can be understood only by reference to the relationships of the group to a surrounding dominant culture.[25]

Although many groups in a pluralistic society will be at variance with the dominant culture, the element of conflict is central in the contraculture. These values contradict the values of the dominant culture as well as express the personal qualities of those in the contraculture. To understand the contraculture, it is necessary to understand the unique interaction of this conflicting group with society that sets it apart from other groups that do not become contra-cultural.

Yinger is firm in his belief that people do not join a contraculture simply because they have been socialized to it. Instead, they share some common needs or values in a frustrating environment. This leads to conflict with the dominant culture. Adolescent and delinquent youths, especially, serve as good examples of contracultural groups. Historically, American Indians constituted contracultures in their resistance to governmental attempts to control them. In any case, contra-cultural norms appear to replace the major values reflecting the deprivation and frustration felt by the group.

Yinger's conception of the contraculture is broader than Roszak's, which limits the principle to the sixties. Yinger's theory stresses the following points: First, contracultures may be found in any period of history. Second, a dominant culture must act as a frustrating situation for a minority group that feels deprived. Third, members of the contraculture have shared values that are more inherent than learned. Finally, the contra-cultural conflict need not be violent, but it will be creative as it develops new norms and values in response to the dominant. Whether the contraculture continues or expires depends largely on historical conditions at the time.

In a brief history of Christianity as a contraculture, W. Stanford Reid notes that the early church was "against the culture on principle."[26] Augustine claimed the kingdom of God was "counter-cultural," and monasticism was a more clear expression of this quality. But it was the Reformation which epitomized a contraculture in its break with society.

With its basic assumption that people came to God through Christ by the Holy Spirit rather than through the church, the Reformation placed itself in a position of direct conflict with Roman Catholicism. The result was not merely a religious movement but a cultural movement that produced a radically different society. If we take the Reformation as a model of a Christian contraculture, we understand the radical nature of conflict. In this case, the Reformation produced a completely different set of assumptions that extended into every corner of society. Definitions of work, sex roles, and wealth were all changed. These assumptions were based on biblical principles but applied to social life.

Contraculture is an important sociological concept with particular meaning for the Christian. It is a hidden thread exemplified in biblical principles. As an analogue of the Marxist revolution, it represents a non-violent, non-ideological form of conflict. It is also non-utopian simply because the Christian does not seek a utopia here on earth.

But both a warning and a challenge is set before the Christian. The warning is to avoid any violent action or utopian and ideological thinking in Christian living. The challenge is to understand more completely the Christian contraculture in all of its conceptual richness and to practice it more effectively.

Revolution

When Marx pursued the hope of revolution, he based it on a certain conception of social reality. The fact that revolution never developed as he expected indicates that his assumption was wrong: class conflict was not the dominant force he believed it was. But this is not to say that revolution, properly directed at the reality of worldly power, would be ineffective or inappropriate. The problem is to determine the source of conflict.

The persistent theme in the works of French sociologist Jacques Ellul is that revolution is not only desirable, but necessary.[27] Arguing that any current attempts to preserve the world merely maintain human structure, he calls for the Christian to be revolutionary. This does not mean vainly attacking the government, economy, or other forms of authority. These are nothing more than useless power struggles. The problem is that there are two different social orders: man's and God's. We make a fundamental error in believing that progress in man's order will solve our problems. Nor will it lead to the order that God has established. Revolution can only occur with a Christian perception of the reality of God's order.

What does this perception require? For one thing, we are deluded if we believe the social world to be real or that it consists of "facts." If we do, we confuse "facts" with truth and allow ourselves to be controlled by them. Such a belief Ellul refers to as "the religion of the established fact, the religion on which depend the lesser religions of the dollar, race, or the proletariat."[28] The Christian is also to realize that the world is dying because of human sinfulness. Since this trend cannot be reversed, Christians need to help preserve the world for the return of Christ, who alone can deal with the problem. Finally, Christians need to understand how they are bound to people. Preservation comes only with our efforts to influence the world through the lives of others.

What Ellul calls for is a permanent revolution, one that continues with the abiding presence of God's kingdom in the world. This means that God's order will be preserved in the world and his Word will be available to others. But it will be a revolution because of its conflict with the world and all that it stands for. By resisting the basic assumptions of our society and challenging its claims over people, this revolution attacks the basic elements of the world's order. In short, it supports God's work by attacking man's work.

History offers no example for Ellul's revolution. For a while, the early church seemed to fulfill the ideal. Since then Christians have accepted the state's authority as valid because it was ordained by God. As long as the church was dominant, it advocated accommodation to society and remained a force in society. Even Calvin and Luther accepted this view and seemed to prefer tyranny to the disorder of revolt. Even though the Reformation altered Western culture forever, it was not a revolution, in Ellul's opinion, because the world's structure was left intact.

When Christians like Oliver Cromwell tried to use violent means, their efforts at revolution were not successful. Faith merely supplemented their political action and did not replace it. Even the use of non-violence, as radical as it might seem, has never successfully changed the world. All of these views are unsuccessful, Ellul claims, because they assume "there must be a Christian 'solution,' a valid way of organizing society or the world."[29] Such a "solution" is not possible because of the irreconcilable gap between the world's values and those of revelation.

Yet Christians attempt such solutions, and when they do, violence results. "Apart from Christ, violence is the form that human relations normally and necessarily take."[30] This is because violence is the natural condition of society. Even the state, Ellul claims, is established in violence and legitimated over time. Superficial idealism and morality merely act as a cover for the reality of violence. Consequently, Christians may be lured into unwitting violence in their attempts to do good.

Ellul is firm on this point and argues that violence forces a person to do what was not intended. Violence is then justified, leading to a recurring pattern of more violent actions to solve problems. "Recourse to violence is a sign of incapacity: incapacity to solve the fundamental questions of our time . . . and incapacity to discern the specific form Christian action ought to take."[31] Violence, then, is a symptom of human weakness and ignorance, qualities we try to repress with our efforts to remove the effects of human sinfulness. We are weak when we believe, as humans, that we can radically alter the nature of the world and solve its problems. We are ignorant when we fail to discern the complex nature of problems and rely on violence rather than on God's means. In effect, violence is a sign of human hypocrisy.

Ellul's argument is telling as it unravels the nature of social reality. Once we accept the fact that God's work is the only reality shaped in creation, all human efforts are merely illusions of reality as we think of it. Without that understanding, we are wrong to believe our actions have some impact on eternal questions. All we do is use the wrong means to attain God's ends, wrong because they are human means, which can never accomplish those ends.

As a former Marxist who accepted Christ in his college years, Ellul turns Marx on his head. Revolution is not violent but peaceful. It is not a crisis but is permanent. It is not a class conflict but a personal struggle. It is directed not at social power but at spiritual evil. This is a radical view of reality, one which makes no sense to the unbeliever. But once accepted as the only valid form of reality, it invalidates any final answers offered by functionalism or conflict theory. Their insights and analyses are important and necessary but always inadequate to unveil the world's structure.

Ironically, Ellul taught at the University of Bordeaux where Durkheim had taught the first sociology courses ever offered at a French university. And yet, Ellul brings all of Durkheim's empirical tradition in social science into question. It simply offers no hope for the world's problems. But that is not to say that modern social science is to be ignored. What it does offer is a basis for understanding problems so that we might live more effectively as "a presence of the kingdom" in the world. Without that we are naive in our simplistic view of society. Some even quickly flock to those false prophets of the modern world who call for battle against social evil. For them, their faith may become an ideology justifying their conflict but never resolving it.

Conclusion

Functionalism did much to move social thought away from the naturalistic and historical determinism of the nineteenth century and into limited social contexts. In response, conflict theory rescued people from those contexts and gave the person a new importance in social thought. But both functionalism and conflict theory expressed different forms of the same concept of social reality. Even Marx, for all of his radical qualities, saw religion as a product of society in a fashion reminiscent of Durkheim. Conflict theorists challenged traditional social realities but never with a transcendent and radically different view of the world.

That is why a Christian like Ellul offers a real hope for a radical social science. More than any social theory, Christianity can explain those universal social and human problems of concern to sociologists like Dennis Wrong. They are the products of both God's work and man's work and combine a unique blend of spiritual and social realities. The result is a conflict of mammoth proportions, one which transcends space and time. It also models conflict on the micro-level of human relations. For these reasons, the Christian as social scientist needs to come to this conflict with study and prayer.

Chapter 7

Social Action Theory

Some thirty-five years ago, C. Wright Mills the enthusiasm of a prominent gadfly. In his large classes of undergraduates at Columbia University, he effectively pushed his Marxist, humanistic bias on eager, receptive minds. What puzzled the outsider was Mills's willingness to take on a heavy teaching schedule when his national stature would have allowed him to work with a small coterie of senior graduate students. Pushed for an explanation, Mills would respond that he preferred to shape the thinking of open, immature minds than attempt to influence those that had settled on their professional goals.

It would be unfair to dismiss Mills's attitude as simply ideological and propagandistic. He might have had those particular biases, but he also knew that people needed meaning in life to give them direction and purpose. Without that meaning, their thoughts and actions could be neither predicted nor influenced. They would be incomplete social beings without direction or purpose in society. Mills's intention was to instill in his students the humanistic viewpoint that had meaning for him, and he accomplished his goal quite well.

If we were to focus on Mills's intent, we would have to say that he was a conflict theorist in the content of his teaching. But in his tactics he showed that he was also a social action theorist. He knew that people are goal oriented and motivated by values even though they might fail in their efforts and be led astray despite good intentions. If there were no meaning in their lives, something to shape their future plans, they would find or invent one.

The Background

Throughout the nineteenth century, naturalistic thinking dominated American social thought. This deterministic view of humans and society reduced people to automatons who acted in response to historical or environmental influences. With such a view of reality, sociologists had little to do but describe the causal factors influencing passive human beings. Linked with dominant theological views of the day, naturalism became identified with a beneficent God who influenced human progress. As natural phenomena, people and society became part of the process of cosmic evolution destined to lead into some future state of moral and social perfection. One would think that the early American social thinkers with their orthodox views would have reacted adversely to such naturalistic thought. This was clearly not the case. It is true that advocates of the Social Gospel, as well as others, presented views that opposed the naturalism of their day. But these men were not highly influential on the future development of social thought. Instead, the major reaction to naturalism came from European thinkers who fostered analytical sociology with its attempts to analyze, describe, and interpret social phenomena. These thinkers provided the clearest cultural context for the development of an alternative to naturalistic social thought.

Describing these early attempts to counter naturalistic thinking in American social science, Hinkle claims that certain common features stood out in their arguments.[1]

1. Men's social activities arise from their consciousness of themselves (as subjects) and of others and the external situations (as objects).

2. As subjects, men act to achieve their (subjective) intentions, purposes, aims, ends, objectives, or goals.

3. They use appropriate means, techniques, procedures, methods, and instruments.

4. Their courses of action are limited by unmodifiable conditions or circumstances.

5. Exercising will or judgment, they choose, assess and evaluate what they will do, are doing, and have done.

6. Standards, rules, or moral principles are invoked in arriving at decisions.

7. Any study of social relationships requires the researcher to use subjective investigative techniques such as *verstehen*—imaginative or sympathetic reconstruction, or vicarious experience.

These suppositions were the key elements of what has come to be known as the social action tradition. This tradition gave greater importance to the person at the beginning of the twentieth century. In contrast to naturalistic views, which stressed that society shaped people according to its will, the social action tradition sees people as social beings who make society. In their social commentaries, Ward, Ross, Cooley, Small, and Giddings all increased the value of people and their capacity to reason and to will their social actions. People gradually became determiners instead of the determined.

Compared with earlier naturalistic views, social action theories gave new meaning to humans. People were now seen as conscious beings who acted within the bounds of rules and moral principles. They were responsible beings who understood their limitations as well as their possibilities. Although human error was not defined in terms of sinfulness, the possibility of its existence gave a new dimension to the human personality. People now began to resemble their ancestors in the Garden of Eden.

It is a curious fact that religious assumptions were never included in these early American social action theories. Orthodox Christians were concerned about the social and moral problems of an industrial society and not the problems of human consciousness and willfulness. Consequently, Christian views foundered on the ideology of the Social Gospel while some of the most important work done in American sociology in the early part of this century reflected mostly humanist thinking. Once set, this pattern has not been easy to overcome.

European sociologists, however, were more sensitive to the religious implications of social action theory. Max Weber, especially, is known as a social action theorist who began with the religious meaning of human behavior. As a critic, Weber provided an interpretation of Marx's work that conceived of religion as related to economic actions and not some epiphenomenon of them. Indeed, the claim that Weber hoped to establish his own reputation as a scholar by refuting Marx's work is probably not far from the truth.

Weber himself described the Protestant Ethic as "Protestant asceticism [which formed] 'the foundation of modern vocational civilization.'"[2] His problem was to understand whether human ideas about cosmic matters and religious interests could influence their concrete actions—specifically, worldly activities such as economics, politics, and science. After entering into an extensive study of comparative historical materials and using religion as the independent variable, Weber concluded that religion did influence the development of social relationships and institutions. In fact, Weber claimed, this influence has shaped Western society ever since the Reformation.

Weber's work has come to be known as *Verstehende Soziologie:* "a system of sociological categories couched in terms of the subjective point of view, that is of the meaning of persons, things, ideas, normative patterns, and motives from the point of view of the persons whose action is being studied."[3] This method of analysis had two major emphases.

First, it took a subjective point of view by putting oneself into the place of the actor in order to interpret the motives and actions of the actor. Second, it attempted to understand how these interpretations could lead to systems of meaning in society that could be linked to the interests of individual actors. In short, it tries to understand how people were motivated to gain particular ends because of the influence of certain cultural meanings in society.

A crucial element in Weber's social action theory is the opportunity for choice on the part of the actor. Instead of merely responding to stimuli, the person could choose among various possible actions with the realization that some choices may be deviant and unsuccessful. The opportunity for such choice implies that action is "normatively oriented"; the actor tries to comply with certain standards approved of by society. Weber assumed that people were rational and gained their objectives fully aware that such rationality was not possible. By hypothesizing rationality, however, Weber hoped to understand the irrational factors causing people to fall short of their goals. These were vital questions for Weber, for "he felt that the development and role of certain patterns of rationality constituted the most important problems of our time in the Western World."[4]

As an agnostic, Weber brought no understanding of human sinfulness to his work. Nevertheless, he could appreciate the fact that falling short of some religious goal was the critical element in the development of modern Western society. In fact, he recognized that this trend was characterized by the development of a disenchanted world. Living in such a world, modern man became secularized and increasingly chose worldly ends rather than religious ends.

Weber derived two types of rational action from these choices. *Value-rational action (wertrational)* refers to a choice of means directed at some absolute value. The action is rational because of its effectiveness in attaining subjectively-meaningful values. Even though the values may be transcendental and religious, the deliberate and reasoned choice of appropriate means makes the action rational. *Rationally purposeful action (zweckrational)* refers to the instrumental use of means to attain some end. Since no value dominates motivations, the actor selects a series of means and ends to accomplish his purpose. In this case, utility may become the dominant value used to judge the efficacy of means and sub-ends in gaining some end. In short, ends were gradually deemphasized in favor of means.

Weber recognized this shift in values as a form of secularization. Traditionally, people are religious as they seek common ultimate ends because they know no other alternatives. But as new goals become available with social change, people seek value-rational actions as new forms of religious expression. This had been the case with the rise of capitalism and the development of science as Puritans sought to glorify God with their involvement in these institutional activities. Although they may have used secular means, the ends were always religious in nature.

This pattern changes with rationally purposeful action. In this case, group ends are gradually replaced by individual ends, which come to dominate personal motives. This is not to say that religious values are completely lost. More likely, religious values will remain in the value system to justify worldly activity. As mentioned in chapter 3, Weber agrees with John Wesley's statement of the dilemma: "So, although the form of religion remains, the spirit is swiftly vanishing away. Is there no way to prevent this—this continual decay of pure religion?"[5] Both also agree on the paradoxical solution: the Christian can lay up personal treasures in heaven by gaining success in worldly endeavors and passing on the fruits of that success to others in need.[6]

Despite the clear theology of works found in this proposed solution, Weber's work underscores some important points for the Christian. First, a certain tension emerges when one's faith is applied to worldly activities. Secularization occurs when that tension is lost and personal motives are directed away from ultimate values and service for God. Second, religious meaning may be separated from an action and used to justify that action. According to Weber, "a motive is a complex of subjective meaning which seems to the actor himself or to the observer an adequate ground for the conduct in question."[7] Unless that mo-

tive is submissive to God's will, the pattern of social change leads toward secul10-
rization.

Weber recognized this problem and realized that secularization, historically, is reversed with a religious revival. The source of such a revival was some form of *charisma*, a term Weber used to refer to "the quality of leadership which appeals to non-rational motives."[8] Charisma, then, refers to some form of moral authority that deviates from the pattern of social action representative of the time. Although the charismatic leader need not be religious, he is always revolutionary in his efforts to break the routinization of life. In other words, charisma epitomized Weber's belief that people are not to be understood merely as products of society's whims.

Weber's work remains a purely humanistic effort because it describes social action as a human endeavor. Still, it is a powerful argument that explains well the development of the modern Western world. For this reason, it cannot be ignored. Neither can it be completely accepted by the Christian. Although Weber's recognition of the charismatic spirit implies an open system in which God may work—a unique quality among social theories—he made no attempt to explain how God's will may be accomplished through human means.[9] For Weber, social action remains a product of human willfulness.

The Theory

The emphasis of evolutionary theory and naturalistic philosophy in early American sociology was on certain conditions external to the person—notably, heredity and environment. People had to adjust to these conditions if they were to survive and thrive. Consequently, rules were of less importance. People were human organisms who survived in groups as all animals did. How they made their choices and what they chose were matters of far less importance.

Two major influences gave new direction to American social theory in the World War II period.[10] One was the need to shift from scientific preoccupations to practical utility to meet the crises of the Depression and of the war itself. The other influence came from European thinkers like Weber who believed that theory fleshed out empirical facts. Together, these two influences nourished social action theory as a clear and viable substitute for what had become the ideology of evolutionary thought.

Beginning with the radical observation that people were the critical elements in the social environment, social action theorists clarified the role of these persons. They were perceived as active people who had an influence on those about them. Consequently, their actions were of concern to those with whom they interacted. In other words, people became conscious of others and the way these others might influence the attainment of their goals. This is the fundamental principle undergirding what has come to be known as the *action frame of reference*.

Much of the discussion of contemporary social action theory centers around one book: *The Structure of Social Action* by Talcott Parsons. Here Parsons attempted to give new direction to American social theory by specifically rejecting Spencer and his influence. Claiming that evolution was Spencer's god, Parsons rejected his

> deep-rooted belief that, stated roughly, at least in the prominent economic
> phase of social life, we have been blessed with an automatic, self-regulating
> mechanism which operated so that the pursuit by each individual of his own
> self-interest and private ends would result in the greatest possible satisfaction
> of the wants of all.[11]

Religion, Spencer thought, was derived from these beliefs and would be replaced by science.

Parsons's original goal in this book was to show that people were not locked into such a system but were intrinsically rational in their action. They could make choices among the options open to them. As part of a larger social system and involved with other persons, an individual would make these choices voluntarily. By analyzing the work of Alfred Marshall, Emile Durkheim, Vilfredo Pareto, and Max Weber, Parsons claimed that these thinkers laid the basis for a new generalized system of action consisting of the following elements: (1) heredity and environment as conditions of action, (2) means and ends, (3) an ultimate value system, and (4) "effort" or the motivation needed to accomplish the cultural objectives.[12]

Most sociologists today have little enthusiasm for these elements. In fact, they prefer to think that Parsons's greatest contribution in this work was his popularization of these European thinkers, thereby radically influencing contemporary American social thought.

A major problem with Parsons's theory is the scope of its claims. It simply claims more than it should: "There are no group properties that are not reducible to properties of *systems* of action and there is no analytical theory of groups which is not translatable into terms of the theory of action."[13] Put more simply, properties of a group do not exist apart from the level of interacting individuals and can be explained only on that level. The Christian has problems with this notion, since Scripture clearly notes that Jesus is the Creator of all things, including organizational qualities such as power, authority, and ownership (Col. 1:15-16). Some group properties, apparently, cannot be explained without an awareness of God's creative power. Others, too, recognize the extremity of Parsons's statement and usually reject it on other grounds.

Parsons makes his case for this view by showing how people make choices among the possible alternatives offered to them. Fundamentally, people are subjectively oriented toward each other. In their action, they take others into consideration before acting. In addition, certain norms in a situation predispose action to be of one sort rather than another. What results is the *unit act,* the most fundamental element in the social action system. As part of this system, the person becomes an "actor" who makes choices because of the influence of others and the norms found in the situation.

Several problems are readily apparent in Parsons's argument. First, what happens if the actor finds that the norms and the influence of others do not agree? This happens every time a student wants to follow the norms of studying for a test but is persuaded by peers to go out for pizza. Parsons leaves us with the impression that the norms will have the stronger influence, but he offers no satisfactory explanation why this might be the case.

A second problem has to do with the influence of the other person and how that influence on the actor is derived. If norms are not influential, how might the other person impose a will on the actor? We will discuss this at length in a later section, but it is important now to emphasize the diversity of these two completely different influences on an actor. One, the normative system, is external to the actors and may be effective only when the actor and a partner agree to the norm or when an actor resists the partner's influence. The other influence is internally constructed by the actors themselves regardless of the influence of the norms. Apparently each form of influence is explained by a different kind of theory.

This is a crucial point for the Christian. Parsons believed that norms were derived from some common ultimate ends. These were necessary to integrate the decision-making process among people. In the case of our study of weary students, all of them would forego the pizza if studying were considered to have some ultimate importance for their lives. The religious meaning of action, of course, is usually considered as the basis for such ultimacy. But since religious meaning and all other forms of ultimate meaning fall outside the limits of science, the origin of integrating ultimate ends remains largely a matter of faith. Consequently, one either accepts faith in ultimate ends with its implications for religious belief or accepts a theory based on internal personal influences on behavior.

Apparently, Parsons had a considerable amount of faith in common ultimate ends, for, as noted earlier, he moved in his thought from individual voluntarism to group functionalism. In short, the needs of the group came to take priority in his thought over the needs of the person. His critics, who usually represented more humanistic values, largely dismissed his theory when it reached the functionalist stage. The religious implication of ultimate values, coupled with a downgrading of individual needs and desires, provided a rather one-sided view of reality which was unacceptable to them.

In one sense, the critics had justification for their views. The problem is that people do not act completely as described by Parsons or his critics. Some persons are more individualistic and anti-organizational in their actions, while others are more likely to follow Parsons's model and conform to the norms. Indeed, some people readily move back and forth from one model of behavior to the other depending on the social situation and how they perceive it. In short, it may be necessary to accept *both* theoretical models.

To understand the problem a bit more closely, let's return to the unit act, the building block of Parsons's social action theory. We should remember that Parsons, in his desire to move away from Spencer's influence, wanted to explain behavior in terms of future consequences and freedom of choice, not past causes and some form of determinism. If people were rational, then they would make the best choices for all concerned. Biological or environmental factors would not be necessary to determine a person's behavior.

But since a person is motivated by an unknown future in social action theory, how does one speculate on another's possible motives? How can we know if the person will conform or not? The need is to adopt the view of the actor. We need to understand how that person regards social relations or is socially motivated and what he or she thinks about a situation. This is what Weber meant by the term *verstehen:* to understand the deepest meaning in a situation for a person. Once this is done, it is less important to ask whether the person will conform to the norms of the group or the influence of other actors. The general tendency will be to be influenced by whatever has ultimate meaning in that situation and seems to answer the person's deepest needs.

The actor, then, is the crucial element in the unit act. Parsons does not conceive of the actor simply as an organism responding to some stimulus. This notion of the person is found in behavior theories and differs from Parsons's notion. Rather, the person in social action is a *self or ego* who responds to a situation because of an awareness and experience of it. As a subjective being, the actor makes decisions based on those experiences and then reflects on their merit. Over time, the actor evaluates a series of past events while imagining those that might be in the future.

This is a high view of the person who may judge the self as well as be judged by others. This is not to say that such judgment is always desirable for, as we understand from Scripture judgment maybe reciprocal (James 5:9). It is a view of the person as a responsible being, one who stands in an incredibly complex web of relationships over time and evaluates them. The person has some responsibility for those relationships and their development or demise.

In addition, the actor is responsible for the perception of the surrounding world and how it should be evaluated relative to others and self. Is a rumor to be accepted as valid and true? Are economic trends to be viewed with alarm? How the world is perceived is a clue to a person's thought and behavior. It may also tell us something of the person's values and the meaning he or she attaches to the world.

The second element in the unit act is the end of some action. This goal may be either in the distant or more immediate future. But since it is in the future and outside the realm of current "facts," the end may be imagined and realized only with effort and will. Although the act is completed once the end is attained, another end may be established to initiate a new direction of action. For this reason, a person is always involved in a series of interrelated acts.

Especially as this interrelationship becomes complex, ends may be conscious or unconscious, and motives may be mixed. Studies have shown, for example, that girls, traditionally, have wanted to do well in school work in the lower grades.

Upon reaching puberty, however, their motives may shift as they seek to avoid being too successful in competing with boys. A result is that girls often have mixed motives, conscious and unconscious. They try to please their parents by being good students while also playing down their accomplishments in order to be acceptable to possible boy friends.

There is often tension, then, between what we *want* to do (an end) and what we *should* do for someone (a function). Given that tension, how will it be resolved? The key remains the value attributed by the person to the action and the meaning it may have for him or her. In any given situation, it might be just as sensible to sacrifice self and give to another as it would be to seek one's own end. Unless this perception by the actor is shared by another, there would be no way of understanding why the choice was made.

Since there are always obstacles to gaining some end, these *obstacles or conditions become another element in the unit act.* Although often external to the person, some conditions may be found within him or her. The student who fails a course because of peer pressure has no one else to blame. Submitting to such pressure is largely a self-imposed condition.

Conditions are a constant reminder of human limitations and fallibility in attaining some end. Despite our best intentions, we may fail. Since failure is hard to accept, we try to deal with it in several ways. First, we may rationalize our reasons for failure and displace the condition elsewhere. Witness the student who blames the teacher for failure on a test because the "right" questions weren't asked. Instead of accepting the condition of human fallibility, the student attributes failure to external conditions. Second, we may believe that conditions can be transcended, and our goals may be achieved in spite of the conditions. This may require us to seek new and better ways to gain our ends.

Modern society encourages the view that we may transcend the conditions of life. Increasingly, the means to extend life, improve standards of living, and extend ourselves beyond the earth are given to us. Consequently, we have come to value ourselves more than the old boundaries around us. As conditions blur together, our sense of valued ends and means used to gain them may be altered.

The means used to attain some end is a fourth element in the unit act. Since an end may often be gained by the use of a variety of means, the actor has many options. Ideally, a means will be chosen that is both effective and moral. A student will usually study for a test because studying has both of these qualities.

But pressured for time, it may be necessary to choose between studying and cheating, which may be just as effective but not moral. The choice that is made reflects the student's values.

Means may also act as *conditions* or *ends* for other people. If we are to understand others' motives accurately, we must understand how the means are perceived by them. A computer, for example, may be an efficient means of writing a book for the person who knows how to use one but a condition for the person ignorant of its use. Similarly, a house may be a means for one person to gain status in a community, while for another homeowner a house is nothing more than a necessary form of shelter. Again, values are important for understanding how people perceive means.

Parsons recognized that conditions and means are interchangeable in people's thinking. For that reason, if there were any agreement on the meaning of means and conditions among actors, some prior basis for consensus would need to exist. Society would be chaotic if agreement were not possible. For some persons, cheating on income taxes can be a means to gain a refund; for others, cheating on taxes is a condition which requires honesty. There should be agreement that cheating is either a condition or a means. If people are to get along with each other, it can't be both.

This is why *Parsons considered norms to be an inherent element in the unit act.* As objective bases in action, norms are necessary to keep a check on the subjective possibilities of individual choice. Without norms, society would lack unity and the possibility of integrating individual actions. This is not to say that Parsons advocated any particular normative system. The choice of a set of norms was a problem that Parsons dealt with in other contexts.

Parsons's theory recognizes the importance of subjective meaning in human behavior. But he also tried to balance this with a concern for the objective nature of values and norms.

Some would say his functionalism took him too far in this direction. Nevertheless, this concern for the proper balance of the subjective and the objective aspects of social action is an important problem in the development of social thought. It is also of critical concern for the Christian.

A Christian Critique

It is intriguing to note the similarities in Parsons's theories and those of some early American theorists. Each suggests the importance of individual, subjective choice in the attainment of ends. Each also recognizes the importance of means, conditions, and the moral implications of making a choice. In both cases, social action theory moves away from earlier deterministic theories and describes action in terms of dilemmas with moral implications.

Despite these similarities, Parsons's work is actually based on a European tradition with a high regard for the place *of* religion in human behavior. This was especially true in the work of Weber who tried to explain behavior in terms of the meaning people attached to it. In his development of the increasing rationalization of modern life, a trend described earlier, Weber focused on certain problem areas which are of particular interest for the Christian.

The Calling

Weber believed the Reformation was the pivotal point in Western history simply because it radically changed people's motives. Protestants now shared new values. These, in turn, shaped their choices of goals and the means for attaining them. Freed from the values of the Catholic church, people could choose means and ends previously denied to them. Consequently, science, economics, and the family were three institutions revolutionized by Protestant values.

In each case, Weber demonstrated, new vocations developed as people believed they were "called" to "a task set by God." Science gained new importance as it was done "for the glory of God" and to reveal his handiwork in creation. The acquisition of wealth in capitalistic activity became acceptable as that wealth was turned over to the church for needy ministries. The family became a field for Christian service as parents raised children in "the nurture and admonition of the Lord." In each case, as Weber described it, people sensed the obligations as well as the opportunities of new shared values.

Weber represents social action theory written in the broad sweep of social change. Once religious interests could be applied to secular activities, the old separation of religious and social interests was blurred. A tension developed between religious and social dimensions of social action as people tried to be faithful to God's calling to a worldly role. Since the task was set by God, a person acted because of the authority vested in that office and not because of any personal claim to authority. An obligation to God remains, but always for the purpose of gaining some social end.

Weber described the vocation of science as a tension between two basic motives. The *religious* motive required the scientist to do science for its own sake. This was "pure" science and could honor God with its discoveries. The scientist could also have the *social* motive of providing some utilitarian end. This was "applied" science and would benefit people with its discoveries. Without these two motives, science as a vocation would be a distortion of what God intended it to be.

Merton's study of seventeenth-century Puritan science is a model of Weber's description of science as a vocation. Merton notes Boyle's claim "that the study of Nature is to the greater glory of God and the Good of Man."[14] These men held the sincere belief that people would revere God as they understood the marvels of his creation in nature. But the values of the day also encouraged social welfare. Puritan scientists did not eschew such worldly goals but sought to dominate nature with scientific inventions. In short, Puritan scientists were "in the world" of their culture and accepted its values but were not "of the world" and sought to worship God in their work.

Weber understood that vocations were fragile and threatened by modern forces. "Today the routines of everyday life challenge religion. Many old gods ascend from their graves; they are disenchanted and hence take the form of impersonal forces."[15] These "impersonal forces" are objective and gradually rationalize religious interests until they lose any influence on action. Put another way, the world becomes secularized as it is rationalized and weakens the religious basis of vocations.

In such a world, the *career* is the modern, secularized form of the calling. Commitment to a task because of its religious meaning shifts to a commitment to an accompanying lifestyle and its expectations. People are motivated by a hierarchically arranged pattern of careers, each affording greater rewards at successive levels. The career seeker now conforms to social expectations and accompanying worldly values. As well as being in the world, the careerist is of it.

Weber is not optimistic about the future. "The fate of our times is characterized by rationalization and intellectualization and, above all, by the 'disenchantment of the world.'"[16] What has been lost is the awareness of God's ruling influence in the world. Culturally, Weber does not expect a return of that awareness. The best he can hope for is that people will search for the ultimate meaning of their personal conduct and interpret life in terms of that meaning.

When we turn to Scripture, we find a number of examples of the calling as a form of social action theory. Jesus, of course, provides the clearest example of one who consistently did good for those about him while fulfilling eternal values. He maintained the tension between heavenly and earthly values simply because he demonstrated how they merged in practice. Even when the disciples couldn't understand him, Jesus demonstrated how the kingdom of God could be manifested on earth. In fact, it was only when the disciples came to understand the gospel after Christ's resurrection that they too were able to bring the contradictory values of the calling together and sustain them in their lives.

Paul, too, experienced the calling in his life and struggled with the personal implications of it. Called as a missionary, he supported himself by tent making. He was torn between his desire to be with Christ and to continue his ministry (Phil. 1:23). In the Old Testament, we find saints who were guided by eternal hope in God's provision but struggled with the problems of everyday life. Abraham experienced the wealth of this world but continually sought to please God in his faithfulness. Moses, too, combined the worldly activity of administration and leadership with the eternal values provided by God. Indeed, one can scarcely find an Old Testament saint who did not exemplify the calling as described by Weber.

Ultimacy

Social action theory must deal with two problems if its assumptions are to be accepted. The first involves the unique quality of the calling and the need to maintain a balance between its potentially conflicting value systems. Without this balance, secularization weakens the basis for group unity and predictability of individual action. The other problem involves the dilemma of multiple actors who do not share the same value system. When this occurs, they cannot interact with a clear knowledge of how the other will act. Each is unable to predict the action of the other or to cooperate with that person on similar terms. This problem of how people work together to accomplish certain objectives is the problem that undergirds all social action theory.

If there is to be any order in society, people cannot pursue their own private ends exclusively. Their individualism must be tempered by group ends. On some occasions, these must be considered preferable or superior to individual ends. These group ends imply the existence of some objective reality so influential in people's lives that they repress their subjective desires for them. In some way, then, group ends gain priority over personal ends in some situations.

An extreme example is found in the Harmonists, a pietistic sect that practiced celibacy in nineteenth-century America. Originally, the Harmonists lived in typical family units before emigrating from Germany in the early part of the century. But the founder, Father Rapp, believed their faith commitment should include celibate living as a biblical principle. Some of the families believed this was asking too much of them and left the group. But we know that most accepted the doctrine, separated themselves from other family members, and committed themselves to the commune to live a celibate lifestyle.

Another illustration of group ends gaining priority over the personal is the example of the rain dance as practiced by Indians in the Southwest. The tribal need for rain was caused by arid conditions. As a member of the tribe, each Indian was expected to accept the group's need of rain as a personal heed.

Lacking modern technological means, the problem was to obtain enough rain to provide for adequate crops. At some point in the tribal past, someone must have decided that dancing could produce this result because the gods seemed to respond to the wishes expressed in the dance. If the performance of the rain dance could be associated with an adequate rainfall in a causal relationship, then the rain dance would become the means used by the tribe to produce rain when needed.

We should note two important facts here about the rain dance as a group end. First, the dance would take priority over the personal ends of the individual tribal member. If some preferred to go hunting, they would choose to participate in the dance instead. This choice would be made not only to show tribal unity to the gods but also because their individual needs would be best served by meeting the group's ends. Second, there is no logical connection between the rain dance and an adequate rainfall. In this sense, the rain dance reflects an ultimate value and falls outside the realm of objective fact or scientific testing. Ultimate values may then acquire a religious quality and demand some expression of faith from the people.

We can now summarize four major qualities of the principle of ultimacy as it relates to the theory of social action. First, a relationship between ultimate values and personal needs is expressed in a series of linked means and ends. Personal needs are perceived to be met as ultimate ends are achieved. Second, the sequence of this relationship implies the importance of group ends which are intermediary to ultimate values and individual needs. If the group is to maintain its unity and survive, then its ends must be superior to individual needs and desires. Third, ultimate values find their origins in the super-empirical world simply because they exist beyond scientific proof or thought. They are meaningless to the outsider and only make sense to the group member. Last, ultimate values gain credibility and support whenever they are successfully related to the accomplishment of *some* immediate end. For this reason, the subjective world becomes important as it gives plausibility to the ultimate values.

The weakness of the principle of ultimacy is clearly apparent in a secularized society such as ours. In a world that is "disenchanted"—to use Weber's term—there is no basis for accepting ultimate values. The world is believed to be closed to any spiritual power and influenced only by scientific, empirical means. Consequently, group ends wither and the individual gains priority in a self-oriented society.

But what happens when some inexplicable personal or group tragedy occurs in a secularized society? Let's say a city is destroyed by an earthquake or a person experiences some unexpected personal loss. In these cases, new ultimate values and the spiritual forces they represent may take the place of the former religious faith. This assumes, of course, that by some means the new values can be related to a successful resolution of new needs. Astrology, for example, or some cultic belief in the spiritual power of natural phenomena may gain religious status and provide new ultimate values for new believers. When this occurs, people are again "enchanted" by new gods and build new religions about them.

As long as ultimate values are seen as super-empirical and devoid of any basis in scientific fact, they are vulnerable when faith is weakened. For this reason, the Christian is challenged to understand the empirical basis of our faith in creation. How can we show that ultimate values are more than a matter of faith? What is it about society that can be scientifically demonstrated to be given to us by God for our personal and social welfare? Without such validation, Christian ultimate values remain on the super-empirical level and valid only for the believer. Consequently, there is no unity in society. It remains fragmented as the unbeliever goes another way and seeks those false gods and the answers they seem to provide.

Rationality

Parsons's description of rational action had two major elements. First, any action is rational if it pursues ends that are possible within the conditions found in the situation. Second, means are chosen by the actor best suited for gaining those ends and verifiable in scientific terms.[17] Within the limits of these boundaries, it is apparent that all human action has a rational element; it is either rational or believed to be rational.

But as the actor attempts to be rational by choosing the best means to accomplish his or her best end, it is just as likely that a wrong choice of ends or means will be made. This fact suggests that rationality in social action is more likely an ideal than a reality. Since an element of error is present in every attempt at rational social action, non-rational action remains as likely to occur.

Kingsley Davis, a student of Parsons, has succinctly stated four major sources of non-rational conduct.[18] First are the *super-empirical ends that cannot be proven or disproven by scientific means.* Since these are future states existing outside some present time-space situation, it cannot be demonstrated that *any* means would be appropriate for *gaining* these ends. This would be true of the Harmonists, for example, if they believed that celibacy was a necessary means to gain eternal salvation. Celibacy might just as easily be a condition preventing salvation. Marriage and family living may be a means instead. Hence, rationality is irrelevant to the questions, and the action of following a celibate lifestyle is really non-rational.

A second form of barrier to rational action is found in what Davis calls *the haziness of the end.* Here he refers to the possibility that an actor will not be sure of the effect produced by the means used. This notion is comparable to Merton's concept of unanticipated consequences of purposive social action and implies a certain short-sightedness in choosing a certain means to gain an end. While we may assume an action will have a positive effect, it is just as possible that an unperceived negative effect will result.

The haziness of the end suggests a third source of non-rational behavior: *we are often ignorant of the means available to us.* Since an actor can use only those means that are known (all of the possible means cannot be known), there is always an element of ignorance in behavior. Such ignorance may be forgiven if the knowledge falls outside a person's experience. An Indian, for example, could not be expected to use irrigation as a substitute for the rain dance if he were never exposed to methods of irrigation. This is a matter of cultural knowledge that falls outside the Indian's experience. In a rapidly changing society, ignorance becomes increasingly important as mushrooming knowledge produces a plethora of new means.

A final cause of non-rational behavior is *normative restrictions.* Here Davis refers to the fact that some means are ignored, not because of ignorance, but because they are not permitted. Since moral restrictions are imposed on means as well as ends, the actor will always find the choice of means to be limited. Social order is maintained if means are restricted so that people cannot choose those means that would inconvenience others in the pursuit of their ends. Stealing, for example, is not an acceptable means to be used in our society for gaining something. In effect, normative restrictions produce a social environment favorable for the practice of the Golden Rule.[19]

The fact of limited rationality in social action is important for the Christian for two reasons. First, *it emphasizes the human quality of finiteness.* Unlike God, who is omniscient and omnipotent, people are limited in what they can know and do. Further, human finiteness underscores the limitation of individualism as a social value. How can we highly value ourselves if we recognize our imperfections? Even the defenders of modern individualism have become ambivalent in their support of this value.[20]

A second important fact for the Christian follows: *limited rationality implies the necessity of social order.* People cannot ignore others and their needs if they are limited in meeting their goals in life. The fundamental need to work together in community for our personal, as well as our common, good is underscored.[21] If resources are scarce, individualism must be controlled if all are to be satisfied in meeting their goals.

The illusion of human rationality, then, is a ubiquitous problem. Instead of facing up to their human frailties, people protect their egos with this notion that they are rational. Especially in a modern society which offers so many technological substitutes for human qualities, people are deceived. They assume the qualities of God for themselves and fail to understand God as he is.

Means and Ends

The problem of rationality is really a problem of ends and how means are related to them. If we believe humans are autonomous and act outside of God's influence, it makes sense to speak of rational action. We may assume that we control the means to gain the ends we seek. But when we realize that human action is just as likely to be non-rational—that we are limited in choosing means and ends—we are forced to recognize the possibility that God is involved in social action. Since Jacques Ellul is a major Christian commentator on this problem, his work will form the basis for our discussion.[22]

Arguing that God controls means and ends because they were established prior to the creation of humans, Ellul claims that the choice of our means should be determined by God's purpose. Since this is an ultimate end, any ends we may seek must either fit into the will of God or fall outside of it. In short, our rationality must be on God's terms.

Although the problem of means and ends was exemplified by the Fall, it preceded that event. In modern times, the problem has taken a new direction, one which emphasizes the problem of technology and its influence on human behavior. Ellul simply claims that in the development of new and powerful means we have forgotten our collective ends. In his words, "everything has become 'means.' There is no longer an 'end'; we do not know whither we are going."[23]

Here Ellul echoes the sympathies of social action theorists and the notion of *displacement of ends.* With the weakening of ultimacy in a secularized society, people shift their goals to a lower level of immediacy. What had been an end in the past has now become a means. Thus, everything becomes "useful" in a utilitarian society. If people had once sought to please God in their work, for example, they now seek to please the organization and the claims it makes on them.[24] The Protestant Ethic with its concern for the calling now becomes the "Social Ethic" with its emphasis on the career and its usefulness for social advancement.

In addition to the *ubiquity of means* and the *dissolution of ends,* another characteristic of means and ends has emerged in modern society: *means seek to justify themselves.* According to Ellul, the idea that "the end justifies the means" has become an outmoded notion that doesn't fit with the reality of today's world.[26] Because people no longer control society, their rationality is limited by the dominant technology of a modern world. Instead, anything is justified if it is effective and, today, technical means are effective or they are replaced by new techniques. Thus, the technical process, whether we find it in machinery, politics, or some other form of social activity, will justify itself. Ultimately, people are limited in their choice of means, and they are forced to choose only that which is effective. In such a world, as we have come to realize, even the question of morality becomes subservient to the question of success.

A final characteristic of means, as described by Ellul, is that they have become *totalitarian.* Ellul claims that "means have become so exclusive that they exclude everything which does not help their progress."[26] Consequently, our ultimate values are little more than an illusion to mask the sterile nature of the technological world in which we live. Worse, our spiritual values are under the influence of means and placed at their service. Put more simply, it is the nature of totalitarianism that it extends to everything, even the people who are controlled by the forces "they have made,

Ellul paints a gloomy picture that is difficult to deny in our society. The Christian, especially, is trapped in a world made by others but in which he or she must live. While not directly at fault for such a world, the Christian is not completely without responsibility. In day-to-day decisions, we have chipped away at God's world and left it in fragments. If we can find any hope, apart from the redemptive work of Christ and the promise of his return, it is in the realization that God has established the end and will bring it to pass. In the final analysis, there is nothing we can do except to be what God would have us to be.

Conclusion

Known for his atheism, C. Wright Mills was asked by a student whether he believed in anything. After a moment's thought, Mills replied, "Yes, a BMW engine." In his honesty and forthrightness, Mills exemplified his own belief that as an atheist, technology was the only object of his faith. He was conscious of who he was and how he fit into the world. Social action theory helps us to develop a consciousness of self and to understand the meaning it should have in a modern society. This means that the Christian has a special burden when faced with the principle of ultimacy. Living in a modern society, our self-consciousness differs from Mills's. As our history extends into eternity, we need to understand the world and its times as God does. We must understand the limits to science and rational thought when dealing with these ultimate ends. In this context, social action theory provides only a hint of how we are to proceed. But it also helps us to look at our neighbors and their needs and how to relate to them. Social action theory encourages a sympathetic perspective on people and highlights our personal shortcomings. In this sense, social action theory picks up some of the threads of biblical truth for us to follow.

Chapter 8

Exchange Theory

We have looked at three different ways of studying social reality. *Functionalism* considers social structures to be real and to have priority over individuals. *Conflict theory* argues that persons are the sources of social reality. *Social action* stresses the importance of the subjective meaning of a person's actions. This meaning is often religious and is considered real if actions are influenced by it.

Exchange theory begins with the question, "Why do people borrow something from others or lend something to them?" The answer is that the exchange itself is more important than what is exchanged. What counts is the social relationship involved in the exchange, not the thing itself. In social action theory, relations with others may be the means to some end. But in exchange theory, relations with others *is* the end.

Exchange theory provides a picture of people who are first social, then acquisitive. Unlike social action theory, exchange principles do not describe the person as a rational, end-seeking actor. Instead, exchange theory supports non-rational behavior as people forego their best interests for some group goal. Social action theory argues that ultimate ends are the main basis for gaining group unity. Exchange theory, however, describes the reality of social wholism and group unity as part of the exchange process. In short, *exchange theory describes people as social beings who place their emotional interests above their economic interests.*

The Background

How people are perceived is often influenced by their setting. In the case of exchange theory, it is important to note whether a complex or simple society is being studied. Weber, Parsons, and other social action theorists concentrated on the modern society and its development from simpler forms. In this setting, people are very individualistic, goal-seeking beings in a highly differentiated society. Early exchange theorists, however, concentrated on simple societies experiencing little social change. There they found a completely different kind of person, one who experienced obligation more than freedom and morality more than individualism.

Early exchange theory divided into two main traditions, one French and the other British. Each employs anthropological methods in the study of ethnographic data gained from primitive or other early societies. Each has roots in the functionalist tradition. They differ on the importance of the person and the group in the exchange process.

Durkheim's nephew and pupil, Marcel Mauss, claims the preeminent position in the French tradition because of his major work, *The Gift*. In this slim volume, Mauss conceived of gift exchange as the basis for a variety of wide-ranging social phenomena. Gift-giving was a part of all personal relationships between individuals and groups, and helped to shape moral, economic, aesthetic, and religious institutional structures. In order to understand these institutions correctly, he claimed, they must be seen as part of the exchange process. Put more simply, Mauss claimed that the exchange of gifts is part of a complex, concrete, social reality that must be studied as a totality if we are to understand it properly.

According to Mauss, the exchange of goods is a moral transaction and not a rational, economic one. "Things have values which are emotional as well as material; indeed in some cases the values are entirely emotional. Our morality is not solely commercial."[1] One aspect of this sentiment is found at Christmas when we are assured "it is more blessed to give than to receive." Even in a world of commercialism and materialism, moral precepts remain embedded in the act of gift-giving.

This is not to say that these precepts have the same meaning in our modern society. Although gift-giving may humanize our economic and rational self-interests, it is often little more than a shadow of the morality found in simple societies. The exchange of gifts at office Christmas parties has become such a ritualized form of behavior that it is far removed from the practice encountered in tribal groups. Similarly, the round of golf among businessmen involves an exchange often designed for manipulation rather than for moral reasons.

Mauss argued that we become rational, economic *beings* only in our modern, Western societies. Only then did a person become, in his words, "a calculating machine."[2]

> I believe that we must become, in proportion as we would develop our wealth, something more than better financiers, accountants and administrators. The mere pursuit of individual ends is harmful to the ends and peace of the whole, to the rhythm of its work and pleasures, and hence in the end to the individual,[3]

To counter this trend toward self-interest, Mauss encouraged a return to an awareness of the social reality of the group and the individual's place in it.

To this end, Mauss concentrated on the different meanings of things when comparing earlier societies with our own. In simpler societies the difference between persons and things was barely distinguishable. Things were not objects as they are today but meaningful parts of the family to be kept and treasured. Possessions gained value as they were passed from generation to generation and not because of their cost. Indeed, wealth was made to be shared or given away. This was the original social principle behind the Protestant Ethic with its philanthropic motives. In giving, a person gave something of self and, expecting something in return, was bound in dependence upon the other. Consequently, social relations developed in which the recipient was socially linked with the donor.

By contrast, a sharp distinction between person and thing exists in our culture. In a world of rapidly changing values, the value of anything is determined by its price and not by tradition. Wealth may be hoarded because it lacks any moral meaning in society. There is no norm requiring that it be shared with others. Without such expectations, social relations, especially across class lines, suffer. And where the traditional meaning of gift-giving is found, as in the giving of Thanksgiving baskets to the poor, it is usually trivialized by the limited and ritualized conditions surrounding its approval.

This quality of dependence in the exchange of gifts carries with it another quality—power. In simple societies, one always has an obligation to give, receive, and repay. Failure to continue the gift exchange may result in loss of social status or ostracism. The potlatch as practiced by the Indians of Northwest America, for example, is a ritualized practice of gift exchange. Since the Indian who spends recklessly gains social prestige and honor, a fierce competition to outdo each other ensues. Huge fortunes may be lost as people are caught up in the exchange and destruction of gifts. In turn, power is given to the victor in any potlatch.

Mauss concluded that the power found in the process of gift exchange comes to reside in the things themselves. In the tradition of Durkheim, he shows how such power has a spiritual quality. Stated differently, things gain religious meaning due to the power they have in the exchange process. Ultimately, people and things are linked because of the common meaning they share. Mauss describes how this common meaning is sharpened by the exchange process. "But in addition in giving [gifts], a man gives himself, and he does so because he owes himself—himself and his possessions—to others."[4]

Here we see again the unity of person and thing so characteristic of simple societies. But we also see a new social reality: *people* may be gifts. Mauss's countryman, Claude Levi-Strauss, developed this notion as a basis.for his theoretical approach of *structuralism*. This view claimed that certain universal forms were basic in the human cultural experience and paved the way for the establishment of various social structures. In other words, one structure, such as an institution, exists because it is related to another structure, which, in turn, gives it meaning.

Structuralism continues the idea that reality consists of social facts that are superior to individual facts, a notion that goes back to Durkheim and characteristic French social thought. Following this principle, Levi-Strauss claimed that marriage existed because of the incest taboo and a principle of reciprocity. A man would give up his sister or daughter only if his neighbor gave up his as well. Women, therefore, were meant to be exchanged and not kept as sexual objects. This principle of reciprocity acquired a powerful hold on the moral conscience of society, requiring the institution of marriage in place of incest. In Levi-Strauss's view, the superiority of marriage and the exchange of women as gifts established the importance of other rituals of exchange: the dowry and the giving of wedding presents.

In contrast to the French view of social collectivism, the British held to a more individualistic tradition. Bronislaw Malinowski, for example, rejects the idea that all religion has a social basis. Magic exists in primitive societies to "bridge the gap" between the known and the unknown. This is primarily a personal need, which magic fills, and is performed mainly outside the tribal context of religious rituals. The native fisherman, for example, would rely on magic when suddenly beset by a storm on the open sea. In this view, magic supplemented religion and existed as a personal, rational act intended to gain some religious end important to the individual.

Malinowski, as the foremost exponent of the British tradition, accepted a "principle of give and take" in exchange. But this principle carried with it personal as well as social benefits. "The real reason why all these economic obligations are normally kept, and kept very scrupulously, is that failure to comply places a man in an intolerable position, while slackness in fulfillment covers him with opprobrium."[5] For such a person, exchange met important personal and psychological needs as well as social functions.

Malinowski's classic description of the Kula Ring in the Trobriand Islands illustrates well the importance of psychological need in exchange. As natives traded among islands scattered over a wide expanse of ocean, they always exchanged armlets and necklaces in a prescribed manner. Malinowski interpreted this practice as a way of structuring a distant network of social relationships. He concluded that the Kula satisfied the natives' psychological needs to develop ties of friendship as well as to provide for social solidarity.

The history of exchange theory offers a fine example of the corrective tendency found in social thought. Early thinkers, operating from an economic, utilitarian framework, assumed that humans were merely rational, acquisitive beings. When the exchange process was studied in a different setting, the preliterate tribe, that notion was corrected. Depending on your preference for the French or British views, natives from simple cultures exchanged goods for either social or psychological reasons. In either case, it was clear that motives extended far beyond the economic, providing a new awareness of the social reality found in the exchange process.

It is important to note that the moral implications of primitive gift exchange broke down in modern society. As things acquired new meanings, they became impersonal and were separated from old values. Money, especially, was more widely used to determine the value of something and gradually weakened the personal and social meanings of exchange relationships. This did not mean that the rudimentary forms of exchange theory were obsolete. Instead, it suggested that some of the traditional exchange principles may still be applicable but in new settings and with different meanings. The task of modern exchange theory is to locate those settings and interpret those meanings.

The Theory

In the period from 1927 to 1932, a pioneering study in industrial sociology was completed at the Western Electric Company's Hawthorn works in Chicago. This study resulted in a series of books, among them the influential *Management and the Worker by F. J.* Roethlisberger and W. J. Dickson. This became a classic work and one of the first attempts to interpret the behavior of factory workers under both normal and abnormal conditions. Its contributions had a wide impact on sociology as well as the study of industrial relations.

The most famous study in this book was that of the bank wiring room with its description of relations among a group of men responsible for the assembling of telephone equipment. A major insight from this study was the realization that workers are not motivated by monetary rewards alone. Although these men could have increased their pay by working harder under a piecework plan, they set and maintained an upper level on production which was constant and below their maximum potential. What influenced them was a vague but firm notion that their traditional production level was "right" as well as beneficial for the group. Put more simply, the social and psychological values of their work were more important to them than its economic values.

The director of this series of studies, Elton Mayo, was a psychologist at the Harvard Business School. In one of his classes, Mayo assigned readings from the work of Malinowski and other British anthropologists to illustrate how rituals supported productive work in simple societies. A student in those classes, George Homans, perceived that social institutions were repeated in societies that could not have learned about these structures from each other. This suggested that cultures were not unique but were formed because human nature was the same around the world. He concluded that people working in similar situations could independently form similar institutions in very different societies.[6]

Homans illustrated this principle in a book that outlined the rudiments of his early exchange theory: *The Human Group.* Concentrating on an analysis of five diverse human groups—one of them the bank wiring room—Homans tried to understand the common features found in each. In other words, he pursued his earlier observation by showing how groups with very different purposes nevertheless had similar qualities. The result was a series of elegant propositions that have left their mark on modern sociology. In addition, Homans conceived of what he considered to be the critical problem in sociology: how people, under certain conditions, could develop and maintain certain structures that were never intended to be formed in the first place.

Whether this problem is as critical as Homans thinks is unimportant. What counts is the implication that people unintentionally construct new forms of social reality. They interact for a particular reason without noticing the social implications of that interaction. This was the case with the bank wiring men whose group social activities discouraged them from seeking higher monetary rewards. Further, human behavior may be controlled by these new social forms. The Trobriand Islanders, for example, became compulsive in their Kula activities for the purpose of maintaining some patterns of friendship.

Homan's bias against the French collectivist approach is also important. He believed a social fact could not be explained by another social fact as Durkheim had argued. Social forms could only be explained on the individual, psychological level. According to Homans, it was on this level that one would find the underlying psychological reality of all social life. In future work, Homans increased his study of this level of reality.

Before looking further at Homan's theory, we should note his emphasis on the human group as the major setting for social exchange in modern society. This was in contrast to earlier descriptions of the exchange processes in simple tribal life. He may go too far when claiming that civilizations decay with the weakening of group structures.[7] Nevertheless, his suggestion that individuals need group links with one another is a basic—if obvious—conclusion.

What kinds of links are these? How are people involved with each other in groups? Homans lays out the elements of his theory in *The Human Group* with three major concepts: *activity, interaction,* and *sentiment.* Homans considered these *first-order abstractions* because they are observable. Other concepts such as status and role constitute *second-order abstractions* because they are less observable. A mother, for example, is a second-order abstraction since this merely describes a person with many different responsibilities. Feeding children, however, is a first-order abstraction because it is an observable activity usually done *by* a mother.

Homans approached the study of exchange in group settings with a fundamental observation:

> When a number of persons have come together to form a group, their behavior never holds to its first pattern. Social life is never wholly utilitarian: it elaborates itself, complicates itself, beyond the demands of the original situation. *The elaboration brings changes in the motives of individuals.*[5]

Stated differently, more is exchanged in a group than is intended; the surplus of that exchange changes the members and even the group itself.

A key reason for this elaboration effect is the mutual dependence of action, interaction, and sentiment. Each affects the other and, in turn, is influenced by the others. In the bank wiring room action and interaction were dependent oil each other so that men could not work alone. As interaction increased with their mutual cooperation, each man found it necessary to cooperate. Similarly, sentiment and activity were linked causing men who liked each other to help each other. Reciprocally, helping others caused them to like those men more. At each point in the exchange process, the group and its members differed slightly from what they had been.

Homans describes these elements of action, interaction, and sentiment as parts of an *external system.* This was the social means provided by a certain group to deal with some specific problem. In a work group, it is simply the behavior needed to get a job done; connecting, soldering, etc. But an *internal system* results from the external system and influences it. A worker who doesn't approve of his partner's soldering methods will develop negative feelings about him. Two men who frequently work together will gradually exclude another member of the team simply because their interactions will increase their sentiments for each other. Elaboration occurs as these two systems, the internal and the external, are in gentle friction with each other. The result is a constantly changing set of activities, sentiments, and patterns of interaction.

It is unlikely that the Apostle Paul had this process in mind when he described sin in Romans 7. Still, one can readily see why people might "do that which they would not do" in a group experiencing elaboration. In such circumstances people say things they would not otherwise say or vote differently from their original intentions. People do not necessarily act rationally in a group. Nor is there anything special about Christian groups that insulates members from the elaboration effect. For this reason, it is important to see groups as places of potential tension and dissatisfaction as well as peace and unity. As one Christian leader has suggested, groups can be places where Satan sits among the members once the door is closed.

Homans systematically works through the studies he analyzes, noting the characteristics of each and how they influence the exchange process. In a study of street corner behavior, he describes some of the effects of social rank on behavior: "The higher a man's social rank, the larger will be the number of persons that originate interaction for him, either directly or through intermediaries."[9] That proposition implies a service element in exchange; people come to the leader for help. But since the elements are reciprocal, it is also true that "the higher a man's social rank, the larger the number of persons for whom he originates interaction, either directly or through intermediaries."[10] That proposition implies a power element in exchange; the leader gets the followers to help him. Put more simply, service and power are opposite sides of the same coin.

Scripture has much to say about service and power. We are told "to serve one another" (1 Peter 5:5) and "not to think of [ourselves] more highly than [we] ought to think" (Rom. 12:3), presumably to avoid a destructive power relationship in the church body described later in that chapter. Apparently, an awareness exists here that service and power are, indeed, opposite sides of the same coin. The human tendency would be to see these two qualities as morally comparable and equally desirable, depending on the situation. Scripture, however, alerts us to the superior quality of service over power and encourages us not to think of them as reciprocals. Exchange theory helps us to understand the elements in the problems of service and power and aids us in choosing the service side of the coin.

Homans is a good example of the scientist using the inductive approach in the study of data. Since all of the studies he analyzes were done by others, they constitute secondary data. Nevertheless, he doesn't come to those data with known biases or preconceptions. In his later work, however, he attempts to find explanations for his earlier findings. To do this, he turns to deductive method: abstract principles are applied to empirical data. Since these principles cannot be arbitrary, they need some consistent framework to hold them together.

Homans found his framework in behavioral psychology, especially that of B. F. Skinner whom he admired as a colleague at Harvard. This was a shift from his earlier years when Homans had been involved with Parsons, Merton, and other functionalists. Indeed, Homans's *The Human Group* may be as good an example of functionalism as of exchange theory. He broke with functionalist thinking, believing that the *person* should take priority over *social facts* when explaining social phenomena. What people did, he came to believe, was more important than what they experienced.

Homans made several assumptions in this deductive approach to human behavior. First, he assumed that Skinner's principles of behavior, derived from his study of pigeons, applied to people too. This meant that people entered into exchange that was more or less rewarding or costly to them. Another apparent assumption is the belief that people constitute the only form of reality. Any form of social organization, such as groups, results from human relationships and is more nominal than people. Finally, and perhaps most importantly for our consideration, his theory assumes that people are self-motivated, rationally evaluating every exchange for its rewards and punishments. Here Homans explicitly and openly recognized economic motives in the exchange process and implied a return to the earliest forms of exchange theory.

Which of Homans's two theoretical approaches is more accurate in its description of human behavior? Are people largely influenced by group processes that shape their relationships with others? Such a view suggests that people are primarily social beings who, unlike most animals, build their worlds with the help of others. Are people primarily individualistic and responsive to environmental stimuli that are evaluated as rewards and costs for the purpose of maximizing self-interest?

This second view suggests that people are mainly economic beings and not unlike animals who live for self-gratification. It may be that these two contrasting views are drawn too sharply and fail to do justice to the implications of Homans's work. Then, too, it may be that these differing views only exist because of the differing approaches used by Homans—one inductive and the other deductive. It may also be that both views are correct and represent humans accurately as complex and even contradictory beings in their social behavior.

Homans's work is admirably suited for an understanding of how exchange works in small group settings. But it does not explain how human relationships lead into more complex social structures. Even on the group level Homans does not account well for the negative aspects of human relationships. He says little about conflict, for example, and nothing about power. Nor does he give adequate attention to the role of the other person in the exchange process. Especially in his later work, behavior is the singular activity of one individual.

Peter Blau, writing at the time of Homans's later work, did much to deal with these questions in his expansion of exchange theory. Unlike Homans, who saw all activity as a form of exchange, Blau limited exchange to relations with others from whom rewards are expected and received. But since people are involved in many exchange relationships at one time, success in one relationship may produce strain or failure in another. Consequently, individuals experience dilemmas as they try to maintain balance and stability among relationships.

Blau uses the concept of social attraction to describe how exchange relationships are chosen. Social attraction explains a process whereby person *A* assumes the perspective of another, person *B as A* learns B's needs and values, then A presents himself to *B* as being attractive; *A* meets *B's* needs by displaying the values desired by *B*. In this way, *A* focuses on an exchange relationship with *B* who is encouraged to do the same for A.

We don't have to scratch too far below the surfaces of our own fives to understand how frequently and effectively we use the principle of social attraction. Ultimately, our objective is to gain some reward from *B* under the norm of reciprocity; if I meet B's needs, then he or she is expected to meet mine. And if I can maximize my reward from *B* with a minimum of cost on my part, so much the better. Self-interest is still a highly motivating factor, though less direct than in Homans's behavioral approach. Nevertheless, since we are always involved in a variety of exchange relationships, self-interest is heightened by the competition for social attraction. In short, *A* must always appear more socially attractive to *B* than *C or D*.

Blau explains how people compete with his description of four classes of rewards: money, social approval, esteem, and compliance. Ranked in terms of social value, money has the least value and compliance the most. Since power is the ability to gain compliance in an exchange relationship, power is highly valued as a social reward. Here Blau shifts to the group level by noting that groups provide different types of social rewards. Some groups offer all four types of rewards to their members while others provide fewer rewards. If we seek the greatest social values, then we will also be involved with those groups providing the most rewards, especially power.

The problem is that power is not distributed equally among group members. This is a potentially unstable situation that may provoke conflict unless group members accept the inequality of power. On the other hand, power may encourage group integration when group norms are placed over self-interest. This means that members willingly accept the inequality of power distribution and give priority to the social value of social stability. As stability continues, subgroups form and the larger organizational structure is accepted.

Here Blau moves beyond Homans's small group exchange theory and asks the question: How does exchange produce stability in larger organizations? In response, he stresses the importance of *shared values* instead of interpersonal attraction as the dominant feature of individual exchange. This means that certain group values involving exchange need to be accepted by the members. Such values would define expected rewards, stress the norm of reciprocity, or clarify fair exchange in the group. Without such values, Blau argues, social organization beyond the level of individual relationships would not be possible.

Finally, Blau is concerned with the role played by institutions in organizations. Since institutions represent traditional values, they clarify how new values fit into the exchange system. Fashion, for example, helps to define those values in clothing, automobiles, and other consumer products that grant power to members of society. In this way, Blau moves away from Homans's behaviorism and recognizes a level of reality beyond the individual. On the other hand, he does not move to Parsons's argument of ultimacy as the basis for shared values. He remains something "more" than an exchange theorist, in the sense of Homans, but "less" than a functionalist, in the tradition of Parsons.

A Christian Critique

Exchange theory raises problems of a different sort from those found in earlier theories. The questions it deals with involve individual attitudes toward people and things. Homans's discussion of the elaboration process, derived from the works of the Italian sociologist Vilfredo Pareto, is vital for Christians. We cannot assume, as we like to do, that we control our attitudes by associating with people like ourselves. Elaboration occurs because of the exchange process itself and not because of the persons involved in the process. This means that Christians may have as much unintentional self-interest as the nonbeliever.

Another important problem for the Christian is the confusion between people and things that may occur in the exchange process. Mauss pointed to the frequent and even necessary occurrence of this tendency in simple societies. Today, we dislike the idea that people may be treated as things or that things may be loved like people. Those with a high view of creation, especially, wince at the thought that the meaning of people and things may be reversed. The abortion issue may provide a clear understanding of the meaning of life. On other issues, however, the distinction may not be as clear.

Since the exchange process is influential in the shaping of human attitudes and actions, Christians cannot take their motives for granted. We cannot assume our best intentions will be fulfilled once we are involved in relationships with others. Each type of exchange must be analyzed for its particular meaning as well as for how it might influence our attitudes and actions.

Money

The classic sociologists understood how the use of money changed relationships in modern society. Weber, for example, considered money to presuppose bureaucracy.[11] Simmel had more to say about the specific effects of its use on people. "Money has carried to its extreme the separation... between man as a personality and man as the instrument of a special performance or significance."[12] In short, money causes people to become different socially from what they are personally.

Money is not something we readily control. Therefore, the meaning of money changes in a society that comes to rely on it. Using money puts us into the economy and we are controlled by it. Exchange is no longer personal and limited to human relationships. It now acquires the national, and even global, meaning that money has in a modern economy.

This is Jacques Ellul's view in his penetrating analysis of the meaning of money for the Christian. Written in 1954, *Money and Power* has a prophetic ring for today. Ellul claims, first, that *money has become abstract* because people can no longer understand the fixed value that it used to have. With rapid inflation, for example, its value may change daily. Also, *money has become impersonal* as the international economy has become more important. Oil prices are set in the Mideast and not at the corner service station. Consequently, much responsibility for the use of our money is taken from us.[13]

In this situation, we are more concerned with the condition of the economy than its morality. "Thus we subordinate moral and individual problems to the collective problem, to the total economic system."[14] People are not held responsible for their use of money except in the most blatant cases of greed and misuse. They are merely seen as victims of a dominant economic system. People tend to assume that once inflation has been reduced or the unemployment rate goes down, morality will enter the marketplace again. Of course, it rarely does.

Ellul claims that when people stress the systemic importance of money, they may argue for one economic system over another. But instead of siding with capitalism or socialism, it's more important to understand the spiritual reality of money. As a spiritual entity, money can be a blessing. It may have other spiritual qualities when used for stewardship purposes. Since these qualities are usually symbolic, it is more important to understand what money may stand for than what it may be used for. Referring to Ecclesiastes 5:10-11, Ellul says "a person's hunger for money is always the sign, the semblance of another hunger—for power or rank or certainty. The love of money is always the sign of another need—to protect oneself, to be a superman, for survival or for eternity."[15] To understand the true meaning of money, Ellul turns to Jesus' reference to money as "mammon" and the idea that money is a power. Specifically, *money controls us when we subordinate people to it in a buying-selling relationship.* We value money more than people, for example, when fair wages are not paid for work. In any such case, the value of a person is denied as he or she is further dehumanized as objects. Instead of glorifying God, their true Creator, people are now subject to money and its owners.

In addition to the economic meaning of money in exchange, there is a social meaning as well. As money dominates a relationship, a competitive attitude develops that seeks to establish one person as superior to another. Gradually, competition becomes a norm and money the basis for it. Although the world may encourage, such a relationship, the Christian cannot. As in so many other forms of social relationships, the believer must be in tension with the world and resist its controlling influence.

For Ellul, exchange is not merely an economic or even a social process. It has a spiritual meaning that pits the person against spiritual powers in human relationships. We might see this spiritual meaning as part of the elaboration process described by Homans. Ellul prefers to see it as a form of reality we cannot master: "[We] still cannot dominate the love of money, for this is aroused by a seductive power which is far beyond us, just as it is maintained by a force that is outside us."[16] Here, as elsewhere, Ellul is in the structuralist tradition of Mauss and Levi-Strauss but always with a clear awareness of the biblical basis for the structured spiritual reality found in exchange.

Power

Although Ellul is clear that money is a power in human relationships, it is not the only power to be found there. "Power is something that acts by itself, is capable of moving other things, is autonomous (or claims to be), is a law unto itself, and presents itself as an active agent."[17] One finds power in a relationship wherever he or she enjoys domination or control of another.

Ultimately, all legitimate power was authorized by God in creation (Col. 1:15-20). The Christian gladly accepts and submits to its authority. All other power is a human construction devised for worldly purposes in human relationships. Ultimately, the intent of such power is to maximize the gain and minimize the loss of self. In each case, the will of one person is subordinated to the will of the other.

With the multiplication of the means of exchange in modern society comes a comparable increase in the forms of power. A doctor has power over a patient when tests are required to make a diagnosis. Budgets convey power to whoever controls them. The person controlling time in a relationship also gains power over the caller "put on hold." In a modern society, the forms of power are increasingly available to all of us.

Another type of power is found among persons of influence, those referred to by C. Wright Mills as the *power elite*. These are people who have the means to transcend the environments of ordinary people and insulate themselves against the shocks of daily life.[18] These are leaders who, like Adam and Eve, seek to escape the confines of their world. And like Adam and Eve, they experience and spread the corrupting influence of power.

Ironically, we admire their achievements and their success in gaining "the American dream." If there is a problem here, it need not be with success itself. The problem occurs when power is used to gain that success and then denies others access to such power.

Two clear symptoms of the use of power are present in an exchange relationship. First, some persons exhibit a "take charge" attitude that places them in positions of dominance. This attitude conveys a false sense of one's ability to control a situation and separates the person from dependence on God. Used in this way, power may strain and even break the relationship one should have with God. Second, some possess a competitive attitude that denies power to another. Since there is a limited supply of anything exchanged in a relationship, the person with power must have more of that commodity than the other. In sports, for example, the winner presumably has more skill than the loser. Put more simply, *power on one side of a relationship requires powerlessness on the other.*

In one sense, the poor and powerless are always with us (John 12:8; Matt. 26:11). They remain clear and abiding indications of sinfulness in the world. In this sense, poverty and powerlessness were not intended by God. A unity and balance in relationships may come only when the weak and powerless are raised to places of equality (1 Cor. 12:12-26). Such equality comes only with a reversal in the way we think about relationships. In brief, the self is to be subordinate to the other person and to the relationship as well. When we fail to reverse our thinking, we ensure the continued presence of the poor and powerless about us. Gradually sin becomes structured in society as it accepts the powerlessness of people.

This resulting sinfulness takes several different forms. First, *powerlessness denies the humanity of the person.* Powerless people are like boxes in a corner, objects, without the will or means to move across the room. As objects of another's power, to the powerful, they appear as less than the object of God's will. This means, second, *they are denied the use of the gifts God gave them.* They are limited as instruments of God's grace in their relationships with others. *Finally, powerlessness seeks power to fill the vacuum in lives.* Denied access to the acceptable forms of power, the powerless turn to those deviant forms of power unacceptable to society. As deviants, the powerless are transformed into threats to the powerful.

Without social power, Jesus was also a threat to the powerful. In response, he sought no new forms of worldly power. To the disciples' dismay, he didn't come to establish new economic, social, or political systems. Instead, he relied on the transcendent power provided by God to his Son. It is this power that now allows the powerless to be powerful.

We can identify with Christ, for we are all powerless in this world. In response, we have several options open to us. Like the power elite, we can find new forms of power in a changing world, forms that give us the competitive edge in our relationships. We may also try to understand the forms of power made available by God to his people. These are the principles found in revelation: the Ten Commandments and the Golden Rule. Ultimately, they are the forms of power that equalize all exchange relationships.

Manipulation

Power implies two things in an exchange relationship: that we have successfully attained what we wanted from it and that we have been efficient in getting it. This is the first aspect of power—the success factor—that makes power so attractive *in* our world. But the other aspect, the efficiency factor, cannot be forgotten. This implies that we want to succeed with the smallest cost. We want to use the best means to gain our end.

Efficiency, then, implies a best choice among alternatives. These alternatives might be external or internal, technical or personal. Instead of employing external means, which may be costly or unpredictable, we prefer, to rely on those familiar means most available to us. That might mean getting more efficient use out of our equipment. It might also mean using personal relationships to better advantage.

Manipulation, in the sense of behavioral psychology, refers to some change in a setting that produces a specified change in a person exposed to that setting. This notion of manipulation fits well into Homans's later exchange theory. Another and more sociological view of manipulation perceives the person as a means to the attainment of some goal. Two questions arise concerning this type of manipulation. Does the person understand that he or she is being used as a means to some goal? Does the person agree to being used in that way? Manipulation implies that people are used without their understanding or consent.

The way people view personal freedom and equality has much to do with their attitudes toward manipulation. Those who believe they have complete freedom and equality have a problem when manipulation is identified. Such persons will rarely agree to being manipulated. On the other hand, those accepting limitations on personal freedom and equality may accept manipulation in certain situations. One finds them volunteering for distasteful tasks shunned by others. When certain ends are at stake, such people may gladly submit their wills and even their lives in a cause.

Christians are also among those who may accept manipulation in certain situations.[19] First, Christians accept the fact that people are not completely free or equal. They know that God's plan bounds their lives and requires their submission. Children, for example, are not as free as or equal to their parents. Second, Christians should want to fit into God's plans for their lives. This would include being used as a means to attain a certain purpose. The crucial problem, of course, is to understand that purpose and how to fit into it.

Fortunately, there always seems to be others to provide spiritual counsel and help our understanding. In such cases, a counselor helps the counselee to understand God's will for his or her life. Usually the relationship is honest and the exchange is open. The counselee gives up some freedom while accepting the superior judgment of the counselor. But even under these ideal conditions, manipulation, in its human sense, is possible if the counselor inserts his or her own desires into the process. In manipulation, the will of the counselor may appear to be substituted for the will of God.

The point is that manipulation is ubiquitous in our relationships. Even in a benign situation such as counseling, we may fall into a manipulative attitude toward others. Thinking as the world does, we often use others to solve our problems. This means that we think simplistically. We like to believe that people are like the machines we master in a host of daily activities. We push the right buttons and they give the proper response. What we try to avoid is a complex relationship in which the other exerts his or her will in a threatening manner. Consequently, we try to deny the will of the other at the same time that we magnify our own. In this kind of competitive situation, reciprocity is weakened and the relationship is threatened.

Reciprocity is one of those principles found in Scripture as well as in sociology. We find it whenever people share equally at some level in a relationship. The encounter between Jesus and the woman at the well, for example, was a reciprocal relationship. There was no attempt to manipulate the woman for some ulterior purpose. At each point in the discussion, the woman's curiosity and understanding was aroused. Her humanity was nourished until as an act of her own will, she accepted Christ as the Messiah and told others about him.

If we are to preserve the best qualities of the exchange relationship, we need to understand our motives. Our worldly attempts to be successful or efficient in a social relationship may strain or even break the relationship. The Christian also needs to be God's means to accomplish God's ends. In sensitive and perceptive ways, the believer must be a faithful instrument of God's will. Resistance or insensitivity at this point strains the relationship with our Lord. Finally, exchange is always improved when the person is enhanced as a subject. This means we understand the other as a human being, as one created by God, and not as an objectified being.

Altruistic Love

We have noted that power and service are two sides of the same coin. If A initiates action for B and controls ZJ's behavior, then A has power. A's will is dominant and B is subordinated to it. In service, the process is reversed. Here B initiates the action for A who becomes a servant as he or she responds to S's initiation. In this case, B's will is dominant and A subordinates his or her will for B's sake. As a servant, A is willing to be used as an object by B whose value as a person is then enhanced.

Homans, remember, referred to these principles in the context of leadership. It is the person with high social rank who has the greatest potential for power and service, because high status provides the authority for power and the attractiveness for service to others. It is important, then, to have high social rank but to think and act in terms of low rank. For this reason, a Christian is told in Scripture "not to think of himself more highly than he ought to think" (Rom. 12:3). This means ignoring our own high social rank and thinking in human terms, as the equal of others.

Jesus represents the best model for such thought and action. Giving up his high rank, he became equal to humans (Phil. 2:6-8). He became a servant as he subordinated his will on the cross to the will of the Father. As an object of rejection by the Jews, he confirmed their human willfulness. Further, he acknowledged his acceptance of the Father's will when he prayed "not my will, but yours be done" (Luke 22:42). Finally, he subordinated his will and became an object of sacrifice for all who willingly put their trust in him.

Jesus is also the model for altruistic love as described by Pitirim Sorokin, an eminent sociologist.

> Real altruism begins . . . when an individual freely sacrifices his rightful interests in favor of the well-being of another, refraining from harming him, even though his legal right entitles him to do so, and helping him in various ways, though no

law demands of him such action. In this sense altruistic conduct is always above the purely legal conduct exacted by statutes. In contrast to obligatory legal conduct, altruistic conduct is always free from any external compulsion. It is freely chosen and it is also the purest form of free conduct known.[20]

As a perfect, sinless being, Jesus was completely free to become thoroughly equal with human beings. By comparison to this, human altruistic love is always faulty.

Nevertheless, Sorokin finds in altruistic love a necessary antidote for the world's problems. A Christian in the tradition of Leo Tolstoy, Sorokin left Russia after the revolution and emigrated to the United States. He helped found the sociology department at Harvard in 1930 and was a key figure in establishing its prestige. Although his thought and personal style often made him a renegade among his peers, Sorokin's prophetic work is gradually being rediscovered.

One of Sorokin's major interests was the study of social change. He believed that in modern Western culture all values are denned in sensate terms: nothing is real if it doesn't appeal to the senses. Consequently, our culture is fundamentally materialistic, hedonistic, and utilitarian. Even people have been reduced to the level of mere sensory objects. To counter this pattern, a definition of reality based on supersensory, religious values must be fostered. Sorokin believed that Western culture had passed its sensate peak and needed these new religious expressions to replace the old forms. Altruism was the most important of these expressions.

Sorokin was fascinated by the impact that revolution and social crises seemed to have on interpersonal behavior. He believed the normal tendency to moral indifference found in routine forms of social exchange was intensified in periods of crisis. This meant the majority of people sought self-oriented gratification while only a minority of people sought altruistic, religious activity. If sociology were to prepare for this post-sensate period, it needed to understand the forms of altruism and how to encourage them in social relationships.

These are intriguing thoughts. One can understand why Sorokin was considered a curiosity in the field. He was advocating the kind of social morality and group consensus found in Durkheim's work at a time when his colleagues were describing the self-interested, competitive spirit of their day. They were talking about reality as they saw it while Sorokin described reality as he thought it should be.

Which view is correct? In one sense, exchange theorists like Homans and Blau are correct. Their analyses describe a competitive human nature with its manipulative approach to social exchange. As far as it goes, this is an accurate picture of much human behavior. Since the picture is more complex than that, however, Sorokin offers a reasonable alternative. Remember, he believed a minority would still be inclined to altruism in a crisis. Referring to the kind of altruism found in Jesus, Francis of Assisi, and other saints, he claims that altruism could provide a viable basis for future relationships. To that end, he established the Harvard Research Center in Creative Altruism in 1949. His goal was to show what altruism might look like and how it might be fostered. Sorokin simply tried to describe a side of the coin we do not often see.

Conclusion

Nevertheless, there is a problem here: Can we be sure that altruism and other forms of exchange are always what they purport to be? Is it possible that altruism may simply be an illusion? Herbert Schlossberg claims that altruism is "best interpreted as a counterfeit of Christian love."[21] In a sense this is true. Certainly Sorokin's attempt to capture the spirit of altruism for the masses in some institutionalized form doesn't comprehend the nature of biblical altruism. In its institutional form, altruism is closer to an ideology.

But all forms of social exchange have this built-in fake factor. As with any social reality, the possibility of self-delusion always exists. Unable to understand or accept the corrupt nature of the world, our perception of ourselves may also be darkened. In modern society, especially, the potential for illusion in human relationships is heightened by the forces of change about us. One of these forces is a major topic of concern in the next chapter.

Chapter 9

Symbolic Interactionism

In the word was the beginning . . . the beginning of Man and of Culture."[1] Even for the mid-twentieth century, Leslie White has made a rather audacious statement. At first, the aphorism seems to parody Scripture and nothing more. But this celebration of the "Word" actually attempts to give new meaning to the symbol as the origin and basis of human behavior. As the cell is the basic building block of living tissue, White contends, so the symbol is the basic unit of civilization.

In one sense White, a modern American anthropologist, is correct. The ability to use symbols is a key point of distinction between humans and anthropoids. This is a high view of people whose minds are fundamentally different from lower animal forms because of this ability to form cultures with symbols. At the same time, White offers a low view of creation and God's work in it. He does not recognize that this Word has been expressed by God in specific, tangible form (John 1:1). Nor does his view recognize that God used symbols to give specific meaning to his creation (Gen. 1:5) and accepted the names given by man to creatures (Gen. 2:19). In White's view, people interact with symbols instead of with God.

White defines a symbol "as a thing the value or meaning of which is bestowed upon it by those who use it."[2] This means that people, through the use of symbols, can give value or meaning to anything. Since God is not in the picture, it is pointless to ask whether a human meaning is in agreement with his. A married couple, for example, may accept the meaning of a binding relationship implied in the symbol of a wedding ring. If they do, they would accept the symbolic meaning given to marriage by God. But if there is no absolute basis for marriage as a binding relationship, then a couple may define it as they will. A symbol may mean nothing more than what we agree it will mean. By consensus, it appears we give the symbol the meaning we want.

The Background

Symbolic interactionism describes the kind of social reality found in the interaction of people with the symbols they make and use. It is one of those theories usually referred to as *interpretive sociology* because the person is considered dominant in social life. In such theories, people shape the meaning about them with their social action. By contrast, naturalistic sociological theories conceive of social structures as the dominant form of social reality. In these theories, people are subservient to the group and shaped by it.[3]

Interpretive sociologies are increasingly popular because they appear to do a good job of explaining the place of people in modern society. In this sense, social action theory qualifies as an early form of interpretive sociology. At a time when earlier theories were foundering on emerging issues, social action theories provided new ways of interpreting a person's place in society. As a leading theorist in this school, Weber looked away from the stable social structures of traditional societies to the problems of an emerging modern world. The result was an appreciation for the importance of the actor who could choose among a host of options. But Weber never completely accepted the German philosophical tradition that led to sharply defined interpretive sociology. He realized that humans were not as free as this tradition implied; freed from one social bond, they were trapped in another. In this sense, Weber held to a naturalistic view of social theory.

Symbolic interactionism is well suited for dealing with the problems found in the vague, shifting social setting of our world. Modern problems are not readily studied by measured, empirical means. This is especially true in the informal and more intimate social relationships found in contemporary life. In urban settings, for example, rapid change has eroded the traditional means of behavior. Gestures, words, and even clothing have been transformed by the new settings in which they are found. For this reason, symbolic interactionists turn to the process of social interaction itself to find and interpret social meanings.

It is not surprising that symbolic interactionism has been identified with the Chicago school of sociology and its concern for urban problems. Studying society's deviants and emerging enigmas, these theorists concentrated on the new social problems found there. Minority groups, for example, offered a tapestry of symbolic cultures for interpretation. With little understanding of the dominant culture, these minorities acted on the new subjective definitions for life as they found it. In a very real sense the Chicago school showed that people shape their communities and, in turn, are shaped by them.

Though not a professional sociologist, George Herbert Mead had an enormous influence on the development of symbolic interactionism. Teaching philosophy at the University of Chicago almost from its inception, Mead was part of a group of thinkers including William James, William I. Thomas, and Charles Horton Cooley who tried to show the linkage between consciousness and the objective world. Thomas, remember, had stated that if consciousness defined a situation as real it was real in its consequences. It was the mind, then, that influenced the objective world and not the other way around.

Looking to language for a link between the mind and social action, Mead found it in the *significant symbol*. Of all the gestures located in a social setting, some were understood by all. These significant symbols referred to objects and called out a common response among persons much as a Santa Claus draws the attention of children at Christmas. As people interpret symbols with common meanings, they interact. Further, they can take the point of view of someone who gives the same meaning to the significant symbol and make adjustments to agree with that person. Finally, it is possible, once significant symbols have been identified, to consider various routes to some symbolized object, mentally practice which of these routes should be pursued, and then take the appropriate action. All of this assumes, of course, that the interpretation is correct and that problems will not occur when action is taken.

This process of mentally putting oneself in another's place or "taking the role of the other" allows for great efficiency in behavior. The person chooses among alternative actions instead of responding to stimuli. Thus, individual will, not environmental conditions, becomes the basis for action. At the same time, human action is a fundamentally social phenomenon; the presence of others must be considered, not ignored.

Mead's idea of "taking the role of the other" was a key building block in the development of what has come to be known as *role theory*. In Mead's day, social evolutionary thought was still arguing for the objective nature of society and its determining influence on behavior. As these ideas gradually slipped in popular appeal, Mead's views offered an alternative. Social structures became nothing more than networks of human expectations requiring different types of role performance from people. This meant that society was little more than patterns of coordinated activity maintained by people in interaction with others. This was, indeed, a radical shift from evolutionary thought.

Mead was especially concerned with the problem of individual and group interaction. Why should a boy, for example, be influenced more by a father than by a Little League coach? Would the family or the team be more important for the boy? Each group conveyed expectations to the boy that demanded a response. Mead explained that the boy would give priority to the significant other: either the father or the coach, whichever provided the significant symbol for the boy. In short, the control of symbols could lead to the control of people.

The illustration also shows that significant symbols may change the structures of groups. If social structures are networks of expectations, changing those expectations changes the structures. If the boy, for example, expects the father to spend time with him and the father knows it, the father can maintain good parental relationships by playing ball with his son. But if the boy knows that the coach expects him to play ball for the team and the boy shares that expectation, he might as well play ball for the coach and not with the father. Gradually, family relationships as well as the structure itself change as the son moves into non-family roles and relationships.

Mead saw this pattern of institutional change as a normal part of social life. If society is nothing more than a constructed phenomenon resulting from adjustments made among people's expectations, then society undergoes constant change through the influence of those persons. Some choose to continue with traditional institutional expectations and fulfill those responsibilities. Others choose different expectations, thereby changing traditional institutional patterns. Change is unpredictable, Mead would argue, simply because people are unpredictable, especially as they interact with others.

Even though Mead recognized the unpredictable nature of human beings, he also believed the self could be a stable, predictable personality. Stability resulted from people taking another's point of view. For instance, Mead claimed that significant symbols aroused in the user the same response understood by the receiver. If A shook a fist to intimidate B, A also experienced the power of intimidation directed at B. Consequently both persons could predict and share the meaning of the symbol and its effect on the other. What they also shared was the attitude of the other toward one's self.

Mead saw this process of self-evaluation proceeding through three stages: *play*, the *game*, and the *generalized other*. In loosely-defined forms of play, the child takes the role of several others and gradually develops a self-image based on their expectations. The game is a more highly structured form of cooperative activity in which the child tests those self-images against the expectations of others. Self-conceptions are more stable and reliable forms of self-image that develop as they fit expectations of others in structured situations. Predictability in behavior and self-awareness increases as the child conforms to some generalized other—community of attitudes that the child personally accepts and conforms to. At this level, the child has developed a self-conception that fits with the expectations of a larger community. The resulting behavior is shared by the community as a whole and not just by significant others.

This description of the socialization process fits well with much of what we have come to accept in modern social science. Mead's theory, however, does raise several problems. The first has to do with the exclusively social nature of mind, self, and society—Mead's major concepts. Do they share some part of a larger form of reality, or do they constitute a separate form of reality? We will develop this idea later.

Another problem has to do with the effectiveness of the process *of* self-development. Can children be socialized into society if generalized others are weak and unstable? Accustomed to the traditional family structure, Mead did not envision today's weak families and the barrier they would cause for self-development. People struggle with self-evaluation when social forms of reality offer little basis for the development of stable selves. With no other form of reality to turn to, people develop weak and unstable selves.

In one sense, Mead did recognize this problem of unstable selves in his description of the two parts of the self. The "I" is the acting part that is creative and spontaneous in its social responses. The "me," however, is a composite of all the internalized attitudes of others accepted *by* the self. In interaction, the "me" conforms to expectations while the "I" is impetuous and unpredictable. In simple societies, the "me" tends to dominate while the "I" is more prominent in complex societies. Together the "I" and the "me" allow for balance in personality as well as in society.

For Mead, social organization cannot exist without personal awareness of others and their views.

> It is only insofar as the individual acts not only in his own perspective but also in the perspective of others, especially in the common perspective of a group, that a society arises and its affairs become the object of scientific inquiry. The limitation of social organization is found in the inability of individuals to place themselves in the perspectives of others, to take their points of view.... In the field of any social science the objective data are those experiences of the individuals in which they take the attitude of the community, that is, in which they enter into the perspectives of the other members of the community.[4]

Reality, then, is objective as well as subjective and to study it, we must enter into the proper perspective on it.

The Theory

With this statement of Mead's as background, we should note the difference between an *attitude,* as it is used in most sociological theory, and *& perspective,* as it is used in symbolic interactionism.[5] An attitude refers to a person's expected future action. If we know a person's attitude toward some object or person, then we can make a good prediction as to that person's behavior. A perspective, however, links the person to some reference group instead of a future action. This means the person will act depending on the perspective used by the group to which he or she refers behavior. How the person has acted in the past relative to that object is unimportant.

Since we all have many such reference groups, the perspective could be quite unpredictable. A church member, for example, may vote quite differently from other members if he or she is influenced by an occupational group instead of the church. Put more simply, *perspectives are more subjective and less measurable than attitudes.*

Perspectives are also more flexible and unstable. A perspective changes as interpretations of a situation change. Even if a person's perspective is known, a change in the situation as it is perceived could change a person's response to that situation. An attitude toward a friend for example, will always be positive because a friend is, by definition, always viewed positively. A perspective on a friend, however, may change that attitude, depending on the situation. In short, the meaning of a friend depends on the interpretation given to the situation.

Despite the unpredictable nature of perspectives, we can make two rough assumptions about them. Since things are not necessarily perceived as they have been but sometimes as they might be, there is a creative quality to perspectives. The stress is on the new or potential meanings of things rather than the old or traditional. Another assumption we can make is that perspectives will often be pragmatic. This means that objects or people are defined according to their usefulness for us in some future situation. Extending that assumption a bit, we could also say that the meaning of something is dependent on a person's involement in a situation. A friend, for example, has no meaning until he or she is given meaning by another. The creative and pragmatic quality of perspective, then, directs the interpretation given to the meaning of things.

To illustrate the symbolic interactionists' point of view, consider the role of a catcher in a baseball game. Generally, the catcher is governed by certain rules requiring the giving of signals to the pitcher, *receiving* the pitch, returning the ball to the pitcher, and so on. But some situations are not clearly structured and may require a creative and pragmatic approach. If a base runner is sliding into home, no rule demands that the catcher must block the plate. If the situation is interpreted symbolically by the catcher as a blocking situation, then he will block the plate. In a game, the catcher does what he believes needs to be done. Put more simply, *if the rules allow for interpretation of meaning, symbols shape that meaning for interpretation by others.*

In situations that are open to interpretation, then, symbols communicate meaning to others. As social objects, symbols may be used in any way people might choose. When a vendor throws a bag of peanuts to a customer in the stands, something that would not ordinarily be done, we may conclude the situation is flexible and the behavior acceptable. If a coach slaps the rear of a player circling the bases after a home run, approval is communicated and nothing more. Since the crowd shares the same meaning, it accepts the slap as a significant symbol and applauds to show its approval of the player as well.

Since symbols are abstractions, they may be used to construct reality as well as communicate it. This is done when the meaning usually associated with some concrete act or object is separated from it and given to a different concrete act or object. The symbol *gay,* for example, has been disassociated from the feeling of joy and associated with homosexuality in some situations. The problem is to interpret the meaning of the symbol correctly in any specific situation. This is done when the word becomes a significant symbol and gains the social approval of others. In this way, humans construct a new social reality.

But people also symbolize in interaction with themselves. They do this when berating or arguing with themselves. This means that the self is also a social object open to interpretation. Charles Horton Cooley used the descriptive phrase *looking-glass self* to describe this quality. We look at ourselves as images placed on a mirror by others. In this way, we become objects to ourselves just as others are objects to us. As mirrored selves, we have time to evaluate those images and, if desired, change them symbolically. If we think we're unattractive, a new hair style or teeth braces may be enough to change that image. In every situation, we see ourselves as we think others see us and then adjust accordingly.

A radical view sees the self as a process rather than as an object. Like other social objects, the self is constantly changing with every social interaction. In one situation, I am confident; in another, timid and afraid. In this radical view, the self has no tangible quality that continues, unchanging, throughout life. Nothing can define such a confidence or fear; no abiding uniqueness can give it meaning or direction. In fact, we may learn to see ourselves as objects that don't really exist. Or we may see ourselves merely as products of social interaction, always becoming and never complete.

Others take a less radical view and recognize an enduring, consistent aspect in the self. Although this aspect may result from interaction, it also influences interaction and contributes to the enduring self-conception. Someone hoping to be a great actor in the future does not readily accept all contrary opinions. The looking-glass self is adjusted depending on who is holding the mirror. A movie producer's opinion may be accepted when a family member's may not. In this view, the self may be flexible but not fluid. There is an indelible quality that limits its adjustment to any situation, and that quality gives a different meaning to the self.

It is easy to be critical of the radical view of the social self. The possibility that some enduring spiritual quality may be part of the self is simply nonexistent in this view. But if we see the self as a key to understanding life in a modern world, the idea of a social self, at least as presented by the second view, gains merit. A major integrator of contemporary symbolic interactionism, Herbert Blumer, states: "The possession of a self provides the human being with a mechanism of self-interaction with which to meet the world—a mechanism that is used in forming and guiding his conduct."[6] Attempting to interpret complex and often contradictory situations, a person uses the self to call out all that has been experienced about similar situations. In addition, interaction with the self allows for mental reconstruction of circumstances and how to deal with them. By means of the imagination, situations are rehearsed in the mind for the best approach to be used before putting it into action.

This process of self-interaction leads to two prominent values characteristic of symbolic interactionist thought. The first is the value of *self-interest*. Whenever we analyze a situation to understand how it affects us personally, the self becomes dominant. It then replaces others as a major object of concern. The second value is *self-manipulation*. We control ourselves by the same symbolic means we control any other social object. The objective is to anticipate and solve future problems so as to enhance our self-concept. Those who embrace symbolic interactionism simply believe they can become all that they want to be.

Since symbolic interactionism always recognizes an interplay between the self and society, collective values are shaped by individual values and vice versa. The mass media shape these values by choosing heroes who solve problems with a "take charge" view of life. In real life, these are often sports heroes whose self-motivation and directed discipline have made them successful. In fiction, heroes are painted more broadly as outsiders, the Rambo types, who justify their individualistic and often anti-social behavior. With these stereotypes firmly embedded in our minds, the values of self-manipulation and self-interest gradually become part of our cultural thinking.

Of course, people are never completely consumed with their own needs and desires. As symbolic interactionists are quick to remind us, the formation of a self-concept depends on a relationship with others. If we develop a strong social self, it is because we have learned to interact and cooperate with them. Gradually, we take on the perspective of some larger group—in Mead's term, the generalized other—and learn to solve problems through the control of self. In Mead's thinking, the self and society are two sides of the same coin, simply because they share the same social reality.

Society, then, is not necessarily a hostile place. There is no clear "struggle for survival," to use Spencer's term, or "war of all against all," to use Hobbes's phraseology. Society consists of people who act by taking each other into account. As people interact with symbols, they come to share a common perspective in interaction. Communication allows them to fit their acts together, solving problems in the process. Gradually they come to understand their differences and share their similarities. But only by taking a holistic view of society can we see this merger of individualism and social responsibility.

Herbert Blumer uses the *term joint action* to describe this general process of developing social relationships:

> To begin with, a joint action cannot be resolved into a common or same type of behavior on the part of the participants. Each participant necessarily occupies a different position, acts from that position, and engages in a separate and distinctive act... Instead, the participants fit their acts together, first, by identifying the social act in which they are about to engage and, second, by interpreting and defining each other's acts in forming the joint act.[7]

Whenever people come together, pragmatically and with self-interest, to aid each other in solving a problem, joint action occurs. A committee meeting, students studying for a test, even a marriage are examples of joint action. And, in each case, they are also examples of society.

Blumer does not see society as an established social structure. As a critic of functionalism, he rejects any idea of society as a system that gives rise to human action. Instead, society results from people coming together to meet the conditions of their lives. Through joint actions, they construct the reality of society from what is important to them. Through the process of symbolic interaction, then, society comes into being. In any case, the actor's objective is always to serve the needs of people and not the expectations of society.

In contrast to the functionalist view—that society makes people—symbolic interactionists take the opposite view; people make society. Since society is nothing more than people in symbolic interaction, each person has the capacity to influence and direct society. This is done as social roles are symbolically reinterpreted and society reflects those new interpretations; women move into the professions in greater numbers, marriages become more fragile, and evangelists rely on TV for spreading the gospel. In each case, society is restructured as individual needs are met.

But symbolic interactionists are not one-sided on this question. They acknowledge the influence of society on people as well. Over time we learn to accept some of society's perspectives on problems and use them to define reality for ourselves. Without such definitions, the issues in civil rights or biotechnology could not be clarified. As some consensus forms on these issues, a generalized other or shared definition of reality forms and is accepted by the consenting persons.

The key word here is "accepted." Symbolic interactionists resist the idea that some form of reality could determine behavior. Its influence depends on its approval. Since the only form of reality is social, and people control the social world with symbolic interaction, the pattern is reciprocal; people make society, which, in turn, influences them. This is not to say that other factors are not involved. Traditional cultural institutions and social traditions exist to limit individual action. But within those limits, each person interprets a situation in terms of his or her needs, desires, and values, and then acts them out.

It is this "acting out" process that symbolic interactionists seek to understand. This cannot be done by simply observing people or asking them their opinions. It requires an involvement with people, even an intimacy not found in traditional sociological research. To understand people this way means understanding their *covert* as well as their *overt* action. This is no small task. Even though some brilliant studies have been done, the methodology remains flexible and unformed. In fact, the raw ingredients for symbolic interactionist methodology continue to be the unique perspective it offers and the subjective empathy it requires.

A Christian Critique

Symbolic interactionism offers a powerful tool for the analysis of social situations. Especially in a modern society, it provides a very contemporary way of looking at things and interpreting their meanings. As people shift perspectives from one situation to another, it is important to know "where they're coming from" and to interpret that perspective correctly. But knowing all of that, is that all we need to know?

Symbolic interactionists suggest it is, because reality, for them, is social and nothing more. Any form of objective reality is interpreted by symbolic means but not described as influential on human behavior. The complex problems of modern society defy traditional answers and are open to any number of interpretations. In such a setting, there is little awareness of ultimate questions or irresoluble problems. Consequently, the idea of a spiritual reality remains antithetical to symbolic interactionism.

This is not to say that symbolic interactionism remains completely incompatible with Christian thought. Not at all; in fact, it may help us understand social situations that might otherwise defy explanation. It also contributes to understanding the sin of hypocrisy as people do one thing in one situation and another in a different situation. Some aspects of symbolic thinking are even modeled in Scripture and are necessary for our use today.

Dialogue

Christian sociologist David Moberg refers to a dialectic as "the art or practice of logical discussion as employed in investigating the truth of a theory or opinion."[8] Based on the word "dialect," dialectic refers to a way of conversing for the purpose of resolving some problem. "Sometimes the dialectical discourse occurs within the mind of a person, sometimes between persons, and sometimes between groups."[9] Since these persons usually hold differing positions on some issue, dialectics involves understanding the thought of another. As understanding occurs, the person responds to the other's actual thought and not to what he or she believes that thought to be.

Another way of looking at the dialectic is to see it as a dialogue with oneself, or between differing partners, each of whom seeks to solve a problem. Referring to dialogue, Ellul describes it as "a matter of entering a new phase in which the contradictory statements are adopted and make progress possible."[10] The objective is always to grasp the reality and totality of some situation. Since contradiction is found in any complex situation, dialogue must recognize these contradictory elements and interact with them to understand the underlying truth.

Joint action is the counterpart of dialogue as found in symbolic interactionism. In this view, people do not respond to structured social qualities such as roles or cultural norms. They either interact with themselves in some form of mental dialogue or with others by means of symbolic interaction. Blumer refers to this process as "taking each other into account," meaning "being aware of him, identifying him in some way, making some judgment or appraisal of him, identifying the meaning of his action, trying to find out what he has on his mind or trying to figure out what he intends to do."[11] As in a dialogue, the objective is to understand the actual thought of the other. In the cases of self-interaction, we try to understand what the other part of our self might be thinking.

As in the case of dialogue, people in joint action interact from different, not similar, perspectives. According to Blumer,

> a joint action cannot be resolved into a common or same type of behavior on the part of the participants. Each participant necessarily occupies a different position, acts from that position, and engages in a separate and distinctive act. It is the fitting together of these acts and not their commonality that constitutes joint action.[12]

As is true of dialogue, joint action results in a combination of the interests of both partners. Blumer refers to this as

> a transaction—a fitting of the developing action of each into that of the other to form a joint or overbridging action. I would say that the transaction is something other than an addition of the actions of the two individuals; these two lines of action in their developing interrelationship constitute a singleness.[13]

Joint action differs from the dialectic in its conception of reality. In symbolic interactionism, this reality is always limited to the social. For Charon, "Society is made up of individuals working things out in relation to each other."[14] This is joint action and nothing more. As Blumer explains it, joint action "means that the two individuals are brought into a relation of *subject* to *subject,* not of object to object, nor even of subject to object."[15] Since symbolic interactionism emphasizes the social aspect of that person as subject, any joint action is limited to the social. Consequently, transactions are limited to the social as well.

By contrast, the dialectic found in dialogue encompasses more than the social. Quoting Plato, Ellul says: "The dialectician is the one who sees the totality."[16] Specifically, a dialectic "always claims to have to do with the real."[17] For Ellul, as for any Christian, this reality exists prior to the dialogue and was structured in creation. "I believe . . . that the reality is there first, and that the term arises only in understanding it, in taking cognizance of an experienced reality."[18] It is this experienced reality, the objective world that symbolic interactionists fail to include in their perspective.

One way of conceiving of dialogue is to see it as a continuum with joint action at the social end and dialectic at the nonsocial end. Joint action produces communication among persons who share their differing needs and social impressions for the purpose of solving some social or personal problem. A dialectic involves communication among persons who share their differing experiences of reality for the purpose of discovering some ultimate truth. Both forms of dialogue may be used appropriately in their proper places.

The problem is we often confuse these forms of dialogue and how to use them. Much modern dialogue is merely joint action designed to gain consensus for dealing with some immediate social problem. We find this in most bull sessions and committee meetings. We deceive ourselves if we think that such discussions lead us into a knowledge of objective reality. In such situations, we are merely trying to resolve our concerns about personal or organizational problems and nothing more. But on other occasions dialogue allows us to share experienced reality as exemplified by prayer meetings or Bible studies. At these times, it is just as wrong to reduce them to joint actions designed for social purposes only.

This is not to say that joint action is inappropriate for Christians. We need to understand the problems of living in society, deal with those problems by understanding the views of others, and then act upon them. There is always a unity, a wholeness, in God's plan for the world that requires a dialectic among all its forces. Moberg claims this is especially true of the church, which is often polarized on issues: "Lopsidedness and imbalance result from many of the choices made when Christians fail to recognize the wholeness of the world or of the gospel and are impaled on the horns of various dilemmas."[19] All too often hypocritical Christians and church conflicts result from an inability to maintain the dialectical tension inherent in God's complex world.

Illusion

What we have been experiencing for the past one hundred years or so is a gradual shift on the continuum of dialogue from dialectic to joint action. The idea that something must be patently true or false to be believed no longer grips us as it once did. Instead, any claim to truth remains open to interpretation. Os Guinness sums up the problem in this way:

> It doesn't take a cynic to see that, since the truth requirement has been lifted, a climate has been created in which flagrant nonsense or complete error can be believed, and incontrovertible truth, in turn, can be disbelieved *without the question of their being objectively true or false being raised at all.* In short, we have created a climate in which a thing's *seeming* to be true is often mistaken for its *being* true.[20]

The change in climate referred to by Guinness includes a change in the communication process in this century. The revolution in electronics has placed new filters between the person and the experience of reality. Instead of accepting facts for ourselves, we now rely on predigested presentations of those facts by the mass media. As Ellul states, for the average person, "a fact becomes true when he has read an account of it in the paper, and he measures its importance by the size of the headlines!"[21] By comparison, even personal experience of that event may be colorless and perhaps suspect.

Of course, the complexity of the modern world has made us dependent on the mass media. We simply cannot experience starvation in Africa at the same time we want to experience congressional hearings in Washington apart from modern technology. Television uses this technology to give us powerful symbolic forms of these experiences: the bloated stomach of the starving child or the aggressive manner of a Senate counsel. Unless other experiences can be captured with comparable symbolic richness, they tend to be ignored or, just as likely, disbelieved.

Ellul refers to the facts hidden from the average person as *real facts.* He calls those facts that gain public support and credibility *surface facts.* Support is given to these surface facts because they solve a fundamental problem—they make sense out of an otherwise chaotic world. In a society filled with contradictions and ambiguities, surface facts provide apparent answers to problems. They seem to balance the current budget or resolve a crisis in foreign affairs. It is unimportant if surface facts provide only temporary answers. The important thing is the sense of group satisfaction they provide.

The noted historian Daniel Boorstin describes the religious nature of the problem in more graphic terms. Barely a century ago, he says, journalists recorded events as though God were communicating to us. Since then, the definition of news has changed from whatever God allowed to occur to whatever editors chose to print. But the journalists' attempts to play God are flawed. "The news they make happen, the events they create, are somehow not quite real. There remains a tantalizing difference between man-made and God-made events."[22]

Boorstin refers to these man-made events as *pseudo-events*. These are the events covered by the media that replace non-media events by their interest and conviction. A political rally carries a weight of authenticity often lacking in a personal statement made by a candidate. The staged value of "striking it rich" on a quiz show implies a morality surpassing that of hard work. In other words, pseudo-events change our ideals. Whatever had been valued has been altered in meaning by the illusory nature of pseudo-events. In place of these familiar values we find only pseudo-ideals of the images of our time.

The symbols that stimulate our social interactions are found in these images. Boorstin emphasizes the synthetic quality of images and the way they reduce reality to the simple and believable. IBM or USS, for example, convey a personal quality otherwise lost in the corporate giants they represent. As symbols, logos have restructured the meaning of the world as we perceive it. Advertising, especially, uses symbols to cover the flaws in its clients' products and make them attractive for public consumption. Persons, institutions, and merchandise are supplied the unique images that people can share and; interact with. And these images are simply the necessary ingredients of symbolic interactionism.

Consequently, our penchant for logos and the packaging of public heroes has created a world that doesn't exist. Nevertheless, this world competes successfully with the real world for public appeal. Boorstin maintains that these images have replaced the traditional dreams that stirred our country in its early days. The effect is striking.

> A dream is a vision or an aspiration to which we can compare reality. It may be very vivid, but its vividness reminds us how different is the real world. An illusion, on the other hand, is an image we have mistaken for reality. We cannot reach for it, aspire to it, or be exhilarated by it; for we live in it. It is prosaic because we cannot see it is not fact.[23]

We have become accustomed, then, to a world of illusion. We find it in the statistics always available to sports announcers for fleshing out their commentaries. We are left with the impression that the batter is a .350 hitter instead of someone who was arrested on drug charges. With symbols, we limit our experiences of people and events to those we want to remember. As with the looking-glass self, we turn a mirror on any object to gain the most favorable image.

This quality of deception, if not deceit, influences anything it touches in a world of illusion. Ellul has singled out "the political illusion" as an example of the effect illusions have on institutions. Since political "facts" have been altered for public consumption, the political world is not real. Only those facts with which the public can identify are emphasized. "To become 'true' in the eyes of the crowd, fact must be social... in the sense that everyone can recognize himself in it."[24] Thus, we are deceived into believing that both our political views and the political news are true.

If we assume that political facts are true, we come to believe that all problems are political and soluble by political means. Ellul refers to this assumption as *politization*. We further assume that politics provides for morality by the creation and protection of values. We come to believe we are a moral nation if we oppose communism in Vietnam or Nicaragua. When this happens, Ellul concludes that "political engagement is thus comparable to a religion."[26] But politics struggles only with surface questions—budgetary matters and foreign affairs—and not with the ultimate issues of human and corporate good and evil, which lie at the root of all political concerns. In this way, politics itself is deceived concerning its effectiveness in the real world.

It is an illusion, then, to believe that problems are solved by politics. But the illusion will remain as long as politics is defined in terms of social reality and nothing more. Believing that political symbols actually represent what they claim to represent, we are blinded by the political illusion that covers the world as God presents it to us. Worse, the illusion takes the place of the reality.

Symbols

Ellul's discussion of politics raises theological questions, which for the most part he leaves unanswered. Gregory Baum, a Catholic theologian, deals with some of these in his discussion of symbols.[26] The first meaning of a symbol (S1) reminds us of past events in our history. The cross or baptism, for example, functions symbolically to link us with our own personal and spiritual memories. These symbolic meanings remain external to us and open to interpretation. Only when we bring something to those symbols—some emotion or memory—will they become real to us.

If symbol (S1) helps us to remember some subjective reality, then symbol (S2) reveals a hidden form of objective reality. Here the symbol is the only means by which we can understand deep truth. When we understand this truth, we understand the hidden meanings of our own lives and how they fit into God's plan for us. Used in this way, the cross and baptism transcend our personal interpretation and guide us to the meaning of salvation in Christ. In this sense, symbols retain an important and even necessary place in the Christian faith.

Baum's description of symbol (S3) suggests that those of this type are less representative of the concrete world and ignore a part of our mind's structure. As patterns of our personal imagination, they help us to bridge the world as it is and the world as we experience it. In addition to helping us remember the world (S1) and revealing it (S2), symbols (S3) also provide us with a response to the world. In this case, symbols form a dialectic between our minds and the structured, objective forms of reality understood by (S2). How we respond to reality largely depends on the way faith employs (S3) in our minds. If the cross and our baptism as symbols (S3) are prominent in our minds, we will be motivated to action by them.

The last meaning of symbols provided by Baum is (S4): "the reflection of society in the mind."[27] This is the meaning of symbols conveyed by symbolic interactionism to the exclusion of the first three meanings. It is the kind of symbolic meaning Mead had in mind when he described the reciprocal relationship between mind and society. Since reality is only social, symbols (S4) reflect this reality on the mind, which, in turn, confirms it in the social world.

Baum believes that the meanings of symbols (S2) and (S4) are not separate but dialectically linked. Symbols (S2) do function to provide some persons with an understanding of hidden reality. But since society is a social construction, this fact is also reflected on our minds by symbols (S4) and joins with (S2) in our perception of reality. This is not to say the two forms of reality are synonymous. Baum is quite firm on this point. "Yet since the Christian gospel sets itself off from the society and transcends it, it is impossible for Christian symbols to be wholly identified with the symbols of the social order."[28]

What this means for the Christian should be clear. *We need to understand, first, that the influence of social symbols extends into our minds and shapes our understanding of religious truth.* Social issues concerning abortion, womens' rights, and other social questions may be symbolized (S4) to the extent that their social and religious meanings are merged. Second, *we need to understand the social context that gives rise to such symbols.* In our secularized society, illusions dominate. This means that any imbalance in the dialectic will favor the social response and its meaning of symbols (S4) and not the spiritual revelation of symbols (S2). *Finally, it is necessary for the Christian to understand correctly his or her personal response to this dialectic and respond correctly.* In general, this could mean resistance to the reflective symbols (S4). But for those who live apart from the world, it could also mean a better understanding of those symbols is needed, as well as an awareness of symbols (S3) to clarify our response to the world. Baum makes the same point this way:

> Since every person is religious, the question that preoccupies the theologian is not whether people believe in God but what kind of divinity they actually worship. The gods are universal. From a Christian point of view, however, people have only two basic choices—either they believe in the true God or they are idolaters.[29]

The sociological distinction, of course, is not that sharp. Symbols (S3) may lead to idolatry when the difference between God and idols is blurred in our thinking. In some situations, true believers may, indeed, be false teachers.

Idols

Two meanings of *idol* are of interest to us here. The first states "an idol is something which is good in itself but which becomes evil and alienating when set up as the highest good and as a religious absolute."[30] J. A. Walter's idea here is that idols are neutral in meaning until they meet a basic human need. In other words, the person interprets the symbol in terms of personal need. At that point, the meaning becomes exactly the opposite of what was intended; it becomes evil instead of good. Instead of pointing to God, the idol, as symbol, points to itself. The second meaning of idol comes from Christian thinker Herbert Schlossberg: "Idolatry in its larger meaning is properly understood as any substitution of what is created for the creator."[31] When we come to rely on the idol as the highest good, it then points to itself as God. Even in an apparently secular society, we find the *sacred* in diverse social forms. By some common agreement, people come to believe that some thing or, just as likely, some principle or idea becomes an essential part of their culture. When such a principle or idea replaces God as the object of our trust, it becomes an idol.

As a sacred object, an idol may bring order to an otherwise confusing world. It provides meaning and answers for the problems found there. Walter, for example, suggests that security, not money, is an idol. Although money may bring security, it is the desire for security that motivates us.[32] This desire may carry over to jobs, marriage, even children, which become idols if we are insecure without them.

Walter describes the family as a modern idol that demands more of us than we can give to it. Although we spend much time escaping from the concrete family, we worship it as an idol. We assume that the family should be highly valued because it agrees with biblical principles. But the family as we experience it today is not always as we conceive it or as it is presented in Scripture. Certainly the biblical model is not the taskmaster that the modern family often is. Nor does it convey the romantic notions that are associated with the ideal family. To resolve the distinctions among these types of family—the ideal, the biblical, and the experienced—in our thinking, we treat the family as a social abstraction. We value it as a social ideal and even worship it as an idol even though it is far removed from our mundane experience or biblical principles.

The point of the modern family as an example of an idol is simply this: our social interpretation of any biblical principle can lead to idolatry. This is especially true when the symbols associated with that principle are powerful and highly valued. Walter, for example, describes work as an idol in our society. In an earlier day, as we saw in a previous chapter, work had a religious meaning because of the prevalent notion of calling in the culture. In that context, a proper balance was maintained between the social and religious meaning of work. But with the loss of that religious meaning, the exclusive social meaning of work elevated it to the status of an idol. Today, for most of our culture, work is a social necessity to organize our world and remove the insecurity lurking in it.

But as we noted earlier, an idol doesn't just point to itself; it points to itself as God. In the case of work, it becomes an idol when, as Walter suggests, work equals worth. At one time, human worth was assured by one's relationship with God regardless of social position. "Work was a response to being valued, rather than a means to being valued."[33] Today, work has reversed the process; the social meaning of work becomes the means for attaining human worth. Work, as an idol, has replaced the Creator.

If we think of a balloon at the end of a string held by a child, we have some idea of a symbol: the balloon pointing to reality, the child holding the string. There is something right and proper about the symbol of that child holding a balloon. So it is with family, work, and a multitude of other symbols that have a clear biblical meaning. We understand that the symbol properly points to what it refers. But when social change alters that meaning, the symbol is like a released balloon, pulled from the hands of the child by the wind and free to settle where it will. Similarly, any symbol, when abstracted from reality, may refer to anything we desire. Like a *balloon, we* pull it from the air and hand it to the god we choose.

The making of idols is a social process. It begins by giving something a value not consistent with God's intention for it. If idolatry is to be avoided, two things are needed. We need, first, to measure the value of something and, second, to compare it with biblical standards. Unless this is done, group consensus changes the meaning of something and sends it, free floating, into the air. We also need to resist such group control of symbolic meanings. Like a child, our grasp of the cord should be tighter as the wind grows stronger.

Conclusion

Robert Bellah's recent analysis of individualism and commitment in American life describes the self as separated from its traditional roots.[34] Each person is free to seek his or her own self-interests. "In a world of potentially conflicting self-interests," Bellah maintains, "no one can really say that one value system is better than another,"[35] "What is good is what one finds rewarding. If one's preferences change, so does the nature of the good."[36] Consequently, today's morality, as Bellah describes it, is open to interpretation and redirection by personal choice.

This is the kind of thinking that gained considerable credibility about one hundred years ago. But the richness of the modern symbolic environment coupled with a flabby concept of objective truth has multiplied its influence. It is now the kind of thinking that dominates modern culture. Symbolic interactionism describes this thinking well—and that's what good science should do. But a science is only as valid as the reality it describes. Outside that science and outside that description of reality the darkness needs illumination.

Chapter 10

Phenomenology and Ethnomethodology

There is no better way to start this chapter than to look at the title and ask "What do those words mean?" *Phenomenology* and *ethnomethodology* refer to forms of social thought so different from the traditional kind of social theory that they seem imprecise in their meaning. For one thing, phenomenology refers to a group of theoretical approaches and not just to one theory. For another, phenomenology defines reality in very broad and shifting terms. This idea causes no problem for the phenomenologist who looks at the world in very untraditional ways and finds very untraditional and variable meanings. Other sociologists, however, usually prefer more traditional approaches to social thought.

Let's return to the boy holding the string of a balloon and the idea that such a scene is "right and proper." The phenomenologist would challenge that notion as absurd. Why should we believe it is better for a little boy to hold a balloon than for an old man to hold one? Even a balloon tied to the ear of a horse could make sense to the phenomenologist. If there is any reality in the world, it is found in the immediate experience of the actor. In short, reality may be anything that feels good at the moment.

It's easy to see how these ideas have moved us to one end of the objectivity-subjectivity continuum of realty. The under-girding idea of all phenomenological sociology, including ethnomethodology, is that *subjectivity is the basis for scientific methodology as well as for subject matter*. In symbolic interactionism, language represents a reality that lays some constraint on people. Through *joint action* they agree on a certain meaning and act accordingly. In phenomenological theories, such constraints may not even exist. Like balloons, people are free to float where they will.

The Background

Phenomenology has its origins in German idealism, the philosophical tradition that also gave rise to Weber's interpretive sociology. Both Weber and the phenomenologists rejected Durkheim's positivistic view of the social world: social facts have to be interpreted and may not be taken as givens. Weber, however, was never as radical as the phenomenologists on this point. He envisioned an "iron cage" in social change that would constrain people and prevent the greater personal freedom perceived by the phenomenologists. The theory takes its name from Kant's notion of phenomenon.

> A phenomenon, then, is no "substantial" unity; it has no "real" properties, it knows no real parts, no real changes and no causality...To attribute a nature to phenomena, to investigate their real component parts, their causal connections—that is pure absurdity, no better than if one wanted to ask about the causal properties, connections, etc. of numbers.[1]

The only reality of phenomena is found in the way people act so as to confirm their existence. Stated differently, reality in the world is simply the result of humans routinely acting out their interpretations of the world and nothing more.

If we accept this idea that human interpretations of social events are the only reality, there is no external world to study, no social facts or empirical data to research. Suicide, for example, has no meaning as a social problem because it does not exist as a group phenomenon. Suicide can only be understood as an interpretation given to the act. In another society, suicide could produce a completely different personal interpretation and, thus, a completely different meaning.

If social facts do not exist and empirical science fails to get at reality* the phenomenologist faces two basic problems: What is to be studied? And, *how* is it to be studied? The thinker who gave the earliest fundamental answers to these questions was Edmund Husserl, the German philosopher who defined consciousness as the object of phenomenological study. If social facts do not exist, then the object of study becomes the individual's subjective definitions of those facts. Husserl did not see this approach as a retreat from science to philosophy. For him, a philosophical method could be just as scientific as any natural or physical science.

Husserl described phenomenology as a "science of essences." This essence was the central reality of anything, uncorrupted by other meanings attached to it. This was the meaning of something in its "pure" form. In other words, the *essence* of anything is what it signifies. This essence cannot be found in the external world but only in the consciousness. The essence of friendship, for example, is not found in relationships that are distorted by various meanings brought to them by the friends. The reality of friendship is simply the consciousness that friends have of the relationship.

Admittedly, essence is a very ambiguous notion, not readily translated into familiar terminology. Some of the ambiguity, however, is removed by reversing the thought process. Since reality is found in consciousness instead of some external world, it is necessary to "disprove" that world rather than to "prove" it. Instead of accepting it as a natural and well-ordered world, it is to be questioned and critiqued. People are deceived if they believe the social world to be anything more than a figment of their imaginations. In addition, Husserl claimed, they contribute to that deception with any belief that the world is natural.

Husserl referred to this idea—that society is accepted because it is natural—as the *natural standpoint*. Since the resulting *natural attitude* masks the truth that society is merely a human construction, a major objective of phenomenology is to study how society is ordered and distorted in the process by people. This meant that the phenomenologist had to "think away" this natural attitude or, in Husserl's term *bracket* it. Only by such bracketing could one arrive at the essence of anything.

Let's look at friendship again to understand how this process might work. If we believe that we gain friendship when we ask someone to do a favor for us, we take a natural: standpoint on friendship. We assume this is a principle for . developing friendship because scientific studies have said it is true. But it has become a principle because people have looked at friendship that way and acted accordingly. Phenomenologists would say this is a distorted notion of friendship, the essence of which is something else. To understand what the essence of friendship might be, we must bracket the principle and not accept it as true. Put more simply, we must resist and even reject the common-sense notions of society concerning friendship.

Traditional thinking takes a different view of friendship. Because it is part of the natural world that can be accepted with confidence, friendship makes an impact upon our consciousness and influences our behavior. By contrast, Husserl thought of consciousness as *intentional*. "Mind or consciousness is viewed as some kind of relationship between a subject and object and the notion of intentionality is an attempt to describe this relation."[2] Consciousness always interacts with some object and gives it the meaning we perceive there. In short, consciousness, as a process, must be studied to understand the meaning found in friendship and not vice versa.

We take it for granted that friendship as presented by society is friendship as it should be. We assume that the interaction of our consciousness with friendship as an object is the only option available to us. This naive attitude becomes a common-sense view of the world as people accept it without question. Phenomenologists not only question this attitude but study it to understand how the mundane world is constructed.

Phenomenologists study intentionality to understand what the consciousness has "in mind." It is this quality of "being in mind" that was the only reality for the early phenomenologist. This is the essence, or idealized intentional object, of anything. Although an essence may exist in the mind, it does not exist in the real world.

The essence of suicide as conceived by the phenomenologist, for example, would be quite different from Durkheim's study.[3] Durkheim's conception of society as a vast network of social unity suggests that suicide is a symptom of a breakdown of morality in the relationship. Measured in terms of suicide rates, it is nothing more than a social fact related to other social facts. Phenomenologists argue that Durkheim is wrong to take his idea of morality for granted. We cannot assume that the person committing suicide holds to any common-sense idea of morality. It is more important to understand the person's intentionality—how he or she conceived of suicide and its related social meanings. Without such understanding, the essence of suicide remains hidden.

Existentialists have always claimed that "existence precedes essence." This means the essence of anything does not exist until it is given meaning through intentionality. Ultimately, the *person* is the source of all meaning. The other approach says that "essence preceded existence." In this case, meaning exists *before* there are people to interpret it. For the Christian, God is the source of all meaning laid down in Creation. So we are tempted to argue for either one side or the other. The problem is that both sides might be valid. In some cases, essence precedes existence because God did create meaning that humans cannot alter. In other cases, people must properly supply meaning in a modern society left undefined by God.

To illustrate, we might return to the discussion of culture found in chapter 5. Since chopsticks are a culturally relative item found in certain cultures, we have no reason to believe their meaning is defined by God for some absolute purpose. We may accept the idea that Orientals define chopsticks as eating utensils just as we use a knife or fork for the same purpose. In this case, existence may properly precede essence. But marriage is a completely different matter simply because its meaning is not culturally defined. In both the West and the Orient, faithfulness in marriage is the ethical norm, though it may be interpreted differently, even as it was in Scripture. This implies that the meaning of marriage is not open to casual interpretation. Its essence transcends human existence because it preceded it.

It's easy to confuse these two levels of reality by failing to recognize the existence of each. Early phenomenologists are especially sensitive to the problem and correctly oppose unconscious efforts to raise the mundane to the absolute level. They are critical of the natural standpoint and encourage a subjective, intentional perception of the problem. But *their exclusive concern for the subjective level blinds them to the possibility of an absolute level.* Consequently, phenomenologists err by ignoring God's created reality and conceiving of it only in terms of the mundane. In either case, reality is distorted by limited, human perception.

The Theory

Although Husserl's work spawned a variety of sociological approaches, most were limited in influence and concentrated on the continent. Any claim to a sociological theory in phenomenology would have to be associated with the work of Alfred Schutz, who emigrated to the United States from Vienna just before World War II. It was not until his major work was translated in 1967, however, that his influence was felt in this country. This was a time well suited for a new sociology that could challenge old structures and discover new realities, and Schutz made a notable contribution to it.

Two students who responded to that challenge were Peter Berger and Harold Garfinkel. Berger, currently the most prominent advocate of the sociology of knowledge, has had a wide impact on the field, especially on the thinking of Christian sociologists. Garfinkel, who, like Berger, was a student of Schutz, took the theory in another direction and attempted to give it a methodological foundation. Known as *ethnomethodology*, Garfinkel's work tries to understand the way reality is constructed in mundane, daily social encounters. The distinctive approach of each theorist has enriched sociological theory and influenced the direction of American sociology in the last two decades.

In contrast to Husserl, who tried to understand reality in the consciousness of the abstracted, single individual, Schutz defined reality in terms of interacting parties. This assumption, known as *intersubjectivity*, was the crucial concept in moving phenomenology from philosophy to sociology. Schutz's work also moved phenomenology from the study of essences to the study of the practical, ongoing social life of people. The objective was to study the reality of this everyday life and the meaning that people brought to it.

These two assumptions, that the world is intersubjective and that there should be a practical interest in this world, were fundamental for Schutz's conception of reality. Although other realities exist, it was this paramount reality, the reality of everyday life, that became the object of sociological inquiry. For Schutz, this paramount reality was Western life as we experience it today, the cultural expression which shapes the social lives of all of us in a multitude of ways. Although there may be reason to lapse into other realities, such as non-Western culture or the world of drug-induced fantasy, we always return to the paramount reality of our mundane world. For this reason, it becomes for us a tacit, taken-for-granted world.

Schutz claimed people experience social reality both indirectly and directly. Direct experience occurs by personal involvement with another in a face-to-face situation. At such times, actions are unpredictable as people interpret another's behavior freely and often in unprecedented ways. Schutz realized that such unpredictable behavior fell outside the scope of scientific inquiry. Since he sought to move phenomenology from its philosophical tradition to a scientific basis, he discounted direct experience as valid data for scientific study.

What was more important for Schutz were the indirect ways we experience life through interaction with others. By *indirect*, Schutz means we deal with people as "types" rather than actual persons. These types are comparable to the social roles we all play in prescribed situations. Instead of perceiving each new situation as a problem requiring specific interpretation, we discern the social roles and behave as we have in the past. Our first encounter with a Swiss train conductor, for example, should pose no particular problem for us if we have been on trains before. The conductor is a type of social role requiring responses similar to those given to other conductors in the past. Even a child who has never been on a train has experienced a conductor indirectly if a parent has told him or her about conductors and what they do on a train.

The point is we are socialized to think in terms of types of persons and situations instead of specific persons and situations; then we fit ourselves in accordingly. In subtle ways, we develop what Schutz calls *stock knowledge at hand,* a host of rules and social practices by which we are able to act in unfamiliar as well as familiar social worlds. This stock knowledge acts as a compass to give us cues in unfamiliar situations, interpret events appropriately, and then act in an acceptable manner. Gradually, this stock knowledge becomes part of the paramount reality used to interpret social events and the people in them.

Since this stock knowledge "works" in the sense that we successfully adjust to our social worlds, we rarely evaluate its claims to truth. We simply take its assumptions for granted and, without questioning, use it to interact with others. A further assumption we make is to believe that others share the same stock knowledge and will use it accordingly. Treating others as social types, we create a predictable social world for our convenience and for the scientist's inquiry.

The social world of race relations illustrates the point well. Traditionally, the expected social relations between blacks and whites were understood by both groups. Stock knowledge outlining social etiquette for social interaction was shared within each community and distributed, subtly, across racial lines. Racism became the paramount reality for the two communities as tacit agreement resulted from the acceptance of stock knowledge. Minor adjustments in thinking could be made about those who did not fit the racial types perfectly as long as they didn't challenge the paramount reality of racism. But when blacks seen as pushing beyond their "station in life," did challenge it, some major public adjustments had to be made in the lives of both communities to restore the tacit nature of the social reality of racism. This could mean lynching the black or ostracizing the white. In either case, the community learned that the paramount reality had been questioned and needed to be restored.

Schutz used Husserl's term "life-world" to refer to this cultural, taken-for-granted world shared by a group of consenting actors. Here we find all the typifications of social types expected in that social setting. Since one college shares the life-world of another, we are comfortable in moving among colleges, always finding students and professors acting as expected. The paradox is that in such a constrained situation we also feel more freedom; we think less about our behavior and are less anxious about the responses of others. Consequently, we have more freedom to modify behavior and challenge the life-world. Put more simply, we are more likely to break the rules when we know them well.

Schutz acknowledged that any stock of knowledge has a private component and used the term *biographically articulated* to refer to this condition. This means that each person brings certain unique qualities to his or her life-world. But since these qualities do not facilitate social adjustment, people usually rely on typifications or *recipes* to interact with others in the life-world. As long as the life-world is stable and predictable, the recipes allow for effective adjustment to it. But in modern society, life-worlds are increasingly dynamic and unpredictable. To fit into such a world, people either compensate by developing new and creative ways to adjust to unfamiliar social situations or else move to another life-world. In either case, their actions become less predictable and less open to scientific inquiry.

Schutz considered these situations that defined the use of recipes to be problematic situations. This meant that some discrepancy existed between the knowledge of types at hand and the situation to be understood. For one reason or another, a person or situation doesn't fit into our repertoire of experiences of that situation. How do we explain a Samaritan who tenderly cares for a beaten Jew? How do we explain the radical change of Paul's attitude toward Christians in human and traditional terms? In fact, we don't. Instead, we choose some logical response and, in faith, act accordingly.

In a modern world, replete with problematic situations, the problem of interpreting situations increases greatly. The phenomenologist recognizes this problem and accepts our freedom to choose among available responses when our stock of knowledge doesn't fit a situation. Consequently, our stock of knowledge increases through the use of this and other learned responses. Gradually, more situations and the preferred responses to them become typical. Without any norms or external constraints, the response is accepted by others who then define it as normal and moral.

Here we shift from phenomenology to the study of ethnomethodology and its definition of reality. Put simply, *reality consists of the actual everyday life of people in social situations*. For the ethnomethodologist, traditional sociology masks or, worse, distorts this reality with its description of an abstract social world that doesn't exist. One sees this distortion in sociology's conception of values and norms. In the real world, these are either poorly stated and require interpretation or they don't exist at all. In short, all social norms are necessarily incomplete in the real world.

Ethnomethodologists have focused on rules systems in their efforts to understand the forms of reality. Rejecting the traditional sociological notion that norms are separate from people and that they exist as external and objective social constraints, ethnomethodologists argue that rules are defined by people in specific situations. Remember, for example, the catcher in the last chapter who had to define a plate-blocking situation before he could act? By blocking the plate, he defined the reality of the situation for the runner, the teams, and the fans. Unless the umpire rules otherwise, the reality is accepted.

This example illustrates a fundamental principle of reality construction: *reality is reflexive activity.*[4] This means that people support any claim by approving of it. Even in talk, which is a form of reflexive activity, people create a world that can be taken for granted. By signaling "safe," the umpire displays reflexive activity that approves of the catcher's definition of reality and makes it acceptable to the crowd.

Ethnomethodologists recognize another feature of reality construction: *reality is a coherent body of knowledge.* This means people use reflexive activity to construct a set of propositions for their lives and then act upon them. Some of these become *incorrigible propositions:* those "which you would never admit to be false whatever happens."[5] Cultic leaders, for example, form an incorrigible proposition for their followers by determining the end of the world from some calendar event. Such declarations are unquestioned as statements of reality for the group. As part of the coherent body of knowledge, they are continually justified by reflexive activity.

Another feature of reality is its dependence on social interaction. Reality doesn't exist apart from the interaction of those who construct it and then sustain it with explanations and rationalizations. Further, this interaction requires some social context to give it meaning. The four-year-old may accept his grandmother's definition of himself as "a sweet little boy." Eight years later, however, he may not tolerate it. Interaction between grandmother and grandson during that period is needed if reality is to be defined correctly.

This leads us to the fourth feature of reality as conceived by ethnomethodologists: *reality is fragile.* Whenever reality is questioned it may be broken and even dissolved. Ethnomethodologists have studied this feature with *breaching* experiments designed to test reality by questioning it. They find that reality is fragile because people interact without listing the rules for their conduct. This is especially true for the mundane activities of everyday life where the rules are left implicit. By disrupting this life with questions, ethnomethodologists come to understand the rules and the reflexivity needed to sustain its reality.

A final feature of reality is its permeability. People can move from one reality to another, even when radically different from each other. As one moves into a new reality, it may seem immoral and unacceptable until adjustment to it is complete. At that point its rules have become acceptable through reflexive activity.

Mehan and Wood refer to Schneebaum, an explorer who lived for some time with cannibals in the jungles of Peru.[6] A participant in cannibalistic rites, he eventually realized he had experienced a new reality and accepted its values, as repulsive as they were. Increasingly he realized that his sense of the reality of civilization was gradually weakening, so Schneebaum left the jungle to save himself from being absorbed further into savage ways. Schneebaum explained his reason for leaving the tribe this way:

> I saw within myself too many seeds that would grow a fungus around my brain, encasing it with mold that could penetrate and smooth the convolutions and there I would remain, not he who had travelled and arrived, not the me who had crossed the mountains in a search, but another me living only in ease and pleasure, no longer able to scrawl out words on paper or think beyond a moment.[7]

Nothing here suggests that Schneebaum was concerned for his own moral behavior or that of his native friends. He states neither a preference for civilized life nor an awareness of its superiority. He returned to civilization to protect his sense of personal identity and nothing more. In short, his sense of reality was centered in himself.

Mehan and Wood agree with this claim and argue "that all persons have elegant knowledge of their own reality. That knowledge is absolute within realities."[8] Unlike Schutz who believed that everyday life constituted the one paramount reality from which all other realities were derived, Mehan and Wood argue that each reality is as real as any other. "No single reality contains more of the truth than any other."[9] For this reason, Schneebaum could move easily between civilization and cannibalism with no apparent guilt.

This creates a disturbing picture of reality for the Christian. The idea of truth being located in some absolute, transcendent reality is foreign to ethnomethodologists and other interpretive sociologies. But it is also true that reality (in the sense of behaviors and beliefs), as described here, is what we find in much of modern society. People do move casually from one marriage to another with little sense of remorse or regret. Relationships are fragile and easily broken because the rules that govern our behavior are so weak and do require interpretation. Constructed by humans, these realities are subsequently heir to human error and sinfulness. We could not expect it to be otherwise.

A Christian Critique

Phenomenology and other interpretive sociologies are correct to challenge traditional sociology and its conception of objective reality. Consciousness does construct a subjective reality that overlays the objective. Consequently, new meaning is given to behavior. Consider, for example, Jesus' comparison of anger with murder (Matt. 5:21-22). He tells us that both the objective act of murder and the subjective thought of anger are equally worthy of judgment. Together, they constitute a new reality, one that Jesus would have us interpret correctly if we are to understand the kingdom of God.

But Jesus never rejects the objective reality of life. He did not come to destroy the law but to fulfill it by interpreting it correctly (Matt. 5:17-20). This meant living in such a way that social conventions are questioned or, more radically, ignored, disobeyed, and superseded. For example, Jesus calls the believer to oppose traditional behavior by loving enemies (Matt. 5:44) and praying in private (Matt. 6:5-6). These forms of behavior fulfill the law but with a new meaning that transcends the social and the conventional.

Everyday Life

The idea of everyday life is at the core of a variety of interpretive sociologies. Each case centers on the notion that basic social reality is located among persons interacting in concrete social situations. Any practice is meaningless without interpretation. As these practices are interpreted, the actors construct a world of reality and maintain it by the constant reassuring reflexivity of intersubjective behavior. The result is a world of contradiction and inconsistency that the sociological study of everyday life hopes to unmask and lay out for evaluation.

Interpretive theorists differ in their views of this everyday life. Some are critical of it and seek to understand it so as to change society. For them, everyday life is a relatively modern phenomenon, separated from the traditional world of meaningful day-to-day actions. With increased technology and modernization, the radical says, the world has given way to an everyday life of facts and figures, a world of tyranny in which everything is planned and controlled. For these theorists, the contradictions of society are inherent in everyday life. There is nothing to unify society, nothing to bring it all together. For this reason, everyday life must be critiqued. It must be penetrated and unmasked if change is to produce the kind of continuity and style found in earlier times.

Other theorists, like Schutz, accept everyday life as the ever-present world in which we must live. More consistent with phenomenology, this view emphasizes the mundane quality of everyday life. Schutz's life-world comes to us from the past, organized and continuous, bringing its pragmatic motives into our lives. It provides the natural attitude that includes not merely a world of facts but also a world of values that shapes our view of everything about us. Unlike more radical views, phenomenology seeks to unveil everyday life in order to understand the source of *all* of our knowledge. If it tries to get at the roots of the problem, however, it doesn't try to pull them out as the radical theorists do.

Following the lead of phenomenology, ethnomethodologists believe that all knowledge, scientific as well as commonsensical, begins in everyday life. Since all realities are equal, scientific and commonsensical thinking are different but equally appropriate ways of explaining reality. Rather than describing everyday life, ethnomethodologists try to discover how it is accomplished. Immersed in everyday life, they deal with the world on its own terms. This means seeing interaction as the *only* basis for any meaning in the world. Indeed, the interaction of people *makes* everyday life.

Christians will probably find much to agree with in this discussion of everyday life. Some may approve of the radical position and be critical of modern society in order to change it. A few may risk deep involvement in the world and join the ethnomethodologists who try to understand what makes it work. Most can at least agree with the phenomenologist's desire to understand the social basis of knowledge. Without such study, the human construction of reality cannot be understood or questioned.

Phenomenologists believe this kind of study of the world requires a suspension of belief in the world as objective reality. They counter one faith position with another and argue that belief in the natural attitude cannot be suspended until it is quite clear we are living in this life-world. This is because we are so much a part of the life-world that we can't comprehend what it means to step outside it and be objective about it. Consequently, the phenomenologist assumes it is necessary to believe the world is nothing more than a product of human social interaction if we are to study and critique it objectively.

The Christian has a distinct advantage over the phenomenologist on this point. Unlike the phenomenologist who has only a natural attitude, the Christian, ideally, also has an "unnatural attitude." Although he or she lives in the everyday life of the natural world, the Christian never makes a full commitment to its values. Other values have priority simply because they are not from the natural world but are derived from God's revelation. Put more simply, the Christian always views the natural world as one who is "in the world" and yet "not of it."

This quality of dual citizenship counters the need to suspend belief in the world as an objective reality. Unlike the phenomenologist who must attribute exclusive subjective qualities to something before it can be studied objectively, *the Christian gains objectivity from his or her unnatural attitudes.* This is not to say that all of the Christian world remains untainted by the natural world. Far from it. As part of that world, historically and currently, the Christian world view cannot be completely set aside from the natural attitude and its influence.

This means that the Christian's task of critiquing society differs from the phenomenologist's on at least two points. First, *the Christian world view is a blend of subjective and objective reality.* If this view is to be studied objectively, it is necessary to take an unnatural view by maintaining intellectual distance from it. Without such distancing, any attempt at objective study of the natural world may be contaminated by the forms of social reality brought to it by the Christian world view. Second, *it is necessary to see the natural world as a blend of objective and subjective reality.* The natural world cannot be completely rejected, for remnants of objective reality as revealed by God undergird much of it. In short, the Christian lives in and is influenced by two worlds of mixed reality.

Reality Distortion

"In reflecting upon the results of social research, the ethno-methodologist has come to the conclusion that *the imposition of one reality on another necessarily distorts the reality studied.*"[10] As a reality system, science distorts other systems of reality when it is used as the basis for measuring them. And if science is deemed the preeminent basis for measuring reality in our society, as it now is, then it distorts everything it touches. For this reason, the ethnomethodologist prefers to treat science as any other reality system and equal to all of them.

Mehan and Wood illustrate this point with reference to studies made of educational test results gained from first-grade children in California.[11] Assuming that children share the adult's conception of reality, educational tests are designed to have children give the same response to a question that an adult would give. When they don't, the response is considered to be wrong. One question, for example, required the child to match the *word fly* with the picture of an elephant, a bird, and a dog. The researchers were surprised to find that many of the children matched *fly* with the elephant. When asked why they made this choice, the children replied, "That's Dumbo." Similarly, many children matched a picture of a medieval fortress with the letter D instead of C for *castle*. The reason: the building was, in the minds of the children, a picture of Disneyland.

Mehan and Wood argue that the reality of the child is distorted when tests designed for adults are used to measure their ability. It is precisely the child's ability, which the test hopes to measure, that gets distorted. Even when children understand information known also by adults, they may bring different meaning to it and organize it differently. In the same way, social science may distort the meaning of its findings. Assuming that people are rational in their daily decision making, social science cannot accurately interpret decisions which do not fit its standards of rationality. Any error in that interpretation represents a distortion of reality. Thus, ethnomethodologists reject traditional social science simply because it attempts to order the world by standards not always found there.

To illustrate the point further, consider a road map and the territory it is supposed to describe. At any one time, the map is not a completely accurate description of that territory. This is especially true if the map is old and the area limited in size. Roads that had been open may now be closed for repairs. Two-way streets may have been re-designated as one-way. Even the huge puddle left from a recent rain that can endanger cars does not appear on the map. Thus, the only accurate map is one being made as it is being used!

People experience the same kind of reality distortion as they approach each new situation with "outdated maps." The reality of the world as they have learned it never completely conforms to reality as they now experience it. By relying on their earlier conception of reality, they inevitably distort the reality experienced. But if reality distortion is inevitable, it need not be ignored. Our awareness of reality distortion should allow us to perceive it in any particular situation and then attempt to correct it.

Mehan and Wood correctly observe that ethnomethodology alerts us to the importance of studying reality distortion.[12] The object of study is never the choice of one form of reality over another, but always a unique synthesis of both, a dialectic of realities different from either one reality or the other. But this unique reality cannot be studied by ordinary means of analysis—those committed to traditional conceptions of reality. The researcher must be prepared to step out of traditional social roles and study reality distortion as a unique and new form of reality.

This idea that social phenomena should be studied from some objective vantage point removed from the biases of society is not new. The highest standards of social inquiry have always advocated the need to look at social phenomena from a value-free position. The question has always been whether this could be done. The modern response has generally been stated in the negative: a value-free social science is not possible. Consequently, the choice was clear: accept traditional empirical thinking and its resultant reality distortion by assuming that social phenomena are organized in some preconceived way; or rely on interpretive methods to understand how social phenomena are organized on the individual level. In either case, the social scientist must believe that reality is of either one type or the other and not a combination of both.

The Christian approaches the problem of reality distortion somewhat differently. It is a unique position, seldom shared by the professional social scientist. As one who lives in everyday life, the Christian, like everyone else, shares its definition of reality. One drives on the legally-designated side of the road, uses standard eating utensils, and follows acceptable marriage practices. But as one who is not completely "in the world," the believer brings another conception of reality to everyday life. Meaning in daily living transcends any social context and benefits from a new personal identity found in Christ that should influence even the mundane tasks of life. This "otherworldly" perception of everyday life necessarily and, from the believer's viewpoint, properly distorts the traditional view of reality. Consequently, reality distortion should be accepted by the believer as a normal quality of social life.

Less apparent is the distortion inherent in the otherworldly view of reality. While it is true that this perception is imposed on everyday life, the reverse is also true: everyday life influences our otherworldly view of it. The fact that we are "in the world" is not completely separate from the fact that we are "not of it." Our social roles as parents, for example, may influence and even distort our perception of the value given to children in Scripture. Our inherent sinfulness further distorts our efforts to implement our otherworldly view of social reality. What we would do spiritually is not always what we do socially.

The believing Christian experiences neither a complete acceptance of social reality as understood by the nonbeliever nor a completely faithful conformity to God's commandments concerning life in the world. Instead, both realities blend in a dialectic of living and thought that encompasses both the worldly and the otherworldly. Together, they provide the believer with a unique platform to observe the world and his or her place in it. This platform accepts reality distortion as a "given," simply because of the commitment to a nonsocial form of reality. In addition, no pretensions support that platform. The believer understands the limitations underlying all human knowledge, social or otherwise. In short, the believer has the potential to become the researcher that the social scientist would hope to be.

Bracketing

For Husserl, the key to phenomenology was to be found in separating the consciousness from the life-world with which it was entangled. As long as there was a natural attitude that provided a common ground of experience for people in mundane forms of social life, one could not get at the essence of anything. What was needed was some way to question the natural standpoint that supported this natural attitude. When this was done, a realm *of pure consciousness,* the object of Husserl's phenomenological question, would be isolated for study.

Husserl believed that this isolation could be accomplished by *bracketing,* suspending belief in, the natural standpoint. This meant that one could not put faith in everyday life. Instead of taking social claims for granted, this naive world of social reality had to be questioned. In addition, the scientist could not assume that people would have the same experiences of social reality if their places were exchanged. Our life-worlds are not interchangeable. Bracketing helps to define the differences in our individual consciousnesses. Husserl's phenomenology stressed the need to study essences and their relationship to human consciousness. For this reason, his objective was to bracket as much of the empirical world as possible so as to isolate the essence of consciousness.

Sociologists, including the ethnomethodologists, are not so radical. Since they seek to study the social world and not exclude it completely, their bracketing is limited to certain problem areas. And since each person brackets from a different natural standpoint, the results of bracketing, or *reduction* to use a synonymous term, will also differ.

Husserl realized that a complete reduction would not be possible.[13] Since our bracketing efforts are part of the world we are studying, they will always be limited by a natural attitude. Involvement in the educational process, for example, keeps a person from being completely objective about it. A cab driver with a tenth-grade education may doubt the value of a college education, but those in the college world don't. Consequently, Husserl constantly questioned the possibility of bracketing as the final form of the phenomenological method.

Nevertheless, the idea that we must suspend belief in a world filled with illusions and social pretensions is attractive for both phenomenologists and Christians. The objective is "not to suppress but to place in suspense, or out of action, all the spontaneous affirmations in which I live, not to deny them but rather to understand them and make them explicit."[14] This requires, first, that we question the meaning of any social phenomenon, then avoid involvement in that meaning and, finally, seek to understand the meaning it should have for us.

For the believer, this means it is possible to be "in the world" but only because he or she is not "of the world." One can interpret the meaning of the world from that subjective distance and learn how to respond to it.

For a brief illustration of bracketing, let's return to the idea that a college education has value because it increases personal employability and income. There is a sense in which this notion is sustained by higher education to encourage parents to send their children to college even if it means going into debt. Potential students are also seen as future customers who have to be convinced of the value of a college education. A sociologist might bracket that notion by questioning the idea that education improves one's social status. Once the social status notion is set aside, the meaning of a college education can be reduced further. If one sees a college education as a means to find a spouse, then that too must be set aside as a social construction. Bracketing continues as long as those social meanings which we take for granted can be set aside as unworthy of our belief or acceptance. In this case, we reduce the procedure to the conclusion that a college education is meant to educate a student; then we proceed to interpret the meaning of education.

Much of the process of reduction involves concept clarification. Since many of our concepts are habitual and treated in loose and ambiguous ways, their meanings need to be questioned and clarified. Take, as an example, the concept of church and the idea that it is a place of worship removed from any secular influence. The Christian may properly question this concept, knowing that the world's influence has penetrated his or her otherworldly intentions. Attempts to reduce the concept to its nonsocial elements quickly suggest that the church is often a place where one does business or arranges a weekly social calendar. The concept of church must either be clarified to include these social meanings or be reduced further by eliminating them before the biblical meaning of church as a place of worship may be reached.

The problem is that people rarely clarify such concepts. The mundane world of church worship is an intersubjective world that always affirms the importance of sociability. All parishioners experience certain qualities of worship that shape their natural attitudes toward the church and worship. To bracket the meaning of church worship requires some distance from other parishioners and the inherent sociality of their consciousness. One must step outside the circle to bracket a reality they take for granted. In short, it is necessary to be "in" the church to understand the meaning it should have, but it is also necessary to be "outside" the church to discern it objectively.

Breaching

As a parishioner, of course, one cannot step too far outside the bonds of church fellowship. But it is difficult to be part of a fellowship while still being objective about it. Ethnomethodologists approach the problem differently with their use of *breaching* techniques. Working with the belief that people construct reality by interacting without knowing the rules of conduct, ethnomethodologists disrupt that reality by breaching it. Put more simply, they ignore the rules of conduct and expose the social conventions that are usually taken for granted.

We are all familiar with the courtesies involved in greeting another person. The question "How are you?" could be either a form of social greeting or a concern for the other's health. An ethnomethodologist might expose the question as nothing more than a social convention by breaching it. Instead of replying "Fine," and letting it go at that, the response could be more honest. "Well, I didn't sleep too well last night, and when I got up this morning my back was aching. To make matters worse, the ingrown toenail on my left foot is acting up again." Invariably, such an unexpected response takes the greeter aback. Usually it is apparent that he or she was really not interested in the ethnomethodologist's health. Breaching exposes the question as a social courtesy and nothing more.

On this level, breaching offers a harmless way to liven up an otherwise un-eventful day. It penetrates our mundane and often mindless participation in defi-nitions of social reality with little personal inconvenience. But on another level, breaching may expose a new morality of emerging rules of conduct and the so-cial values they suggest.

Assume, for example, that an unmarried friend confides that he or she is having a sexual relationship with another person. Can we take the confession for granted? Should we accept the definition of relationship that it implies? Po-lite acceptance of the statement or even silence provides condescending support for the relationship. Here breaching could do more than question changing rules of conduct. By questioning the relationship itself we deny the intersubjective support it needs to continue. In addition, breaching implies another value sys-tem, one that could be chosen over the one breached.

Jesus was a master at breaching, especially in dealing with the Pharisees. He exposed their social pretensions as corruptions of God's law. When the Pha-risees criticized the disciples' picking of corn on the Sabbath, he responded with a question; he breached their traditional view of the Sabbath with a reference to David's breaking of the law. Breaching the Pharisees' easy assumptions con-cerning the law, Jesus introduced them to a higher law: "The Son of Man is Lord even of the Sabbath" (Mark 2:23-28).

In the case of the Samaritan woman, Jesus used breaching to reveal himself as the Messiah (John 4:1-26). When he asked her to bring her husband, he ex-posed the sinfulness in her life. Forced to respond, she had to confess that she had no husband. This put Jesus and the woman in a completely different rela-tionship, one which forced her to see Jesus in a new way. Once she realized he was a "prophet," Jesus could then lead her to an awareness that he was the Chr-ist.

Breaching is not a popular practice for an obvious reason: it turns a social situation around to expose its hidden side. Consequently, it disturbs the social order with its honesty. Breachers are deviant because they question what others take for granted. But when society is built on false assumptions, breaching is needed before another reality can become acceptable. Jesus knew this and ac-cepted the rejection that led to the cross in order to present a new reality—the kingdom of God and his place in it.

Conclusion

Society is a vast complex of shifting, ill-defined meanings. We need to in-terpret these meanings for ourselves if we are to make any sense of them. But it is not enough merely to interpret these meanings. We also need to organize them for others and give them some durability for the future. If stocks and bonds are meaningful to us, we accept the stock market as a form of social reali-ty. It becomes one of those social institutions that guides us in our daily deci-sion making. For a broker or investor, the stock market is a tangible form of reality in which confidence and trust may be placed in the future.

Phenomenologists are correct to interpret reality and the meaning it has for people. They provide us with the means to analyze our own misconceptions about society and our place in it. But what phenomenologists overlook—and what the stock market doesn't illustrate—is that God has already ordered reality. At Creation, he organized from nothing all the meaning that life could have for us. Consequently, phenomenological interpretations are always faulty and incomplete. They provide us with limited human interpretations of reality and nothing more.

Chapter 11

The Sociology of Knowledge

Although much of the sociology of knowledge has links with Marxist thought, it remains the most popular interpretive theory among evangelical sociologists. This is largely due to the popularity of Peter Berger and the insights he provides for Christian thinking. Probably more than anyone else, Berger explains how modern everyday life is accepted as an ordered reality separate from human will. We tend to adopt this life as our own and believe it to be true. The sociology of knowledge, however, offers a means to understanding and challenging that assumption.

In his fictional work, *The Gravedigger Files,* Os Guinness describes one of Satan's henchmen going about his nefarious tasks. Writing as a deputy director for Satan's Central Security Council, the demon describes the sociology of knowledge as a major threat to Satan's work in our world because:

> It deals with the modern world and insists on seeing it from the perspective of ordinary experience. . . . Once Christians see it as a simple tool and begin to use it, our position is at risk. When people can trace a line from a thought to the thinker and then to the world in which the thought arose, they are halfway to seeing how ideas are influenced by their social contexts.[1]

And this is halfway to understanding the relative nature of the world to which we commit ourselves.

It is essential to understand our ordinary experiences in an everyday world. We need to know that these experiences can be deceitful if taken too seriously. We cannot trust a tinker-toy world assembled by others for their own enjoyment. But the sociology of knowledge scarcely moves beyond the analysis of that world. Like all interpretive sociologies, its analysis is incomplete and its conclusions limited to the social constructions of reality.

The Background

Though well suited for the analysis of modern problems, the idea that thought is framed in a social context is not new. The mere fact that people could not live alone has always been the basis for social knowledge. As long as they relied on others for survival, consciousness could not be individual. Thought would always be couched in an influential social context that would shape any truths it encountered. Merton explains, "The sociology of knowledge came into being with the signal hypothesis that even truths' were to be held socially accountable, were to be related to the historical society in which they emerged."[2]

We find an example of such historical society in medieval Europe and its domination by a Catholic interpretation of society. The authority of the church and the pope had been accepted as the legitimate basis for ordering medieval society. All social institutions were cast in the traditional model of Thomistic thought. Even the mundane details of daily life went unchallenged by peasant and prince alike. In this context, there was no room for any new form of consciousness, individual or social, that would deviate from the assumptions that dominated the Middle Ages.

But deviation did occur with the advent of the Reformation. Predating the liberating spirit and critical attitude of sociologists of knowledge, the Reformers introduced Europe to modernity. They brought a new perspective to the world, one based on Scripture and only Scripture, and it was this religious consciousness that shaped Western society and all of its institutions. In turn, the Reformation formed its own definitions of reality. Under the influence of the Protestant Ethic, capitalism became a dominant form of economic expression for many. The family had new meaning, and children gained new value. Even science was revolutionized as the search for truth was brought under the will of God. In short, a new social consciousness produced a new world.

The Reformers, of course, did not intend to create such a sweeping revolution. They began with two simple assumptions: first, that the Catholic church had shaped the medieval context with its many social and doctrinal improprieties and, second, that any new interpretations should be based on scriptural standards. The first assumption is firmly in the tradition of the sociology of knowledge because it questioned the right of the church to construct social reality for the individual. The Reformers could not see how society, as they experienced it, was in agreement with biblical principles. It is this second assumption, the idea that Scripture provides objective bases for daily life that falls outside the sociology of knowledge. In the interpretive tradition of sociology such objective bases are either nonexistent or irrelevant.

But the Reformers could not consistently apply their analysis of medieval society to the world they constructed. They could not see how "the world," not Scripture alone, now influenced their own thinking. Consequently, institutions that had been liberated from medieval thought gradually succumbed to the weight of their own traditions. The Protestant Ethic of capitalism also gave way to new social forms. The search for God's truth that had energized the early brilliance of the scientific revolution slowly degenerated into a search for technology. Even the nuclear family, a social keystone of the Reformation, did not always live up to expectations. In Europe and the New World as well, many of the social dreams of the Reformers went unfulfilled as they were increasingly influenced not by religious conviction but by social convenience.

Although practice of the sociology of knowledge was not commonplace in

Western history, it did occur, as illustrated by this brief review of the Reformation. But until Karl Marx appeared on the intellectual scene, the sociology of knowledge lacked solid theoretical foundations. More than any social thinker of the time, Marx provided that theory by critiquing the origins of Western consciousness and the effects it had on society. The result was more than the bare bones of a sociology of knowledge. It was a nicely fleshed-out skeleton, garbed with its own radical attire, ready to strut into history.

For Marx, all human behavior and consciousness were derived from the human relationship to nature. This was a fundamentally materialistic and economic relationship, one involving human dependence on the land and the means of production. All social relations stem from the means of production and create social contexts for thought and consciousness. The dominant context for Marx, of course, was social class. For him this meant that people's ideas were tied to the class structure. "It is not the consciousness of men that determines their existence, but on the contrary, their social existence determines their consciousness."[3]

Perhaps "determines" is too strong a word here. Marx did realize that persons of one social class could be influenced by the thought of another class. But ideas themselves are not separate from social contexts. Even religion, he claimed, is a form of consciousness shaped by social forces. Remembering Marx's assumptions as a materialist, his conclusion that religious sentiment is a social product appears logical. Since for him only the material world is real, religion is a social byproduct that represents human alienation from this world. Consequently, human potential is projected onto gods, which are then used by the state to maintain control of the people. In a capitalist society, Marx claimed, bourgeois religion protected class interests by maintaining authority over the proletariat.

According to Marx, then, all thought is functional; it is interpreted in terms of its functions for some social context. But this does not mean that people understand how thought functions. In fact, people tend to have an incorrect understanding of their consciousness and its relationship to the real world. We know this as *false consciousness,* the tendency of the mind to have a false notion of the true social conditions influencing it. Marx believed the bourgeois class could not clearly understand its class interests as economically determined. Consequently, the bourgeoisie fostered the illusions stimulated by class interests only.

These illusions gain a prominent part in Marx's sociology of knowledge when conceived as ideologies designed to distort the thoughts and actions of the lower class. As a system of thought that may not describe reality, an ideology may be used by its adherents to coerce dependent groups and to gain their support for dominant groups. As illusions, ideologies do not represent reality. They are an inversion of reality and a mere reflection of truth. Hence, ideologies do not emanate from some materialist base. They have an independent existence that cannot be understood until placed in the correct socio-historical perspective, something Marx believed could be accomplished only by the proletariat.

Marx believed the *real* motives behind any thought were always hidden and masked by *apparent* motives. To understand real motives, it was necessary to step out of some social context and interpret the meaning those motives had in that context. Specifically, this meant rejecting the bourgeois interpretation of history and society along with its social construction of reality. Since Marx believed that only the proletariat could reach this state of interpretation, society would be controlled by the erroneous and distorted conception of reality fostered by bourgeois thinking until the proletariat ruled.

The sociology of knowledge is so diverse that it can include the thought of Durkheim, which differed radically from that, of Marx. This is possible because Durkheim's conception of reality started with the social and not the material. Thought, he believed, began in group structures and varied with changes in those groups. Durkheim's explanation was based on the belief that people are more directly and forcefully influenced by the groups in which they live than by the physical environment about them. Social relationships provided the significant experiences shaping thought and knowledge.

While Marx rejected this functional quality of thought, Durkheim accepted it as a necessary and even desirable form of social expression. He referred to the totality of beliefs among people as a collective conscience, shared by a group of people but different from their individual consciences. Like Marx's ideology, the collective conscience was a separate, determinate cultural system. Unlike ideology, however, the collective conscience was not some illusory distortion of reality. Durkheim claimed it presented social facts in its description of the moral cohesion of reality even though it was not based on the material world.

Durkheim would not accept Marx's conception of false consciousness as "false." Since the social was more "real" than the material, thought that contributed to some group need was functional and desirable. What did trouble Durkheim was the breakdown of society into separate, independent groups. Consequently, the collective conscience was fragmented, and people lost much of the moral consensus for their beliefs and thoughts. Increasingly, they came to rely on those in other social groups and the services they performed. In any case, changes in the collective conscience led to changes in social norms with subsequent social problems.

Another attempt to apply the sociology of knowledge to the problems of modern society was made by Karl Mannheim, a German who fled to England with the coming of Nazism. Like Durkheim, he conceived of the modern world as significantly different from the past. It "is a world in which social groupings, which had hitherto lived more or less isolated from one another, each making itself and its own world of thought absolute, are now, in one form or another, merging into one another."[4] In such a world, knowledge was the means used by people to adjust to their environment. It was also the means used to defend themselves against other groups.

Mannheim called such a period the "age of equalization." Such an age is characterized by people "talking past one another." People "overlook the fact that their antagonist differs from them in his whole outlook and not merely in his opinion about the point under discussion."[5] Mannheim considers this "whole outlook" or "perspective" to be the basis for group conflict in modern society. Instead of concentrating on the immediate issues of some dispute, the sociology of knowledge seeks to go behind group assertions and claims to uncover the underlying differences. Put another way, one must remove oneself from the influential knowledge of an immediate experience to gain objective understanding of one's own knowledge or that of another group.

Using Mannheim's reference to two country boys, we may illustrate the point. The boy who lives his life in his village takes for granted the way of thinking and living found there. But the one who leaves his village and goes to the city no longer takes rural thought for granted. Detached from it, he learns to distinguish between the patterns of thinking found in the village and those found in the city. Consequently, in his detachment he no longer accepts the rural lifestyle as absolute. According to Mannheim, the sociology of knowledge needs to develop this ability to use detachment, both mental and physical, to make distinctions among knowledge systems.

The Theory

As with any discipline, the direction of social thought is shaped by questions and how they are phrased. Durkheim helped set the tone for much social thought by claiming that social facts should be considered as things. But he never considered the origins of these social facts to be a problem worth studying. Society was to be studied but not questioned.

Modern sociologists have not taken these social facts for granted. Peter Berger, especially, considered their origins to be the crucial problem for modern sociology. He asked: "How is it possible that subjective meanings *become* objective facticities? In other words, an adequate understanding of the 'reality *sui generis*' of society requires an inquiry into the manner in which this reality is constructed. This inquiry, we maintain, is the task of the sociology of knowledge."[6]

Berger conceived of social thought as a seesaw with social facts at one end and subjective social interpretations at the other. As a student of Schutz, Berger stressed the intersubjective nature of the social world. But he gave a new dimension to Schutz's work by codifying his conceptualizations and by expanding his notion of objective social truth. Consequently, Berger showed how objective facts and subjective interpretations were reciprocal in their influences; people were influencing society at the same time they were being shaped by it. The result was a dialectical view of society as a teeter-totter that never balanced perfectly. Berger refers to one end of the scale as *objectivation:*

> that process whereby human subjectivity embodies itself in products that are available to oneself and one's fellow men as elements of a common world. This process... has its roots in the fact that human subjectivity is not a closed sphere of interiority, but is always intentionality in movement. That is, human subjectivity must continually objectivate itself. Or, in other words, man is a world-producing being.[7]

This is the *externalization* part of the process.

At the other end of the scale is *reification:* through *internalization* "the characteristic of thing-hood becomes the standard of objective reality."[8] As a result of socialization people accept social rules and live as though they were objectively true and not merely constructions of reality established by others. They learn to adapt to society and conform to its expectations as "normal" members of it. Consequently, if objectivation causes society to be a human product, reification causes people to be social products. Both effects are in a simultaneous, dialectical relationship.

In his early writing, Berger claimed that

> social structure is *nothing but* the result of human enterprise. It has no reality except a human one. It is not characterizable as being a thing able to stand on its own, apart from the human activity that produced it. Any specific social structure exists only insofar and as long as human beings realize it as part of their world. In this capacity, however, social structure is essential to human existence.[9]

Later, however, he seems to be more open on this point and suggests "that *all* human societies and meaning systems have some things in common."[10] Put more simply, the possibility exists of an objective reality not constructed by humans.

At some point in this process of objectivation people become aware of the social nature of their world and respond to it as such. Berger refers to this stage as *objectification:* "the moment in the process of objectivation in which man establishes distance from his producing and its product, such that he can take cognizance of it and make of it an object of his consciousness."[11] This occurs when a name is applied to some object so the meaning of it can be communicated to another.

Up to this point, people feel comfortable in the social world they have made. It is a world they can enjoy and control. But once objectified, the world becomes foreign and separated from human endeavor. This is *alienation:* "the process by which the unity of the producing and the product is broken....In other words. . . man forgets that the world he lives in has been produced by himself."[12] He is responsible for the problems found there. By his own choice, he has made a world which now appears to be constraining and even demanding. This is the reified world to which he now conforms and willingly submits himself.

Although any social phenomena may be reified, Berger clearly states they need not be. Objectivation and objectification are necessary because human subjectivity always finds some social outlet in the world. As ideas and thoughts are shared with others, they are objectified and gain new meaning. But alienation and reification are characteristics of the human condition and not of human existence.[13] We can remember that our world was made by us and resist the tendency to reify it. Because of false consciousness, however, we forget how we have objectified the world and assume we have no responsibility for questioning it.

Social roles and institutions, for example, are products of reification. They have become separated from the human will and are accepted as inevitable. People then act with false consciousness, believing their roles require them to fulfill their demands. Indeed, Berger suggests there is a religious quality to such reification that legitimates and mystifies the power of its control. Consequently, human resistance is lost as people become de-humanized products of society.

But Berger insists that neither alienation nor reification are necessary. People can recall the means by which they gave assent to their social worlds and submitted to them. They can be responsible for their divorces and their wayward children. They can even choose to resist the claims of frivolous jobs and social calendars. In each case, the process of reification can be reversed with *de-reification*. In his critique of Berger's work, Perkins refers to de-reification as "a cognitive detachment from what others regard as natural."[14] What had been accepted as true without reservation is now questioned and, perhaps, even rejected.

Berger refers to this act of rejection as *ecstasy:* "the act of standing or stepping outside . . . the taken-for-granted routines of society."[16] What others accept as a necessary given becomes, through ecstasy, an option. We can exert our will and take an individual step toward rejecting society's conventions. Berger graphically describes ecstasy this way: "Society provides us with warm, reasonably comfortable caves, in which we can huddle with our fellows, beating on the drums that drown out the howling hyenas of the surrounding darkness. "Ecstasy" is the act of stepping outside the caves, alone, to face the night."[16]

Note two things about this quotation. First, *ecstasy is an individual act.* Because of the intersubjective nature of the social world, any rejection of it must be solitary. Ecstasy allows for self-authentication and the opportunity to re-affirm the humanness distorted by a reified world. Second, *caves are plural.* These refer to the variety of social roles and institutions that need to be questioned. Ecstasy offers the opportunity to seek for new expressions in each of these. It is unlikely, however, that many will take the opportunity. Stepping out of caves is a deviant act that most will not choose to follow.

If that is the case, what happens to Berger's ecstatic cave dweller? Is he or she to continue wandering in the night alone? Berger feels this is unlikely: "Just as the world cannot be constituted by the individual in isolation, so it is not inhabitable by the individual in isolation. Being in the world means, for man, being in the world with others."[17] Once found, these others offer the means for reconstructing a world in agreement with their own definition of reality.

Anyone who chooses the way of ecstasy has chosen to be free of social roles; ironically, that person is now in the business of building new ones. Each new opportunity we find brings an obligation we gladly accept. Berger refers to this opportunity as *alternation:* "the possibility to choose between varying and sometimes contradictory systems of meaning."[18] Choosing to live on a farm instead of in the city, we trade off convenience for solitude. Indeed, any set of social responsibilities we discard is replaced with another. To put it another way, we *move* from the dampness of one cave to the chill of another.

Despite the inconvenience and even the deviance of ecstasy, there are always people who choose this route. Some may remain isolated in a world without caves. Most, however, perform the necessary social act of interpreting their new social responsibilities with others. Together, they challenge society's definitions of roles with their own. Marriage, job, community, organizations all become those worlds in which they hope to find themselves. The paradox is that each world carries the seeds of alienation from it. Through objectivation, each world gradually represses the subjective quality that brought it to life. In short, our caves turn cold and damp as we probe more deeply into them.

There is good reason, then, for people to approach society with some skepticism, for they are always expected to accept its definitions of reality. But instead of accepting society and everything it has to offer, people need to question and *debunk* it to avoid its control. And yet, debunking social institutions produces the fear of isolation in a world of confusion and chaos. Consequently, our cave dweller prefers any cave to the loneliness and terror of the night.

Berger analyzes marriage as an institution that orders our private world for us.[19] People marry, he says, to avoid the anomic condition of society. It is in the family that husband and wife hope to make a reasonable world for themselves, one which they can control for their development together. Consequently, they externalize their wishes in such a way that each partner's desires merge with those of the other. In this way, they define and accept a new reality for themselves. The result is a dialectical relationship, one in which the husband's actions are influenced by the wife and then return in modified form to shape his original intentions. In the same way, the wife's desires are shaped by the husband.

Here the dialectic of objective and subjective realities—concepts always at the core of Berger's work—finds expression in concrete relationships. The result is a marriage which neither husband nor wife could have conceived of at the altar. It is a unique creation, one which shapes them as they shape it. In the process of submitting to each other, joint decisions are made that gradually change them. Any questioning of this process is countered by the legitimating force of marriage. This assures us that this is an "okay world" to live in. Marriage, it claims, is always preferable to the uncertainty of singleness.

The world, then, stands as a vast network of social facts that claims our loyalty. But since we ourselves have made this world, it is wrong to believe it has any objectivity of its own. A blend of the objective and the subjective, a dialectic of social constraint and human resistance must be maintained. An accurate understanding of the world requires an acceptance of this dialectical quality. More than that, action must be taken if the dialectic is to be renewed and clarified.

Social thought, according to Berger, provides the insight needed to unmask the pretensions of society. Sociology of knowledge is the theoretical means by which we may gain this insight. But theory is not enough. It is equally necessary to live out that insight, to question the distortions conveyed by society with *praxis,* a way of living out the freedom gained from sociological understanding. As Berger states, "there is a close connection here between theoretical insight and practical application—a 'unity of theory and praxis.'"[20] It is this dialectic that must be maintained and focused if people are to resist effectively the corrupting influence of society.

A Christian Critique

It is very important for the Christian to grasp the dialectical, illusory nature of the world as described by Berger. It is the kind of world that gives some meaning to the idea that the Christian is to be "in the world" and yet "not of it." On one hand, this world can be influenced with praxis. On the other hand, it is a deceitful world made for human convenience and use, a world that cannot be taken for granted. Indeed, it is a world that needs the dialectical tension offered by Christians. The problem with Berger's world is its relativity. For him, no objectivity exists outside society's constructed reality, no quality of absolute truth to be accepted. This is not to say that Berger doesn't believe in such an objective truth. The human condition "transcends time and space" as well as the relativity of "historically concrete meaning systems."[21] But the study of such a transcendent order lies outside the scope of sociology as he understands it. He limits the sociology of knowledge to the study of constructed social reality and therefore, it cannot deal with problems of ultimate truth.

Perspective

A major strength of Berger's analysis is its accurate portrayal of modern society. For centuries, the accumulation of human efforts to construct reality for personal benefits has built a hard shell around objective truth. This dialectical network of false notions and distorted perceptions can no longer be phrased in terms of two or more opposing forces. Human attempts at understanding truth have become a knotted tangle of differing assumptions and biases.

Mannheim also understood well the problem of knowledge in the modern world. He, too, perceived the dialectical nature of the problem, believing that opposing viewpoints are not the products of arbitrary will. Rather, they are complementary and derived from specific social situations. As social beings, we conceive of a problem and then proceed to analyze it, always keeping in mind how that problem fits with our own social expectations. When this individual process is expressed by a multitude of persons, the result is complex indeed.

Rather than attempting to understand the epistemological problems in this process, Mannheim argues that the problem must be seen as a totality, especially as it is perceived by those involved in it. What must be understood is *perspective:* "the manner in which one views an object, what one perceives in it, and how one construes it in his thinking."[22] Such a view is determined not by logical thought but by the social experiences brought to that thought. Berger would say that one's social role or institution shapes that thought. In any case, some form of conflict usually results from the differing experiences we bring to our common problems.

At a very mundane level, Mannheim suggests that the differing meanings we attach to words reflect our different perspectives.[23] Freedom, for example, may be interpreted quite differently by conservatives and liberals. The historical and social setting of each group determines the meaning attached to the word. Consequently, it also influences attitudes of each person toward the other as well as their mutual interests. The problem is to understand the viewpoint of the other person, "where they are coming from," so to speak, as well as the historical and social settings shaping their thought. It is the understanding of these various contexts, including the personal, that Mannheim considers to be the major task of the sociology of knowledge.

As noted earlier, such problems are not limited to our day. We need only to turn to Scripture to note the differing perspectives of Jew and Gentile, prophet and king, Greek and apostle.

Jesus, especially, illustrated on many occasions how he took perspectives into consideration when dealing with the Pharisees. He understood the cultural pressures bearing on them as well as their own sinfulness in submitting to these pressures. When dealing with the Samaritan woman, he knew that water had a different meaning for her (John 4:7-26). Accepting that meaning, he acknowledged her perspective and helped her to broaden her understanding to include the wider and even eternal context of her problem. Jesus had this divine capacity to understand the unity of perspectives in their social settings. He also used that understanding in an appropriate and often redemptive fashion.

Other Scripture passages direct us to a more limited view of perspectives. The Golden Rule (Matt. 7:12) tells us to treat the other person as we would want to be treated by him or her. By our actions, we are to create a context for that person's response to us. Also, Paul said he was made all things to all men that some might be saved (1 Cor. 9:22). Here, again, the writer refers to the indirect way we are to understand people's viewpoints, as well as their other needs, if we are to deal with them in a healing way. In these cases, their viewpoints must become our viewpoints.

It is important here to note the relative position of social perspectives. Jesus' divine nature allowed him to take a unique viewpoint when dealing with others. He was never influenced by social roles as we are. Even though he was in Jewish culture, his thought was never dominated by it. By contrast, our problem is that we absolutize those perspectives that should remain relative. Instead of accepting the social nature of our viewpoints, we believe them to be absolute and judge others by them. In short, we try to be like Jesus and fail miserably in the process.

Mannheim claims that a detached perspective is necessary to understand correctly some forms of social knowledge. Detachment comes when a person leaves a social position, experiences changing social norms or institutions, or learns from conflicting social interpretations, which then "establish perspectives with reference to each other."[24] This last form of detachment, based on dialectical principles, Mannheim claims to be the basis for the social origins of the sociology of knowledge. It is in such a marginal social position that we can identify with a particular perspective while, at the same time, standing apart from it to gain a more objective view of that position. We may be in a social world and yet not part of it, both at the same time.

Dialectics

Berger's dialectic centers on the process of externalization and internalization described earlier. Through this process, people are both defining society and being defined by it at the same time. Consequently, society becomes *objective* reality; as a result of externalization, it appears as an autonomous world of facts external to humans. But society is also *subjective* reality; as a result of internalization, it comes to a person in a meaningful and even intimate way by means of socialization. The result is a human marginality that influences our perspectives on society.

On one hand, people see society as ordered and under control. Institutions exist to give security and a sense of meaning to life. We accept these legitimizing forms simply because they solve more problems than they cause. On the other hand, people also see a certain disorder and potential chaos in society. There are always hidden problems that break through our secure worlds to arouse the latent terror that is there. For this reason, people continually defend themselves by shaping new forms of social order and security.

Berger would argue that the individual response to this dialectical process should always be negative. This is the form that praxis takes when pitted against massive social attempts to legitimate efforts to mask problems rather than to solve them. This is the task of sociology, for "the genius of sociology is negative; and, paradoxically, *it is as negation that sociology can make its best contribution to any positive cause.*"[25] Stated differently, in order to be positive on some questions, it might be necessary to take a negative position. The perspective here is neither positive nor negative but a dialectic of both.

Ellul takes a similar position:

> There usually has to be an express and explicit contradiction put in words by someone who contradicts, who bears the negation. In this way the negativity induces and provokes innovation, and consequently the history, of the group or individual. One can see, then, that negativity has a wholly positive side. If there is transition from one state to another, we can thank negativity alone.[26]

Surely the crucifixion of Christ remains as the clearest and most forceful example of the positive side of negativity. By dying, he provided life. And it is necessary for us to have a dialectical perspective, to see the life in death and death in life, if we are to understand how the Crucifixion leads to the Resurrection.

A dialectic of thought, then, can illumine a situation. Paul often used such thought to analyze a troubling problem. When writing to the Philippians from prison, he personally preferred death to his present condition (Phil. 1:23-24). He could understand and even welcome it because he would be with the Lord. But when he realized that such death would not be best for the Philippians, he accepted life even if it meant being imprisoned. The negative, indeed, had a positive quality.

Unlike Berger, whose dialectics are always bounded by social and temporal restraints, Ellul has a wider, even eternal view of dialectics. For him, "there is always *one* history . . . made up of the conjunction, opposition and contradiction of the independent work of man and the 'relational' work of God."[27] This means that everything in society has both a human and divine meaning. The city, for example, is part of human work in culture and changes with its development. In this sense, the city is a passing event in history. But because the city is also a manifestation of God's work in creation, it is also structured in eternity and forms a constant in history as well. Together these two realities form a dialectic which is to be fully revealed only in eternity.

It is this wider view of dialectics that sets Ellul's work off from Berger's in an important way for the believer. Since Berger limits himself to the sociology of knowledge and accepts the constraints of a scientific discipline, objective forms of reality are always socially defined. Ellul refers to this form of reality as "man's work," the attempt to shape society to human will. But Ellul's dialectics includes another form of objectivity, one which transcends the social while mingling with it. This is "God's work," God's revelation laid down in Creation for eternity. It is found at every level of society but is always overlaid by human work that opposes and contradicts God's work. The result is a synthesis, a crisis of irreconcilable forces destined for resolution only in eternity.

Despite the sweeping implications of this kind of dialectical thinking, Ellul's response to problems remains very personal. Like Berger, he firmly says "No" to society. "The only respectable human decision is to refuse all compromise in advance. It is to know, of course, that in action, in practice, in combat, 'evil eventually creeps in,' but never to accept it, never to tolerate it, never to justify it."[28] Here Ellul seems to recognize a spiritual warfare missing in Berger's dialectic. We reject society because it is illusory and oppressive, yes, but also because it is evil. In short, the dialectic includes the conflict between good and evil.

Ellul goes far beyond any social theory in his analysis. By contrast, Berger remains faithful to what he perceives as his sociological task and stays with the problems it poses. But Berger does not lack an appreciation for the transcendent qualities in society. He is, instead, always concerned with the unique view offered by his sociological bias. The result is a different dialectic, one that joins sociology and society in a continuing struggle. Still, it is a classic scientific struggle, a constant process of hiding and seeking, covering and revealing. The result, while still in doubt, will be a world different from what it had been but probably not what it could be.

Debunking

Early social thinkers were as wrong in their evaluations of society as geographers were wrong in their understanding of the earth. The idea of a simple society is as antiquated today as the idea of a flat earth. People still fear to test the social depths, preferring to stay within the shore lines of their limited understanding of what society is or how it should work. Consequently, they approve of much that should be questioned.

Berger understands sociology to be a special kind of science, one that subverts society even as it studies it. In one sense, sociologists have always attempted to shape society to some preconceived, ideal state. They always assumed society could be something different from what it was. That they failed in their attempts suggests they were wrong for either or both of two reasons: their understanding of social science was too limited, or "the world is not what it appears to be."[29] Berger is probably correct in emphasizing the importance of the latter reason.

The point is that the conscious, obvious, official, and public intentions expressed in all social forms do not exist alone. They always blend dialectically with another form of social reality that is unconscious, covert, unofficial, and private. This is the underside of society, a side we rarely see and, indeed, prefer not to see. And when it is seen, we prefer that it would have remained hidden. A form of this reality was described by Edward Alsworth Ross as early as 1907:

> In its reactions against wrong-doing the public is childishly naive and sentimental. It is content with the surface look of things. It lays emphasis where emphasis was laid centuries ago. It beholds sin in a false perspective, seeing peccadillos as crimes, and crimes as peccadillos. It never occurs to the public that sin evolves along with society, and that the perspective in which it is necessary to view misconduct changes from age to age.[30]

Berger again probably correctly asserts that sociology debunks society by questioning the illusions presented to the public. Whether we speak of the divorce rate, political scandals, televangelism, or economic boondoggles, one thing is clear: all is not as it could or should be. It is also clear that attempts at social reform will have little effect on these issues. Unlike most early social thinkers and reformers who understood nothing of human sinfulness, Ross could properly describe how individual sin is structured in society. For this reason, social reform will always remain, at best, partial and incomplete.

It may be, then, that we cannot and, indeed, should not expect the best of all possible worlds. Perhaps we can only hope to punch some holes in society's facades to let the light through. But, as Berger would claim, this requires a way of seeing the world as something that cannot "be taken for granted." It must be questioned and these questions must be directed at its underside. In other words, society should never be trusted and always tested. Berger suggests that sociology offers the best perspective to accomplish this task because its objectivity and interpretation place it in a necessary dialectical relationship to society. Without vested interests, sociology may denounce as it debunks.

But Berger quickly reminds us that the Christian faith may have its own forms of socially constructed reality. The church has always stood as a legitimating institution, ready to stamp its approval on everyday life. The problem is that such legitimation is not always well placed. Too often the church approves of that which is socially functional but irrelevant. As part of the establishment, the church may acquire vested interests that the gospel should not be heir to. Berger correctly claims that scientific integrity requires sociology to examine itself for those social pretenses that cannot be taken for granted. In the same way, the integrity of the gospel requires the same self-examination on the part of the church. Indeed, this may be the proper starting place for any dialectical critique.

God has always used his prophets to accomplish this purifying task. Berger refers to Nathan's encounter with David as a model of faithful debunking, a willingness to pronounce a resounding "No" on David while leaving the door open for God's redeeming "Yes."[31] The point is that Nathan knew what he had to do, and he did it. His indictment of David left no illusions and allowed no further pretense. "You are the man" took nothing for granted and left no social fig leaves for David to hide behind. He was exposed, and he knew it. But he was not destroyed. In the final analysis, debunking produced adialectic of God's judgment and grace.

Nathan, of course, was not unique in his efforts to uncover social and moral corruption. Throughout history, God has used prophets to debunk society. They understood the structured forms of evil in their day and were faithful in exposing them. But did their pronouncements change anything? Was society made any better or people more moral as a result? Not clearly. And yet this faithful questioning was necessary as a witness to God's work in the world. It provided a dialectic for change that was often less than we would prefer but more than we could hope for.

Consider, for example, Jesus' encounters with the Pharisees. As an outsider, he came into sharp conflict with them. More than that, he unmasked their pretenses with all the social fictions they represented. He exposed them to the public and left them with no defense. But scarcely any change in Jewish society resulted. Some lives were changed, but institutions remained virtually intact. What did change was the Pharisees' perception of Jesus and his claims. Instead of accepting him as the Son of God, they called him a fraud and killed him. But this was a necessary attitude and a necessary act that led to the Resurrection and the fulfillment of God's plan.

Similarly, debunking is a futile but necessary act. It is futile because it never gains the desired objectives. It is necessary because it activates the latent dialectic in any situation. But it is also an unpopular act, one usually reserved for prophets and other outsiders. These are people who come from another meaning system to enter into a dialectical relationship with the world. If debunking is our only concern, it matters little who these people are or where they might come from. What does matter is whether they give us a message that is true.

Conversion

In his discussion of American religion, Berger argues for the necessity of personal conversion:

> We also imply in using this term that the encounter with the Christian faith is with something outside Of ourselves. The Christian faith is not a mystical path into the mysterious depths of our own being. Indeed, the Christian faith might seriously question whether we possess any such depths. The mystery to which it points is an external one. It lies in history, not in psychology. It tells us that the God who created the distant nebulae, the God who is other than anything we can imagine, has come to us; that his coming gives redeeming meaning to our finite existence; and that this meaning may be found in the life, death, and resurrection of Jesus Christ. The eyes of the Christian faith look not inward into itself but outward towards this man Jesus, of whom the New Testament speaks and who asked this question of his early followers: "Who do you say that I am?" Conversion to the Christian faith is the answer to this question, the one once given by Simon Peter—the stupendous affirmation that the man asking the question is Christ, the savior. It is the decisive act of God's breaking into history.[32]

Conversion does not bring a person, first, into an encounter with social reality. It is an act of faith that responds to a prior question, one that transcends all forms of culture and consciousness. As such, conversion provides an objective platform for the study of society. Only then may conversion be applied, dialectically, to everyday life.

Berger, however, does not clearly develop this application of conversion. Everyday life remains in dialectical tension, primarily, with the sociology of knowledge. But since he was born in Austria, Berger remains something of an outsider to the American religious establishment and in dialectical tension with it:

> In the American religious-secular continuum of values, Christianity appears embedded in taken-for-granted reality. It does not stand out from the rest of the culture, at least not in its middle-class Protestant forms. Consequently, it can offer no challenge to all that is taken for granted. As we have seen, commitment to Christianity thus undergoes a fatal identification with commitment to society, to respectability, to the American way of life.[33]

Here, Berger correctly describes how conversion may lose the tension it may have with the religious establishment. Instead, the church co-opts the conversion experience for its own purposes and shapes it in cultural ways.

Ellul takes a wider view of conversion and the dialectic with the world it offers. This dialectic is exemplified by Paul's assertion that we are to work out our salvation because we are saved by grace (Phil. 2:12).[34] If we see these as separate statements, they seem to be contradictory; there is no reason to work if we are already saved. But if we recognize the statements as integrated, it is apparent that our salvation is part of a larger process including work. In God's redemptive plan, salvation and work are dialectically tied together. Our responsibility is to recognize this dialectic and five it in our lives.

But living out our conversion requires more than a life circumscribed by our cultural setting. For Ellul, it means understanding the real spiritual problems inherent in any social situation and living in tension with them. These are not the problems of everyday life as Berger describes them. Rather, they are the problems that have become structured in the world, the problems which society covers with false notions and false solutions. They are, simply, the problems of objective reality.

Here we come full circle. For Berger, objective social reality never gains the same meaning it has for Ellul. It remains a social construction of human efforts and nothing more. Conversion is an objective fact realized through the saving work of Christ. But it is largely directed at the church and scarcely extends beyond the wall of the religious establishment. Consequently, a person's social identity in the world is neither synonymous with nor comparable to a religious identity in the world. Put more simply, one's conversion does not clearly extend to everyday life.

By contrast, Ellul ties together more clearly the fact of conversion and the fact of society. He would agree with Berger that our society has constructed a form of reality that is merely illusory. Like Berger, he too would agree that social roles and institutions are the facades of our lives behind which we hide our fear of a chaotic world. But here there is a difference. Berger would have us say "No" to these social fictions, step out of the cave and face the night alone. No transcendent "Yes" is heard. Consequently, any sense of a transcendent objective reality is lost in the social origins of knowledge.

Ellul has a more clear recognition of, and appreciation for, the transcendent quality found in the social world. Granted, it is not readily amenable to scientific inquiry. But he would claim that it is possible, dialectically, to oppose the objective reality of the world with the objective reality of a new life in Christ. In that sense, the Christian has a responsibility to enter into the problems of the world.

> [But] it is not for him to define the problems in the same terms as those who have no faith; it is not for him to tinker with futile attempts at technical and moral "solutions"; his job is to discover the real spiritual difficulties which every political or economic situation contains—In other words, it is in receiving, and in living the gospel that political, economic, and other questions can be solved.[35]

Conclusion

The sociology of knowledge remains a powerful tool in the Christian's intellectual tool kit, another hidden thread with complementarity to Scripture. Guinness rightly claims that "Christians are paying through the nose for their current refusal to think."[36] Too often we fail to see the powerful implications of daily decision making in our everyday lives that are taken for granted. These are trivialized by headline issues and attempts to respond to them theologically. Consequently, we routinely affirm in our homes those things we eschew in the marketplace. The sociology of knowledge brings a new perspective to these questions and offers a way of interpreting them.

But it also tends to relativize the world with this perspective. The dialectic is limited to the social world and includes a transcendent reality that has little, if any, implications for society. Consequently, little basis remains for a tension with society, nothing to invigorate or direct the negative tone of the dialectic. By contrast, Ellul located the problem in a larger context of transcendent truth. It involves a struggle of good and evil, a tension between two necessary and irresoluble forces. Thus, as Ellul proclaims, "we must not weaken the opposition that exists between the Christian faith, the claims of revelation, and life in the world and its demands, its faults, and its compromises."[37]

Chapter 12

Postmodern Theories
Calling Meaning into Question

In the popular sitcom, *The King of Queens*, there is a character played by Arnold Schwarzenegger-era body builder Lou Ferrigno. On the show Ferrigno plays "himself" as neighbor to the main characters, Doug and Carrie Heffernan. Woven through the various episodes of the program is Doug and Carrie's fascination with Ferrigno's former alter ego, the Incredible Hulk–a character he played in the 1980s primetime television drama by the same name. In *The King of Queens,* however, Ferrigno is presented as a real person, simply playing himself. Part of his "real personage" is evidenced in the show's dialogue—he continually has to remind the Doug Heffernan character that he is a real person, and not the Hulk ("That's just a character I used to play; I don't do that anymore.").

Despite Ferrigno's scripted attempts to move beyond his Hulk identity, it keeps creeping back on him. For example, one episode had him purchasing purple pants (Hulk attire) to wear when he attended a science fiction convention. Thus, in *The King of Queens,* he plays *himself,* but does so in reference to a fictitious self which his television character claims is no longer a part of *himself,* even though Ferrigno would not likely be playing *himself* if he had never been the Hulk. Confusing? Most certainly. The viewer is left to ask who the real Lou Ferrigno is, and what the reality is behind the images by which we know him? Phrased another way, what is the truth about him? Is he the sum of these images, or do they somehow float free?

The questions this anecdote raises are typical of those which postmodern theorists grapple with. Some such theorists find that the proliferation of images comes to comprise a reality of its own. So, who is Lou Ferrigno? Through a postmodern lens, he is a pastiche of images which are inseparable from the man himself–in fact his images are larger than he is. Furthermore, our television sitcoms present clear examples of some of the observations and central concerns of postmodern theorists. They manipulate our emotions and increase our appetites for consumer goods. They reduce serious problems to the level of whimsy, and try to both disseminate character-building messages and indulge immorality at one and the same time. In short, they are filled with contradictions—and these are celebrated rather than resolved.

As we will here explore, postmodern theorists are concerned with such things as the explosion of symbols and images, the implosion of meaning, hyperreality, spectacle, and the disappearance of the subject. Despite the fact that a measure of fear and suspicion surrounds it, knowledge of postmodern theory provides an important perspective for the Christian who believes that the scriptures–God's Word–bear witness to the truth found in God and provide a basis for understanding how to live in a world which bends and manipulates that truth. The Christian can thus understand postmodern sociological theory in two ways: either as a description of the contemporary social world where we struggle to grasp truth amidst multiple and competing systems of meaning, or as an expression of despair, which, framed in the light of the scriptural themes of creation, fall, and redemption, reminds us of the importance of faith in a socially constructed world of illusion.

Many people have negative impressions of postmodernism, but it isn't entirely problematic. In the postmodern era we find greater willingness to include voices which were barred from expression in the modern era (for example, minorities, women, and others restrained under modernity's rule). Many sectors of postmodern society emphasize a plurality of voices, and, although there is still resistance to diversity in the community and workplace, there is increasing pressure to include minorities and to listen to what they have to say. This itself represents a shift away from the more narrow and exclusionary tendencies of the modern age.

A great deal of postmodern thought is an extension of work done in the context of earlier sociological traditions. For example, in the field of sociology of knowledge, postmodern thinkers pay a good deal of attention to the ways people use power to construct realities that reinforce their own ideological ideals. Additionally, the reader will recall "breaching experiments" and the "bracketing of reality" presented in the earlier chapter on phenomenology. The phenomenological tradition anticipates postmodernism in so far as it articulates a suspicion about human certainty, about our confidence in our ability to know the world as it presents itself to us.

On the whole, postmodern theorists are concerned with the "new" ways that people are controlled, deceived, and managed through a variety of techniques. Although we sometimes credit postmodern thinkers with advancing relativism, they are frequently concerned to show how the present world leaches meaning from our lives. Much about our world has been trivialized and fetishised– sexuality, humor, religion, relationships, and so on. Postmodern theory can help us to understand how we have been duped by the images, technology, and the various and not-so-subtle allures of the consumer society. Armed with this knowledge, we can more effectively resist the adverse social forces that act on us.

As we explore the questions framed by postmodern social theorists, ask yourself whether their descriptions of the social landscape match your experience of it. What role do images play in your life? Where do you see contradict tory systems of meaning combining, colliding, and co-existing? How have the technologies of communication altered your experience of time, space, and reality itself? In short, whence truth? A number of important postmodern thinkers clearly remind us that contemporary life provides an especially difficult climate for discerning what it means to live in the world, but not be entirely of it.

Although postmodernism unsettles us with its questions about certainty and meaning, when some Christians argue for truth or "absolute" truth, they end up constructing it in accordance with their own ideological predispositions—an ironic fact in itself. Thus, even those who hold to the notion of truth, contribute to its fragmentation as they stake claims in a world of their own making. It is to this world that Jesus says, "And lo, I am with you, even to the end of the age." Truth is still with us, even in these confusing times.

Background

Describing the world as "postmodern" is, in itself, a bit problematic. To understand what "postmodern" means, we must first have a grasp of the term "modern." In our everyday lives, we still describe things using modernist language: we speak of modern conveniences, we may modernize an old house, or when someone finally figures out how to text-message we say "welcome to the 'modern' world." These uses of the word "modern" all imply something hopeful, something that holds promise, a sort of coming out of darkness and into light. They also imply that, as humans progress through history, they will come to see things as they really are, to know more of the "truth" of the world. For example, we speak of "scientific advancements," which come through the exercise of logic and rationality. These give us hope and the feeling that we can access truth.

At first glance, this seems to coincide with what the scriptures teach. Christians speak of "redemptive history," a phrase which signifies the hope we have in the progression from the fall of humankind to its redemption in Christ. Additionally, they think about the notion of sanctification, which also implies that believers are on a certain trajectory of spiritual development–things are getting better in the quest to achieve holiness. Sometimes we even equate progress in a country (like America) with the unfolding of the kingdom of God. This is what sociologists call "civil religion." And, we celebrate progress in all of its forms– in economic matters, in our children's education, in politics, in automobile manufacturing, and in our spiritual lives. It makes us feel sure that we're going somewhere, and that 'somewhere' is good. When the economy regresses, we panic. We feel that we are being denied what was promised to us–by God and by others.

But what of modernity's promise? Is this rationality, logic, and search for truth actually getting us somewhere? Sociologist Charles Lemert opens his work *Postmodernism is not what You Think*, with an anecdote about wondering what will happen to his son when he goes off to college. He then claims that there is good reason to doubt whether the modern world can still deliver on its promise.

What sort of job will his son eventually have? How much will college cost, and can he afford it? The modern condition has become one of doubt and stress, rather than one of reveling in the certainty of promises fulfilled. Presidential debates and elections often hinge on whether a particular candidate can revive modernity's vision and renew the promise. On the question of whether the modern world can deliver on its promises, Lemert says:

1. Personal income, worldwide, is declining nearly at the same perverse rate as economic productivity and cumulative wealth are growing.

2. Continuous working employments, that is: jobs productive of personal income and benefits sufficient to support family life, are disappearing for the majority.

3. Meanwhile, social and economic inequalities are growing worse, not better–most dramatically in the United States to which the modern world had always looked as the land of opportunity.

4. Food supplies are declining to their lowest levels in decades with world grain reserves dropping to just 48 days worth at current consumption levels.

5. Social conflict–ranging from violence against women and children to ethnic, class, and racial conflict–is epidemic.[1]

These strains and tensions are perceptible throughout American culture, and they raise questions about whether or not we are really making progress. In the past decade, the United States has witnessed ecological disaster, devastating damage due to hurricanes and other weather-related phenomena (hurricane Katrina), corruption in business (the Enron scandal), terrorism (the 9-11 attacks), a serious energy crisis and oil supply shortage, fears of global warming, a war (Iraq) and, as I write, an economic recession during which the Dow Jones Industrial Average fell 778 points (September 30, 2008), its greatest decline ever in a single-day. How to understand our lives in the midst of all of this?

It is difficult to pinpoint exactly when this large-scale shift has occurred, but still, the world has changed, to some extent for the better, to some extent not. The rational tenor of the modern age has been called into question, and the boundaries of rational thought have been breached. Consequently, modernity's successor, postmodernity, is characterized by a certain plasticity. If nothing else, these changes give us cause to examine more critically our modernist assumptions. Gene Edward Veith provides a helpful analogy when he compares the modern age with the Tower of Babel. He explains how the tower represented faith in human reason, in the power of the will, and in technology, none of which are inherently bad. However, inside the tower, its builders and inhabitants lost sight of meaningful ends and forgot the God who gave them reason, purpose, and direction. "God judged the pretensions of Babel. Noting their genuine accomplishments and the vast potential of human achievement, the Lord saw that a united, technologically sophisticated human race would be nearly unlimited in their capacity for evil."[2]

Accordingly, the Tower of Babel can be understood as a sort of totem, an idol–for Durkheim, a self-referential symbol pointing back at the collective conscience of its creators. The seeming progress associated with it was less obviously an outward progress (toward certain ends) than an inward activity (development of means). Modernism represented social unity and human progress; postmodernism, by contrast seems to be the "logical" outcome of progress in a world of means without clearly defined ends, of effort which has become turned inward on itself. In Veith's words,

> This is exactly what has happened with the fall of modernism. The monolithic sensibility of modernism, which seemed to have an unlimited potential, has fragmented into diverse and competing communities. People can no longer understand each other. There are no common reference points, no common language. Totalitarian unity has given way to chaotic diversity. Scattered in small groups of like-minded people, those who speak the same language, human beings today are confused.[3]

Christians fall into traps on both ends of the modern/postmodern spectrum. To idolize the modern age–to place our faith in progress, science, and the power of the human will–is to deify our collective conscience and erroneously elevate human ends to the level of the divine. In pursuing the promises of modernism, we often replace prayer with work, and equate progress in the kingdom of God with progress in the kingdom of man. For example, when America advances or prospers, we see the very kingdom of God advancing; when it stumbles, we lament the triumph of evil over good. Civil religion (worship of country frequently seen in patriotism) sets up a parallel between national dominance and the spiritual triumph of light over darkness. In the end, it is simply a form of self-aggrandizement. For the modernist, truth exists, but it is often distorted to support ideological self-interest. It is a truth in search of this-worldly ends, rather than the ends described in the scriptures, those of a transcendent world.

Postmodernism, however, contains traps of a different nature. On the postmodern worldview, truth claims are viewed with suspicion. This is, to some degree, a reaction to those who "hold" or "control" truth, to their failure to recognize that it is to some degree a product of their own social construction. But postmodernism can dissolve into a relativism of the sort that leaves people with very little solid ground to stand upon. Postmodernism elevates emotion, experience, and intuition as forms of truth; truth becomes a mere by-product of the human will, nothing more than a social construction. And we live lives of contradiction. Our unquestioning use of *Wikipedia* as a source of truth is a case in point as is our faith in the accuracy of information derived from hastily constructed internet *blogs*. Both of these suggest that even while we cling to the idea of transcendent truth, at an everyday level we engage in practices which relativize and weaken its impact–or at least call into question our commitment to it. Many Christians rightly see tremendous dangers in the postmodern world-view. Out of a sense of fear, however, they cling to modernist paradigms. Ironically, these paradigms contain equally as many traps and tend to reify particular social constructions of truth.

Structuralism and Poststructuralism
Intellectual Antecedents of Postmodernism

George Ritzer explains that as we move our discussion from modern to postmodern thought, we must shift our focus from *sociological* theories to *social* theories.[4] He says that the former tend primarily to reflect developments that have occurred within sociology proper, and are mostly of interest to sociologists. Social theories, on the other hand, are more multidisciplinary in character. This multidisciplinary approach itself exemplifies the postmodern tendency to attend to plurality of voices.

Because they are not lodged in a single disciplinary tradition, the *intellectual* antecedents of postmodern social theory are hard to definitively identify. Nonetheless, the roots of postmodern theory are to be found in the intellectual debate between two competing, mid-twentieth century philosophies–Jean-Paul Sartre's existentialism and French structuralism; they are also to be found in the poststructuralism of Jacques Derrida. These philosophies are all concerned in one way or another with the deconstruction of conventional notions of power, order, language, texts, and meaning. This culminates in Derrida's *deconstruction of logocentrism* and paves the way for postmodern thinkers like Jean Baudrillard. As we examine this intellectual progression, it is important to note that postmodernism is best understood as a social movement rather than an intellectual one. Thus, while the present section of this chapter helps elucidate some of the intellectual developments which led to the development of postmodern thinking, the next section will draw on examples from everyday life to address the cultural and social implications of postmodernism.

Sartre

The structuralism of the 1950's and '60s, which prompted the development of that of the late 1960s, stands in sharp contrast to the early work of existentialist philosopher Jean-Paul Sartre (1905-1980). Examining the debate between these two philosophies (structuralism and existentialism) helps us understand the intellectual climate from which postmodernism emerged. Sartre saw the individual as responsible for what he or she does, and downplayed the role larger structures played in influencing behavior. This individualism can be seen as a tremendous source of both anguish (freedom implies great responsibility) and optimism (people can control their own fates).[5] As McNeil and Feldman explain, "Sartre's existentialism places a premium on human freedom and responsibility, emphasizing our inevitable entanglements in the concrete world and issues of our times. Human beings not only choose their existence, according to Sartre, but are 'condemned' to do so; freedom, which distinguishes human self-consciousness is also a fatality."[6]

Sartre's later work is more Marxist in tone, and he pays greater attention to the oppressive social and economic structures which constrain human freedom. However, despite his recognition of these alienating structures, Sartre's later work still emphasizes the "... human prerogative for transcendence–the surpassing of the given."[7] The significance of his perspective lies in its suggestion that human beings are *not* ultimately constrained by such structures, social or otherwise, and can thus rise above them. We hear echoes of Sartre in contemporary television commercials which offer such inspiring slogans as "no limits," or the US Army's "be all that you can be." Messages like these communicate freedom, direction, progress, and self-reliance. Additionally, they press the issue of human boundaries, and in this way anticipate some of the central concerns of postmodern thinkers. As we will see, the structuralists take a decidedly less autonomous view of human beings, but the matter of individualism and freedom re-emerges in poststructuralist thought; it appears once again in postmodern thought, where the almost limitless choices confronting individuals have serious adverse implications for the so-called freedom they enjoy.

Structuralism

In contrast to existentialist humanism, the structuralist perspective focuses on *structures* which influence human behavior. When we speak of structuralism, however, we are not referring to the *structural functionalism* of Parsons and Merton. Structuralists are concerned with the discovery and exploration of universal structures which underlie human existence, shape it, constrain it, and give it meaning. One form of structuralism focuses on the discovery and examination of linguistic structures. From this perspective, language constitutes a structure which governs people's lives.

Pioneering the early development of structural linguistics, or *semiotics* (the science of signs), and influenced by Durkheim, Ferdinand de Saussure (1857-1913) developed a formal description of the structure of the sign. He saw signs as the product of two elements–a signifier (a symbol like a word) and a signified (some concept that the signifier references). For example, the word *dog* brings to mind an *ideal type* image of a furry domesticated animal. The connection between the concept "dog" and the signifier or word "dog" is arbitrary–we might substitute an entirely different word for dog. These signifiers are created by a community of language users, though, once created, they quickly move beyond human control and resist any efforts to change them.[8] Despite the arbitrariness of the connection between words and the things they signify, our signs develop relatively fixed and stable meanings as they become institutionalized in language. In other words, signifiers and the objects they signify become inseparable as we use them (every English speaker knows what is meant by the word "dog")

–their arbitrary definition becomes transformed into a universally shared meaning.

In addition to the basic signifier/signified relationship, Saussure developed the distinction between formal language systems and the actual ways individuals use speech. Formal language systems, which are structured and relatively static, he called *langue;* everyday speech, which is more idiosyncratic and dynamic, he called *parole*. Principally concerned with langue, Saussure points out that the meaning of a "sign" in a language system hinges on its relationship to other signs; in other words, meaning is contextual. For example, the meaning of many words derives from their relation to their binary opposites. Cold takes its meaning from the concept of hotness, wellness from sickness, and shallowness from depth. Thus, even at very basic levels, these arbitrary building blocks of language achieve meaning from their contexts, from the structures in which they are embedded. Belsey summarizes, "For Saussure meaning resides in the sign and nowhere else."[9] This does not suggest that it is to be found in individual words, but in the sign as a *relationship* in a structured system of signs.

The main implication of Saussure's work is that, "Meanings, the mind, and ultimately the social world are shaped by the structure of language. Instead of an existential world of people shaping their surroundings, we have here a world in which people, as well as other aspects of the social world, are *being shaped by* the structure of language."[emphasis mine][10] Furthermore, language, which originates in the arbitrary and idiosyncratic, comes to comprise the central structuring agent which defines and regulates meaning in human life; it also becomes a social fact. Saussure, in developing the sign, thus establishes the existence of universal and stable meaning in society. It is this contention that gives rise to the poststructuralist critique of the sign. As we will see, the poststructuralists argue that "The internal structure of the sign has collapsed, with signifiers disconnected from any stable signified, making meaning multiplicative, open-ended, and fragmented."[11]

There are several strains of structuralism. Roland Barthes, for example, extended Saussure's ideas to include sign systems other than those related to language. For him, all types of social phenomena–presidential speeches, movies, jewelry, automobiles, and so on–are reinterpreted as signs, and factor heavily in the meaning systems in which humans are bound. Another school of structuralist thought, anthropological structuralism, associated with Claude Lévi-Strauss, focuses on the structures underlying the operations of the human mind. On this theory, people are seen as controlled by unconscious processes of the mind which operate on the basis of general laws. Taken together, the various structuralist traditions advance a search for *universal structures* which offer a kind of transcendence, and ground human meaning in something outside itself.

Poststructuralism

Poststructuralism shares theoretical ground with structuralism, but also diverges significantly from it. It is sometimes difficult to distinguish between the two perspectives, and theorists like Barthes who are associated with one position are also associated with the other. In contrast to the structuralists, poststructuralist Jacques Derrida, sees language as inherently unstable and unorderly, and thus incapable of exerting controlling power over people. According to him, the structuralist's search for the universal laws governing language (and thus language users) is futile. If different contexts do give words different meanings, the notion of an underlying controlling structure is questionable. "Thus, one of the guiding themes that unify the various poststructural thinkers is their skepticism toward the universality of shared meaning as conveyed as signs."[12]

Poststructuralists argue that the linkages between signifiers and the things they signify have been broken and that the result is a fragmentation of meaning, and the unmooring of language from certainty. Viewed in this way, language becomes en entirely open-ended project—one which has no boundaries whatsoever. Accordingly, "...notions of Truth, knowledge, power, and identity are also challenged."[13] These theories are "post" structural in the sense that they advocate a relativist view of the world where "the patterns, routines, and conventions of social life are inherently unstable and thus only temporarily structured."[14] This intellectual shift has implications for the Christian who believes that the Word of God contains transcendent truth, and that, cultural relativism notwithstanding, this truth is trans-cultural, timeless, not of human origin, and provides regulating norms for human social behavior.

Where the structuralists see stability and universal meaning rooted in systems of signs, the poststructuralists see instability and fragmentation. The evergrowing *liminal* meaning space between generations illustrates the poststructuralist perspective. Many of my students use computer instant messaging and "texting" which contains abbreviations and endless bits of popular cultural shorthand. Were I, a 40-year-old professor, to intercept those instant messages I would be able to decipher some of the meaning intended by them. However, even if I converted all of the abbreviated text, emoticons, and so on, into words with which I am familiar, I would still fail to grasp some of the meaning of their text. If I asked a student to explain it to me, I might still have trouble because some of the ways I must read the text are rooted in a lived cultural perspective from which I am excluded. My students' signs are incongruent with mine and we will never completely achieve a "fit." This incongruency is celebrated daily by *Zits* comic strip writers Jerry Scott and Jim Borgman who derive humor from the fundamental misunderstandings between a teenage boy, Jeremy, and his middle-age parents. In this comic strip we see how language, truth, and beauty have different meanings for parents, teenagers, boys, girls, teachers, students, and so on. What is "true" for a teenager is not "true" for his parents. Where structuralists see the presence of stable language connecting both groups, poststructuralists see a fundamental and irreconcilable disconnect.

Accordingly, the poststructuralists are critical of the structuralist search for the *logos*—the idea that meaning, and thus universal truth, beauty, goodness, and so on, really do exist and underlie everything. "Logocentrism is the belief that there is some stable point outside language—reason, revelation, Platonic Ideas—

from which one can ensure that one's words, as well as the whole system of distinctions that order our experience, correspond to the world."[15] Poststructuralist Derrida, whose work contains emancipation motifs, is "hostile" to the "imprisoning" logocentrism of the West and seeks to deconstruct it. He shares with the structuralists a focus on language, but throws out any notion of an ordering structure.

In deconstructing logocentrism, he favors "writing which does not constrain its subjects."[16] Rather than structural social facts, he sees institutions as nothing more than "writing," and therefore momentary, fragmented, without underlying meaning–and, ideally, unable to constrain people. Rather, they do this, but only artificially. If we think of the world as a theater (recall Goffman's dramaturgy), we can understand people as acting out a kind of text rooted in institutional notions of universal goodness, rightness, and beauty. These notions attain a kind of facticity, and present themselves as true and real. Consequently, people act out their parts, simply repeating the lines (or speech) they are given. In this way they allow themselves to be controlled and they are not free to do their own "writing."

According to Derrida, we live our lives in the "theater of cruelty," where we are enslaved, bound to the "speech" hailing from various artificial, supposedly universal, structures. This theater is "theological" in character, that is, at its center is a text or script, wielded by an author-creator (a god) who defines and regulates meaning. The actors in this theater are "Interpretive slaves who faithfully execute the providential designs of the 'master.'"[17] This theological stage produces a cast of passive spectators, consumers, and satisfied listeners, few of whom challenge the speech.

Elsewhere I have written about the notion of "excellence" in Western culture.[18] Our present cultural fixation with so-called excellence provides a good example of how we passively conform to the *speech* of our institutions. Excellence is somehow thought to be a universal ideal or good. It controls us, especially when our institutions define themselves using this ill-defined concept. For example, just about every educational institution in the Western world (and beyond) does its work over against some ideal of excellence. But, as some sociologists point out, many of us do little more than pursue scripted success through credentials gained in excellence factories–never really stopping to think about what excellence (or success) might look like, or how it might be acted out in countercultural ways. We become interpretive slaves of institutional speech. We follow the script, and our notion of excellence causes us to challenge nothing about it–it is just a word, one that can mean anything we wish.

As we move from structuralism to poststructuralism and beyond, we experience a growing uncertainty about the existence of universal standards of truth, and of the capacity of language to express truth. The deconstruction of language by Derrida culminates in what could be called the "destruction" of language in postmodernity. In the postmodern age, language has become unmoored from any universal standard of meaning–signifiers are no longer connected to only "one" signified. One example is to be found in the way contemporary Black rap musicians use the word *nigger* in their music. It was once a term derogatorily applied to African Americans in the pre-civil rights era–an exclusionary one. Some mainstream rappers now use it to refer to others in their primary groups, almost in the same way they might use the word "brother"–an affiliatory term. In this way, the word becomes dislodged from of its original context and the meaning is altered to such a degree that it means almost the opposite of what it once did. Some rap which protests majority group treatment of Black minorities contains the "brotherly" use of the word 'nigger.' In this way, the word comes to float free from any fixed meaning, and its uncertain meaning varies from group to group, and context to context. This flexibility is the basis for the post-structural critique of the sign, and is typical of language in postmodernity. In fact, as we will see, postmodern language uses the medium of images more than words, and images are infinitely more malleable and resistant to fixed meanings.

Thus, Derrida, who profoundly influenced the ideas of postmodern thinkers, deconstructs language, and challenges the idea that there is any meaning beyond the idiosyncratic. For structuralists, language and other structures account for the stability of meaning; for Derrida, all structures are ultimately arbitrary, artificial, and socially constructed. Consequently, multiple and competing conceptions of what we call truth and reality can coexist and no single one can be privileged over another: There is no *logos*. Like the structuralists, the focus here is on language, but language is understood to be something very flexible, fragmented, momentary, and unstable: We cannot speak of truth, only truths.

In summary, the intellectual developments recounted in this section show social thought and theory moving from a traditional view of reality with an emphasis on structures and stable meanings to a relativist view of social reality based on no unifying *logos*. As we have seen, these philosophical traditions, especially poststructuralism, begin to dissolve the various boundaries (social, cultural, linguistic, and moral) which define human life. They reduce them to mere convention, and set the stage for the more anomic and fragmented experience of humanity in the postmodern age, replete with both grave uncertainties and astounding possibilities. Accordingly, we now turn our attention away from language and toward the almost seamless barrage of images which comprise the *postmodern* world in which we live.

The Theory

What does *truth* mean in a place without boundaries? Our experience of the contemporary social world is frequently such that we shift from illusion to illusion. This masquerade is largely achieved through the manipulation of images by computer technology. Look at an old sepia photograph of a frowning family matriarch. The image, while still a copy of some thing, is largely un-retouched, a representation that faithfully corresponds with the object it signifies. What you see is what you get. These images seem strange to us. Why didn't she smile?

Why didn't she take those awful glasses off? And so on. The basic question we are asking is, "why didn't she manage her image better?" We live in an age in which manipulation of images is everything. We even have image consultants! When a woman has her photograph taken (an interesting phrase in itself), she has often spent considerable time thinking about how she will craft her image. Various dimensions of self and body will each have to be given due considera- tion. Does this make me look fat? Is my hair too poufy? Can I hide this blemish? Does this shade of lipstick match my outfit? All of these decisions will be made with an eye on fashion trends represented in the media–whoever 'they' are. But, she may go still further. Should I have my nose altered? Should I go on the South Beach diet program? How much does liposuction cost? Should I cut and dye my hair red? After all of these decisions with their concomitant modifica- tions to one's physical appearance, a series of, perhaps, fifty photographs will be made; some of these images will then be subjected to various forms of digital manipulation until they are gotten just right. The final result? A sixty-year-old Barbra Streisand who still looks like she is twenty-five. Who is she? She is just who she wants to be, nothing more, nothing less.

While fighting the outward signs of aging is fairly normal in a lot of cul- tures, what about recent trends showing the prevalence of plastic surgery among *young* women? The television show *Dr. 90210* documents this alarming trend through the eyes of its profiteers. Frequently after a young woman has had some body modification or other she will remark, "Now I can be the person I know I'm supposed to be." Or…"Now my outward appearance reflects who I am on the inside." But is there an inside? Or is it, too, just a pastiche of images col- lected from various media sources, which are themselves merely collections of other images from other sources. Are we anything more than images or collec- tions of them? Can we any longer even refer to a "self?"

The writers of ancient scripture, with their warnings about idolatry and the worship of graven *images*, call us to examine the role images play in our lives. Worshipping the true God–for ancient believers, as for us–requires that we set our reality-obscuring images aside, and turn our faces away from the world's video screens. How do we do this in a world that celebrates and seems to turn on mere images, a world where signifiers do little more than represent other signifi- ers, and reality seems to be very much a secondary consideration, or irrelevant altogether? Questions like these animate the concerns of postmodern social theorists who grapple with whether or not anything real does actually exist be- hind the signs we create. Our focus for the remainder of this chapter will be on French intellectual Jean Baudrillard, whose work best exemplifies postmodern social theory and the social implications of the postmodern age. While the struc- turalists and poststructuralists dealt primarily with language, Baudrillard devel- ops the ways in which images themselves have replaced a language of words, and, in fact, have become unmoored from words and the "signified" altogether. His insights are remarkable. For him, ours is a language of free-floating images which move us further and further from reality, until reality itself (if we can even refer to such a thing) is erased.

Born in Reims, France, on July 29, 1929, he was the first of his family to pursue an advanced education. He studied German at the Sorbonne University in Paris and later was professor of German there for eight years. In 1966, he began teaching sociology and eventually moved to the University of Nanterre as professor of sociology. These were tumultuous times in France. The student revolts of 1968 nearly toppled the government of Charles de Gaulle. Though Baudrillard had studied under noted Marxist-humanist Henri Lefebvre, these events produced in him intellectual shift away from Marxism and toward postmodernism. While he has made many varied contributions to postmodern thinking in sociology, he is best known for his concept of *hyperreality*. "Central to his vision of contemporary social life is the notion that our cultures have been thoroughly saturated by the media and entertainment industries such that the differences between the real and the images, signs and simulations, have dissolved."[19]

Sociologist Kenneth Allan describes reading Baudrillard as both "fun and frustrating." He claims that he, better than many other social theorists, exemplifies what he is writing about. As a result, what he says is neither true nor false—his writing defies those categories.

> ... Baudrillard is more than a postmodern theorist; he is part of the postmodern landscape. Just reading Baudrillard is an experience in postmodernity and cultural implosion. Yet at the same time, he tells us something about the society and people living in postmodernity, something very few say with as much insight or art. Baudrillard's writings are thus part play and part purpose.[20]

Accordingly, Baudrillard's insights into contemporary culture are at once, astounding, easy to grasp, perplexing, disturbing, sobering, and delightful. One reason he is sometimes difficult to read is that we tend to approach his text as if it were rational, linear, and progressive—tendencies typical of the modernist frameworks prevalent in academia. In other words, we try to read his texts about the death of meaning, the uncoupling of signs, the fragmentation of identity, and so on, from within a paradigm which celebrates the prevalence of meaning, stability of signs, and unity of identity. However, in certain respects, we must step outside all of this to "get" Baudrillard. In this chapter, we will examine just a few of his many contributions. We begin with the notion of hyperreality.

Hyperreality
A World of Images and Signs

When I was a child I liked to look through the catalogs that found their way to our house. I have fond memories of spotting something I wanted, and then "saving up" until I had enough money to buy it. Among these treasures were a soccer ball, a digital watch (not a big deal now, but they were really something in 1982), and a pocket knife. My parents seemed to understand the notion of delayed gratification, so rather than buying me items outright, they encouraged me to pick up odd jobs when I could, and save my weekly allowance. As I waited for my money to accumulate, I would look at the picture of the soccer ball, which I had torn from the catalog. As I did, I imagined how good life would be when I finally acquired it. Finally the day would come when I would go to the store, unfold a bunch of one-dollar-bills, and bring home the long awaited item. But, while I waited, I fixed my eyes on the image, and imagined the reality behind it. And, the correspondence was fairly close. The soccer ball in the catalog faithfully represented the one on the shelf in the store.

Now, as an adult, I have two daughters–one three, one seven. When my older daughter goes through a catalog, or an advertisement that comes in the Sunday paper, I am amazed at the sheer variety of goods available. Legos have been expanded to include literally hundreds of types of building blocks. Barbie dolls come in an astonishing array of styles, ethnicities, and even social classes. In fact, Barbie has given up marketing ground to the more highly sexualized "Bratz" dolls, which comprise an equally dizzying array of styles. When it comes to sporting goods, the buyer can choose from a full spectrum of running shoes. And, last but not least, electronic goods are as numerous "as the sand of the seashore." To purchase an IPod, you must make at least seventeen choices before you can find the model that will best fit you, your needs, your image, your lifestyle.

My point here is this: In the short span of history since I was a child pressing my nose against the store window, the consumer culture has, quite literally, erupted in a cataclysm of garish delights. And these are mostly concerned with image, not substance. When I bought a soccer ball in the early 1980s, the picture in the catalog might have been accompanied by a soccer superstar, but just as often this was not the case–it was advertised alone. Today, the karaoke machine, made in China, packaged in Hong Kong, and then shipped to the United States is sold with the image of Britney Spears, Miley Cyrus, or some other corporately owned femme fatale of the month prominently displayed on the packaging. But, Britney and Miley had nothing to do with the item, and their presence is all about image–in fact *they* aren't even those images! Thus, while many features of the advertising and packaging associated with "buying a toy" are similar to what they were 30 years ago, important parts of the ritual are very different, both in intensity and in character.

These time-lagged examples illustrate what Baudrillard calls *hyperreality*. He contends that in postmodernitysignifiers have become disconnected from the things they signify. This has a number of implications. For one thing, symbols and images come to have a *realness* about them. When Princess Diana of Wales died in 1997, millions of people mourned her death. They cried, they sent cards and flowers to the palace, and they felt heavy-hearted. But, strangely, these mourners never knew her. Most of us knew Princess Diana only through her media generated images–and there are millions of them. But, we still felt like we knew her–like we understood her likes, dislikes, longings, and so on. In the years following her death, various writers came out with stories about her that purported to describe "the real Diana," the Diana behind the images. Her relatives and friends tried to control some of these stories in an effort to manage her postmortem image. You might even say that Diana's images outlived her.

As strange as this may sound, Baudrillard would say that there was no "real" Diana. He would see her as really nothing more than the sum of her images. In other words, if we strip away all of the media, television, pictures, tabloids, rumors, and other fictions, what is left? Nothing. The same goes for the previously mentioned Britney Spears. She simply doesn't exist apart from the images which comprise her. In effect, these images become more real for us than the supposed reality behind them–the signifier becomes primary over the signified; and, the signified fades in importance altogether or even ceases to exist. This process seems to have culminated in the celebrity culture of our world today–a world of tabloid images where symbolism replaces substance.

How do these images degrade meaning and loosen our hold on reality? Baudrillard makes the point that transferring information always entails some loss of accuracy. It is not the "thing" itself, but is always "about the thing." He offers a simple equation: information = entropy. Anytime we convey information through a medium, we change it in some way, and consequently some of the meaning which it originally conveyed is lost or altered. For example, when you tell a friend about an experience you had, your language-based account never quite captures the "fullness" of the actual event.[21] Remember the expression, "I guess you had to be there."?

Mass media, and mass communication in general, takes the principle of information degradation to new heights. Media prepackages information such that the very form in which it is presented "becomes" the meaning itself – *the medium is the message.* For example, network news programs present so-called "facts" as *infotainment.* Don Henley of the musical group, the Eagles, has a song called *Dirty Laundry* which contains the following line: "We got the bubble-headed-bleach-blonde who comes on at five. She can tell you 'bout the plane crash with a gleam in her eye. It's interesting when people die... give us dirty laundry." And, this media packaging extends to just about everything. When we evaluate the merits of political rivals, we rarely deal in nuance; rather, we easily succumb to carefully crafted images–which frequently claim to reveal the "true candidate." Because the media and mass communication techniques so permeate our experience and transfer information over and over again, we distance ourselves ever further from reality, and, indeed, come to doubt the existence of truth altogether. In addition, so much of our technology is aimed at making information dissemination faster and easier. From Baudrillard's perspective, our technological devices of mass communication dissipate reality. Technological advances can be directly equated with ever diminishing contact with reality.

Advertisements abound, they are present just about everywhere–on park benches, movie screens, television screens, on your laptop computer, even on human bodies (people sell themselves as "living bill boards" to the highest bidder on *e-bay!*). Baudrillard sees advertising as the prime force in reducing objects from their *use value* to their *sign value.* Consider the following example:

Suppose you are a female college student who is taking four classes and lives in a student housing complex just adjacent to the campus. You will need some way of carrying your books to class. There are several options: You might use those plastic film grocery bags you get when they say "paper or plastic?" Or, borrow your brother's old backpack from high school or, buy a Gucci tote bag for hundreds of dollars. Any of these would get the job done. Of the three, the old backpack might have the most utility. But, if you can afford it, you will choose the designer tote, and you may take great pains to let your friends know that it isn't a cheap knockoff... it's the real thing. In making this choice you would have privileged the sign value over the use value of the object, and if it proved too small for your needs, you might put up with the inconvenience for the status you would accrue as a result of its use.

While handbags are one thing, sign value extends even to our bodies. Once dissatisfaction with the Gucci handbag sets in, you might succumb to advertisements about what females should look like. You may decide to "get some work done" (plastic surgery), so that your new image will fit with prevailing media trends. After the bandages come off, your body would work the same way it had before–it would have same use value, but a different sign value. It might even have some of its functions inhibited (thus prioritizing sign value over use value). In drawing these "signs" into our lives, we conform more and more to images which don't actually point to anything to which we are really connected. Who, after all, is Gucci?

In the consumer society, the sign value of commodities frequently supersedes their use value, and, "... the entire society is organized around consumption and display of commodities through which individuals gain prestige, identity, and standing."[22] Consequently, this society conceptualizes prestige and social esteem through the logic of consumption rather than production. For example, we might honor or envy the man or woman who wins the lottery, gets rich quick, and gives away a bit of the money in an act of benevolence over the person who works hard, but never attains the kind of success which would afford him commodities with a high sign value. Thus, Baudrillard's emphasis on the sign value of commodities, is a critique of the conventional view which sees "... consumption in terms of a rational satisfaction of needs, with the aim of maximizing utility."[23] His critique has resonance with Jesus' instruction to take the seat of lesser honor and to place the value of social signs in proper perspective.

"I'm 'Lovin It"
Simulacra and the System of Death

Reality television provides a stunning example of Baudrillard's *hyperreality*–the unreality of a world saturated by signs. A female sociology student in the department where I teach told me that she was part of a group of college women who gathered to watch *The Bachelor*. The show develops around a group of twelve or so young women trying to win the hand of the solitary bachelor.

People in her bachelor-watching support group evidently experience intense emotion and even shed tears in response to developments on the show. They feel triumph, elation, pain, and sadness, when the handsome prince chooses or rejects the maiden (using that term loosely here!) that they're "rooting for." Furthermore, they appear to believe that the emotions expressed by the "contestants" are genuine. If we were to analyze the content of the show, we would undoubtedly find scripted actors, tightly controlled by corporate media groups, which made decisions using weekly ratings produced by yet another corporate entity. When a couple who met on the show got married "in real life" (a distinction we're hard pressed to make anymore), it took *hyperreality* to new levels. It confirmed my students' belief and hope that what they saw on the show was not a series of image, but reality itself. It would seem that their ability to draw a distinction between the two has been greatly weakened or even undermined altogether.

While I suspect that my students, don't "really" believe that reality television is wholly unscripted, what we sometimes fail to see is that neither are television news programs, presidential press conferences, accounts of corporate businesses by CEO's, claims of excellence by colleges, testimonies of product quality by spokesmen, and so on. If we look closely we may see a world of almost seamless images–a world in which we are constantly manipulated by those who are themselves manipulated, and in which nothing really represents "reality." In fact, in a world of image manipulation, reality may be lost altogether. Baudrillard refers to this proliferation of images, which represent realities that never existed and never will exist, as *simulacrum*.

George Ritzer's book *The Globalization of Nothing* [24] and his ideas about the *McDonaldization of Society* [25] provide clear examples of this notion. McDonald's restaurant is a highly visible, global presence. Its image or brand is widely recognized. When we are travelling, we will patronize a McDonald's over a "mom and pop" diner because it represents something familiar, safe, dependable. The image by which we know McDonald's is one of friendliness, standardization, efficiency, and so on. One of their recent slogans reads "I'm 'lovin it!" and their menu signboard invitingly proclaims, "Smiles are free." They have also have a clown, which our children love (despite the inherent creepiness of a gaudily dressed clown-stranger). But, Ritzer asks, who owns McDonald's? When it does well, who profits? Who is the clown (what lurks behind the makeup)? Who makes decisions about what goes on the menu? In other words, much about McDonald's restaurant is a highly staged and tightly controlled illusion that is largely dissociated from space, time, and community. Any particular McDonald's restaurant is thus a copy of another one. But, it is very unlikely that their "Southern Homestyle" chicken sandwich has a basis in anyone's home kitchen. McDonald's is thus a copy of a copy–a *simulacrum*.

On a continuum from the real to the hyper-real, from the original to the simulacrum, we might have, on one end, an authentic Italian restaurant where the owners do the cooking using old family recipes (the real), and on the other, McDonald's which is run by transient workers, many of whom want to move on to other employment, who have no knowledge of what ingredients comprise their food, no real responsibility for the menu, prices, or décor, and who really don't participate at meaningful levels in the so-called community they so readily smile about. By itself, McDonald's is no significant threat to humanity or the "real." But, most of the institutions in which we live out our lives are highly McDonaldized. On a family outing we may start at the Walmart, move on to the Cineplex, grab a bite at McDonald's, buy gas at a pay-at-the-pump station, and wind up the evening watching reality television–all within the geographic bounds of our so-called community. What of this experience has been "real?"All of it, and none of it. We live in the reality of unreality, and our simulacra are, quite literally, everywhere. In Baudrillard's words:

> It is no longer a question of imitation, nor duplication, nor even parody. It is a question of substituting the signs of the real for the real, that is to say of an operation of deterring every real process via its operational double, a programmatic, metastable, perfectly descriptive machine that offers all the signs of the real and short-circuits all its vicissitudes. Never again will the real have the chance to produce itself–such is the vital function of the model in a system of death, or rather of anticipated resurrection, that no longer even gives the event of death a chance.[26]

Spectacle, Simulation, and the Crisis of Meaning

Two summers ago, my wife and I took our daughters to a reunion of our China adoption group (we have two adopted daughters – one from Bulgaria, the other from China). This group contains twelve families, all of whom have adopted infant Chinese daughters from the same orphanage. Our group met in Williamsburg, Virginia, home to one of the families, and proximate to Busch Gardens–a theme park of gargantuan proportions. Theme parks animate Baudrillard's nightmares. They "supersize" all of the elements which characterize the contemporary postmodern world–hyperreality, illusion, images, simulation, blurred boundaries, consumerism, commercialism, and spectacle. The world of Busch Gardens (or Disney, or…) is designed to enchant, to enthrall, and delight. It is a world without boundaries, one in which a beer company sponsors and engineers fun for children! Consider a description of one of their roller coasters:

> Set amid a French village, Griffon carries riders up 205 feet, then hurtles them 90 degrees straight down at 70 mph. And that's just the beginning. Griffon evokes the power and speed of a mythical bird that is part eagle and part lion. It plunges, twists and turns–giving riders an adrenaline-pumping adventure that's unlike any coaster experience in the world.

French villages? Hurtling 205 feet straight down at 70 mph? Mythical birds? Adrenaline rush? Unparalleled in the world? Fantastic!

As I stood near the base of this phantasmagoria, watching my daughter and her "China sisters," I noticed something. As the coaster neared the ground, be ginning to slow before coming to a stop, one of the cars would drag through a pool of water, drenching anyone who stood nearby. I noticed that the little girls gathered below, took great delight in watching unsuspecting tourists get doused. They themselves were, of course, already soaked. Of great interest to me was the fact that they mostly ignored half a million tons of carefully engineered fun for the simple pleasure of getting wet on a hot day. This didn't last long, however, as we, their parents, hurried them away to get on with the business of having the fun we had paid for so dearly. "You can run through a sprinkler at home honey." The kids could not have cared less.

In a world where sign value dominates, and where signs are so proliferated, we actually learn to prefer the unreal over the real. In the story just told, my daughter and her sisters were still young enough that their socialization into the simulated had not yet taken hold. They still preferred the real (unplanned and un-engineered) fun of seeing people get wet. Soon, they will be ushered into schools where they will learn to surf the web, and where much of their experience will be two-dimensional. Rather than going to the zoo, they might look at exotic animals on a screen. By the time they are teenagers they may be deep into video games, or the virtual reality of *second life*, a computer based simulation where you choose and develop a virtual identity. Using the technologies of communication, they will communicate with others who are not present, sometimes ignoring those who are. If they aren't married by age 30 or so, they may enlist the help of a virtual online dating service. Theirs is a currency of signs – of signs, often pointing back to nothing. And I, as a parent, will struggle to keep up with it all.

Baudrillard would decry the inversion of meaning that has taken place in this amusement park, this simulated world; he would see it as imploding on itself. Modernity produced an explosion of signs and was characterized by clarity of difference, clear logic, and a sense of forward direction. For all practical purposes, it seemed to have meaning (not to be confused with justice). Postmodernity produced a reversion of those signs—an implosion of the modernist creations. Gender differences and the roles and responsibilities associated with them are not, for example, so clear anymore. Postmodern sexuality has a plasticity that stands in sharp contrast to the essentialism of the modern era. We see this, for example, in reproductive technologies which extend "natural" birth experiences to infertile and homosexual couples, as well as to unmarried women and senior citizens. The distinction between races has also become less pronounced (something which has some very good implications). Political boundaries have also become amorphous, and national pride, which used to be broadly admired, is viewed by some, as exclusionary and self-serving. In colleges and universities, interdisciplinary studies are common, indicative of the narrowing space between academic disciplines. And in the entertainment field, there are white rappers and black metal bands to be found.

This blurring of boundaries between phenomena—this erasure of classification—culminates in a crisis of meaning. In the modern era, we produce things, and as we progress, these things come to have a sign value. As monopoly capitalism flourished and production increased, as we have seen, sign value began to overwhelm use value. These signs have now proliferated to the point where we can scarcely find any place or any thing that isn't trying to communicate something. I cannot begin to count the advertisements visible through my car window on a simple 10-minute drive to the grocery store. If I happen to have my radio on, I will hear even more of them. Once in the store, signs overwhelm me still further, calling out to me, my wife, my daughters, promising something for each of us. There are so many that we can scarcely deal with them. And, it is even worse during the holidays. In fact, the purpose of the holidays sometimes seems to be merely to re-adorn ourselves with new signage. This crisis of meaning occurs because, in a world where everything points to something, nothing points to anything. Ironically, in a world of signs we end up without a compass, directionless.

Baudrillard, who died before DSL (Digital Subscriber Line) and cable internet connections, would warn us to be wary of technology that enables us to sample and assimilate signs more rapidly. Most of us ascribe a certain morality to technological progression. When we use computers we assume that more and faster functioning equals greater efficiency and therefore better stewardship of information. We don't think much about all those popup ads on our desktops. How many advertising signs do we see in a day? A thousand? A million? A church I visited several years ago had a Nike Swoosh on their Powerpoint presentation which read, "Christianity, Just Do It!" – a good example of the adaptability of signs in a postmodern world. Signs have been destabilized, unmoored from anything "real." Consequently, they may be adapted, modified, and used in anyway anyone chooses. Something secular can be easily transformed into something sacred.

Perhaps you have seen Christian t-shirts of the sort sold at Bible bookstores and on Christian college campuses. On them, signs and slogans developed by advertising agencies working for multinational corporations – often institutions whose moral commitments are dubious–are modified to project "Christian" messages. One such shirt shows a Crest toothpaste ad, modified to read "Christ: Whitens Hearts, Freshens Lives." In another, a Budweiser ad featuring three bullfrogs replaces the words "Bud... Wise... Errr" with "God's... Wise... Errr" and offers reassurance from scripture (1 Corinthians 1:25). What do these signs mean? Have they somehow been redeemed by recasting them into overtly Christian terms? Or, have we simply succumbed to the general meaninglessness that seems to be the hallmark of our lives in the midst of this sea of signs where even an advertisement for mass produced beer is easily adapted to a message about the wisdom of God?

The result of all this is a society which is passive and largely focused on play. Life becomes a game in which we are armchair participants arranging and rearranging signs which have no real meaning. In such a world, Christians flip easily between the secular and the sacred, with little recognition of any boundaries between these two realms. Sunday becomes both a day for church and a day for shopping. And, at Christmastime, we prefer the spectacle of Macy's over the meaning of the manger.

In his book *Enchanting a Disenchanted World: Revolutionizing the Means of Consumption*, George Ritzer develops the ways in which this preoccupation with simulation and spectacle creates a vacuum of meaning, and ultimately leaves people disenchanted. He recounts myriad examples illustrating just how much of our lives are simulated, or fake. A great deal of our interaction with other human beings is, in fact, simulated. The (false) friendliness of the "hello" from the Blockbuster Movie employee, the pleasantries exchanged with the Olive Garden waitress, the hug your children receive from Mickey Mouse during a Disney trip, the "have a nice day" from the Walmart cashier, and even the "God Bless You" from the greeter at church are scripted, simulated, and controlled. Ritzer jokes that even our food is simulated–a McNugget is chicken without bones![27] One of my former students who earned a Master's degree in urban development, told me about seeing simulated communities including a *Lord of the Rings* gated community for those who wished to spend their non-work hours as simulated Hobbits–the fantasy of the child, engineered for the adult.

This matter of the postmodern spectacle bears examination. Ritzer says that one of its functions is to conceal the rationality of the system.[28] The spectacle is thus a sort of opiate that is used to overcome the fact that the commodities we purchase are, ultimately, dissatisfying and disenchanting. He notes that spectacle used to emerge from daily life (such as a local tent revival or county fair), but in our society they do not usually derive from the local. Instead, we travel to Disney or Busch Gardens where, far from our homes, we participate in various attractions in ways that are predetermined by the park's designers, and not at all connected to our lives. Spectacles are tightly controlled, and their purpose is to seduce people into buying commodities. Ritzer writes a great deal about the simulation spectacle of Las Vegas–you may have seen the commercial "What happens in Vegas stays in Vegas." This illustrates just how completely disconnected these spectacles are from our "real" daily lives.

Where does this fetish for spectacle and the simulated leave us? Ritzer ends his book with the following sentence, lamenting the loss of meaning that seems to have overtaken us in postmodernity:

> Those who worry about consumer society, consumerism, the cathedrals of consumption, and the increasingly dizzying array of commodities have genuine concerns and many battles to fight, but the most immediate issue is how to live a more meaningful life within a society increasingly defined by consumption.[29]

His concern is well-founded, but the book concludes with no clear answer to the problem of meaning.

The Death of the Subject
Identity in Postmodernity

If I asked you to come to the front of the room and introduce yourself, what would you say? If I gave such an introduction, I might tell you that I am a man; I have a Ph. D.; I am married; I am a parent; I teach sociology; I am a Presbyterian, and so on. In addition to these affiliations, you would also notice that I am tall (reasonably so... 6'1"), white, and middle class. If I went further, I might disclose some of my political affections or the distinctive features of my theology. Without knowing anything else about me, you would be able to predict quite a bit of my behavior just on the basis of my categorical affiliations. Social identity theorists suggest that we define ourselves by our contrast with relevant outgroups.[30] To be white is to be "not black." To be male is to be "not female." To be middle class (something evident through the signs we display) is to be "not lower class." Being "educated" only has meaning in contrast with those who lack education. Christians often speak of the "regenerate" in contrast with the "unregenerate."

Several years ago I read a novel in which two infants were switched at birth. One, (a non-Jew) went to be raised in a Jewish family; the other (a Jew), went to be raised in a white supremacist family. The families did not learn of the switch until the boys were teenagers and the non-Jewish boy in the Jewish family died of a rare genetic disease. The story developed around the other boy—Jewish in a non-Jewish family—coming to grips with his finding that he comprised the very category he had learned to hate. He was the object of his own opposition, and consequently no longer knew who he was. As a result, he wasn't sure how to live his life—his out-group was gone, his self had collapsed.

Identity and self-concept are often based on exclusionary practices, rooted in out-group contrasts. In the modern era, a time when differences were more clearly delineated, it was relatively easy to establish and maintain. My white, male, middle class identity would be clearly defined and attached to a set of normative expectations. If I acted in ways that were not normative for someone in my categories, I would be sanctioned and perhaps labeled a deviant. My life would be very different from someone who was, say, a black female.

In modernity no one would be surprised to find someone "like me" in a position of authority in some organization. This would have several advantages for me. For one thing, it would limit the number of people I had to compete with for jobs. For another, it would provide me with a strong sense of self or identity. Who am I in this world? I am not those "others." It would be relatively easy to draw clear, strong boundaries around myself and my family. We would largely worship with, socialize with, and marry those who were "like us." Additionally, I would likely feel that this was the way things should be. In other words, I might think that the social arrangements which supported my white male identity were "natural."

Because identity is often rooted in exclusion—in the contrast between "us" and "them"—it provides a basis for group action, especially in the modern era.

White supremacists, for example, see clear differences between themselves and African Americans. When civil rights laws threatened these boundaries and ren dered them permeable, white supremacists were motivated to band together to fight the out-group threat. Or, when women started earning college degrees at higher rates than men, that threat motivated men to circle the wagons in the fight against feminism.

Since culture and identity are interdependent, as culture begins to fragment, so does identity.[31] Accordingly, as we move deeper and deeper into postmodernity, the categories which define our identities begin to break down. For example, I currently work with many women at or above my status. Gender roles are no longer clearly defined. The idea that it is normative for women to stay at home with children is now considered bourgeois–most women work. These changes in gender interaction in the world of work have implications for male and female roles in marriage and the home as well. In general, roles are more egalitarian (although reliable statistics show that women do far more of the work in the home domain, even when they maintain full-time employment). They challenge traditional notions of masculinity and femininity. Additionally, most workplaces are racially integrated, and in many settings we scarcely notice interracial relationships or marriages.

All of these changes give us tremendous freedom, but they come at the price of identity. My daughters are not restricted by the essentialist gender prescriptions of the modern era. The 2008 US Presidential election witnessed both Senator Hillary Clinton and Alaska Governor Sarah Palin campaigning their way to the very top of the political world. The United States just elected its first black president. Thus, it seems that Americans are more accepting of racial and gender diversity in authority positions than it used to be. Still, we are left with the question of what it means to be male or female, black or white. These categories have defined us for centuries, and their dissolution leaves us with an identity vacuum. Because of this we frequently don't know where to anchor our passions–we don't know what to fight for, and even when we do, our social groupings have become amorphous collections of people of different sexes, races, nationalities, social classes, and religions. We can fight for pluralism, but that is not a strong basis for social bonds.

In the end, for Baudrillard, all social categories, classes, genders, political orientations and cultures collapse into each other–everything is absorbed into everything, and the meanings of any and all categories diminishes. He envisions the death of the subject by the object world. This "subject" is modernity itself, especially as it is embodied in the individual who is distinguished by a strong and clear identity. Caving in to the *ecstasy of objects*, the individual exists in a state of inertia and entropy, and is eventually overcome, obliterated by the sheer extremes of object proliferation.

So, ultimately the subject, the darling of modern philosophy, is defeated in Baudrillard's metaphysical scenario and the object triumphs, a stunning end to the dialectic of subject and object which had been the framework of modern

philosophy. The object is thus the subject's fatality and Baudrillard's "fatal
strategies" project an obscure call to submit to the strategies and ruses of objects.[32]

A Christian Critique

At present we are hard pressed to call postmodern sociology a *tradition* in
social or sociological theory. It is simply too amorphous, and lacks the coherence that many earlier paradigms achieved. In many ways, postmodern thinking
represents an extension or culmination of many of the interpretive theories presented earlier in this volume. For example, the symbolic interactionist tradition
elucidates how symbols shape our world, give it meaning, and can represent
distorted realities as humans bend them to their will. The phenomenological
tradition addresses the nature of everyday life, pushes the matter of *reality distortion* to new levels, and suggests that to understand the essence (reality) of
some social practice we must suspend (bracket) what we take to be the truth of
it. From thinkers in the sociology of knowledge, we learn about the importance
of *perspective* in the ongoing task of understanding and debunking the social
world These, and other traditions, teach us that things are often not what they
seem–they call us to more closely examine what we mean by *truth* or *reality*,
and they compel us to move beyond accepting the world at face value. This prophetic task is the central call of sociology. For the Christian, it takes on additional importance because, as we have shown in earlier chapters, the Christian
lives in two worlds, and must suspend commitment to the values and distortions
of the visible, temporal one.

Postmodern theory pushes many of the ideas contained in earlier parts of
this book to new limits. While the early symbolic interactionists explored the
use of symbols and images, they could scarcely have imagined the ways in
which our world has become over-saturated with symbols, or the way in which
these symbols implode on each other, and, in the process, leach meaning from
our lives. They were dealing with problems in the simpler worlds that existed
before the digital era. Postmodern thinkers like Baudrillard seek to understand
the ways in which symbols, the basis for human understanding and the carriers
of meaning, function to exploit and destroy it. He, more fully than his predecessors, grasps the way that symbols can become simulacra. Our idolatry runs much
deeper than we suspect.

If nothing else, Baudrillard, and his contemporary Jacques Ellul, should in-
spire caution about how we use the technologies that facilitate the dissemination
of images. Often we Christians think that if we could just get the right technology to enable us to go farther, faster, and do more, we could convert the masses
and change the world. Baudrillard warns us, however, that the technologies of
information dissemination ultimately narrow our worlds and our understanding.
Ellul cautions us to be wary of using the same technologies to fight the idolatry
they fuel. But we dance on, seldom heeding their warnings.

1 Corinthians 13:12 reads, "Now we see but a poor reflection as in a mirror;
then we shall see face to face. Now I know in part; then I shall know fully, even

as I am fully known." This *reflects* the distorted reality we live within. It calls to attention the role that images play in our experience of that reality, and it expresses the hope we have of redemption in Christ. Christ's return reconnects us to the real. It strips away the distorting images with which we clothe ourselves. The writer of Genesis proclaims that we are made in the *image* of God–images are not inherently bad. In fact, people are called to live as image bearers–we are to *reflect* the glory of God. The problem lies with the source of the images: Who controls them, and to what end? Postmodern theory, perhaps more than other sociological traditions, calls us to consider what it means to live apart from reality, in a world of illusion. And the writers of scripture call us to examine our selves and to ground our identities in Christ, the Word, the Real, and to resist idols.

Hearing and Seeing

If postmodernism is about anything, it is about images. What does it mean that we live in a world comprised of, and defined by, them? Is a picture, an image, really worth a thousand words? The scriptures contain far more references to the Word than to images. Bowing to the Word is worship; bowing to the image is idolatry. Jesus is called the Word. The book of John proclaims the primacy of the Word–the Logos: "In the beginning was the Word, and the Word was with God, and the Word was God. He was with God in the beginning. Through him all things were made; without him nothing was made that has been made" (John 1:1-3). Thus, God is inseparable from his Word, and this Word is the basis for all that is. Furthermore, Jesus was *begotten*, not created–there was no time when the Word was not. When Jesus comes to live among humanity he is called "the Word made flesh." Finally, the Word is eternal–Jesus says "I am the Alpha and the Omega, the First and the Last, the Beginning and the End" (Revelation 22:13).

If you look closely, scripture contains a number of places where there is a "play on the senses." For example, when Jesus begins to preach, he fulfills Isaiah's prophecy, "...The people living in darkness have seen a great light..." (Matthew 4:16). This suggests that the Word brings sight. Additionally, John's gospel gives a detailed account of Jesus, the Word, healing a man born blind (John 9). Here, the Word restores sight, and the apostle John draws our attention to two manifestations of sight–physical and spiritual sight. Those who reject the Word–who cannot hear–are spiritually blind. And, back to the very beginning, when God *speaks*, "Let there be light," the *visible* springs into being (Genesis 1). Thus, time and again, speaking comes before seeing, and seeing depends on hearing–an order sustained throughout scripture.

This emphasis on the Word, and on hearing, is much at odds the conditions of life in the post modern world. As we have seen, we live in a world of seamless and overlapping signs and images. Sight and images eclipse hearing, sound, and words. We might even say that, in postmodern times, the image has devoured the word. Although scripture places the emphasis on hearing the Word, seeing has become, for us, the dominant mode of knowing. For example, one popular Christian song (projected as an image on an overhead screen) reads, "Open the *eyes* of my heart Lord... I want to *see* you." Another submits, "Open our *eyes* Lord, we want to *see* Jesus." While such lyrics are far from inappropriate–for example, Acts 9 records the way that something like scales fell off of Saul's (later the apostle Paul's) eyes thereby restoring his sight–they do belie our preference for the image. They also have implications for the way we approach the scriptures and the very idea of truth. How do we submit to the Word in a world which honors and privileges the image above all else?

In his book *The Humiliation of the Word*, Jacques Ellul explains that while hearing and seeing are inseparable and complementary, they are different and their difference is of fundamental importance. Sight always places the seer at the center of the universe. We see things "before us." "Sight guarantees my possession of the world and makes it into a 'universe-for-me.' Seeing gives me the possibility of action.... Sight is the basis of my mastery." [33] Seeing frequently finds its expression in the artificial ways in which humans take control of the world around them. In this way, sight commits us to mastery, efficiency, and ultimately, self-pursuit. In explaining how the urban age amplifies the visual, Ellul concludes, "The city allows humanity to see its mirror image in the sense of contemplating itself as it contemplates the product of its own work." [34] Human sight tends to circumvent truth as it sees only its own reflection. It is only through deeper reflection, carried out in theological and philosophical terms, that we can possibly get to truth.

The sense of hearing orients us to the world in a very different way. Where images fall into a coherent pattern, sounds do not. The sounds and noises I hear rarely have plain meaning, and always bring uncertainty and questions in a way that visual images do not. Sight, Ellul says, constitutes a universe–we open our eyes and something complete and coherent confronts us. Sound mostly raises questions. We wonder about its origin, while we rarely raise this question with regard to sight. While sight can also raise questions, sound, in a more fundamental way tends to orient us to outward possibilities, to explorations of the imagination. Sight, for all of its outward looking-ness, turns us inward, while hearing has the opposite effect. Sight ends possibilities; hearing opens us up to them.

When the movie, *The Lord of the Rings* came out several years ago, my younger brother, a big fan of Tolkien, refused to go see it. He had read the books several times. His fear was that seeing the director's interpretation of the work projected on a screen would erase all of the possibilities he had imagined during his reading of the books. The words of the books had opened his mind to possibilities that were endless and fantastic. The images contained in the movie would, he feared, present themselves as the reality of the books, thus putting an end to all other alternative interpretations of them. This example reveals a fundamental difference between images and words, sight and sound. Were my brother to hear an audio recording of *The Lord of the Rings*, his experience, though altered, would remain unbounded. Attending the movie, he would have come away with the feeling of, at once, possessing the reality of the book. But, as any book lover knows, the book is better!

The differences between sight and hearing, and our immersion in the visual culture has implications for how we understand the world around us. Ellul says that our civilization tends to confuse reality with truth. For him, the Word (hearing) is related to Truth, but the image (seeing), only to reality. When he writes of *reality*, he is referring to the world we perceive around us, the one to which we must adapt. As we move through this world, manipulating it in various ways, we become caught up in it and begin to take anything empirically verifiable to be truth itself, anything that advances our mastery over reality. Hence, we frequently equate truth with the *proof* we derive from scientific experiments. Ellul says, "Everything is reduced to this verifiable reality which is scientifically measurable and pragmatically modifiable. Praxis becomes the measure of all truth. Truth becomes limited to something that falls short of real truth. It is reduced to something that can be acted upon."[35] In this way, Ellul shows how Truth and the Word belong to an order wholly different from the one verifiable through our scientific, and other, explorations of reality. While Truth resists concrete definition, he says that the questions we ask about it can indicate its nature. The question of the ultimate destination of human beings is a case in point. Also, "everything that refers to the establishment of a scale of values which allow a person to make significant personal decisions, and everything related to the debate over Justice and Love and their definition" belongs to the domain of Truth. [36]

Ellul explains "no image is able to convey any truth at all."[37] He provides the compelling example of a picture of Pope Pius XII in prayer on the cover of a popular French magazine. Does it represent anything true? Is the Pope really praying, or is there no prayer involved in this scene? Was it posed or somehow set up by the photographer? And all this before the invention of *Photoshop*! In another example, Ellul explains that "when we insist on expressing spiritual matters this way through images, something other than truth is always perceived. Even more serious and alarming, truth tends to disappear behind all the lighting and makeup. It tends to vanish where squelched by images."[38] This, Ellul concludes, is the reason why all "spiritual" films are failures. The point is that an image always expresses an incomplete reality and, in so doing, distorts reality. In a way, an image is a lie, for through images we can never come to possess the truth. The Truth comes only through the Word–and it is such that mages can never capture or lead us to possess it.

In this world of illusion where we have left behind both words, and the Word, it is helpful to remember that the Word described in the scriptures is inseparable from the *person* of Jesus. On this point Ellul makes an interesting observation: Jesus never actually wrote anything. The only recorded example we have of his doing so is found in John 8. There we are told how he stoops to write on the ground when asked by the Pharisees what should be done with the woman caught in adultery. The medium here, namely the ground, is important. The soil or sand upon which Jesus wrote would quickly wash out, erasing his markings–the image fades, but the Word remains. Moreover, we don't even know what he wrote. Ellul suggests that Jesus did not leave behind anything written, because to do so would be to convert the Word into an image. An image would degrade it, and we would undoubtedly fetishise such an artifact. In fact, he chastised the Pharisees for turning the living Word into the image of the law. The importance of the "writing" incident emerges in the way the woman caught in adultery was renewed, while her accusers felt suddenly convicted of their own sin. The Word, this encounter with the Truth, opened up new possibilities for everyone present.

As people of the Word, we Christians should consider the implications of our commitment to images. As people of faith, we should consider our commitment to sight. As people of God, we should consider our involvement with idols. Perhaps it is no mistake that for generations Christians have closed their eyes and folded their hands to pray, blocking out images and ceasing the work of their hands. Let him who has ears to hear...

Spectacle

The postmodern age is driven by spectacle. From the thousands of advertisements we see on the short drive to the store, to our Mecca-like pilgrimages to Disneyworld, to our videogames, full-body makeovers, presidential elections, and obsession with televised sports, we are inundated with the images of the magical, mystical, and larger-than-life. Our obsession with spectacle, and with the enchantment of illusion, derives, at least in part, from our need to go beyond ourselves. While spectacle and a sense of magic and mystery are not inherently wrong–we were created to be enchanted–our seemingly insatiable, compulsive interest in entertainment and things "unreal," should compel us to examine the source of our need and longing. In postmodernity, our hunger for something "beyond" seems to grow in proportion to the spectacle designed to satisfy our longings. In fact, our economy is built on the amplification of need, and the suggestion that further spectacle might satisfy that which burns within us.

Postmodern spectacle functions as a kind of sign or totem. As a sign, it both illustrates and exacerbates the hyperreality which characterizes our existence. Given that the postmodern self is comprised of free-floating signs unmoored from their signifiers, involvement may be one way people try to anchor themselves in a fragmented world. We cling to that which enchants us–we look for something significant, beyond ourselves that will provide us with coherence and meaning. Unfortunately, the means by which we seek enchantment for our disillusioned souls often simply reflects, in heightened terms, our own sense of unreality. Our hunger, our need, is spiritual in nature and it can only be satiated with "spiritual" food, satisfied by the real. Although Coca-Cola would have you believe that it is *the real thing*, the illusion fabricated by the consumer culture and the producers of mass media does little more than fill our need with more *nothing*, leave us wearing the emperor's new clothes. Accordingly, spectacle is noisy, garish, visually compelling, and inescapable. But, for all of its excitement and promise, it cannot regenerate our lives, because it is false: it is simulacra.

Spectacle tries to construct a reality out of the image, truth out of falsity. And, by our immersion it, we merely fill a void with a void.

The problem is not with spectacle itself, but with its source and character. Scripture is filled with spectacle, and with the promise of future spectacle, but of a different nature than that found in our amusement parks, casinos, and cinemas. That which it describes reflects the movement of the Word. Biblical spectacle is a signifier which points to–and indeed testifies to–the Truth found in Jesus, the Christ. However, in scripture, spectacle does not float freely, or exist for the sake of diversion or amusement. Rather, it helps tell a story and compels its hearers to consider their place in it. Accordingly, we can *find* ourselves in the spectacle of creation, in that of the parting of the Red Sea and the exodus, that the incarnation, death, resurrection, and ascension of Christ. Most Christian celebrations (Easter, Christmas, and Pentecost) call us to locate ourselves in the story of the Word. Furthermore, the celebrations of the Church are but "whispers" of the spectacle that is to come.

We see several important differences between the simulations and spectacle of the postmodern age, and that found in scripture. Foremost among these is the location of spectacle, whether this-worldly or other-worldly. In scripture, spectacle is mostly, though not always, deemphasized as it relates to a this-worldly orientation. For example, Jesus, the King of Kings, is born to a peasant woman and laid in a manger. Our romantic notions aside, this represents the absence of spectacle. However, the writers of the gospels describe the spectacle that takes place among the heavenly host in relation to this event.

Much of our spectacle functions as an escape from "reality." We escape into spectacle (Disney, videogames, etc.) in order to step away from the reality of our lives, which we frequently perceive as mundane. Jesus, in a number of places, downplays spectacle, telling those he heals or those from whom he exorcises demons to "keep it quiet." This reticence, this hesitation to allow oneself to be revealed through spectacle has been referred to as part of the "messianic secret" by a number of Biblical scholars. Theologians John Donahue and Daniel Harrington provide examples from the Book of Mark where we see Jesus alternately commanding secrecy as well as disclosure.[39] One way of viewing this tension is to see it as reflecting the progressive unfolding narrative surrounding the identity and true nature of the messiah. In this, spectacle can function to either illuminate, or distort the reality of who Jesus is and what he is about. Echoes of this tension reverberate in our Christmas celebrations where in the midst of consumer spectacle we quietly concede that "Christmas has become too commercial," or where we display signs reading "Jesus is the reason for the season." Clearly, our Christmas and Easter spectacles mostly distort from the Biblical texts which position a suffering messiah at the center of reality itself.

The central question, then, concerns the function of spectacle as symbol. As noted in the earlier chapter on symbolic interactionism, symbols in the creation, properly understood, should point to, should reference, the creator. It is for this reason that our thoughts turn to God when we look at a sunset, marvel at the intricacies of a leaf, or are awestruck by the power of a hurricane. These things reference the creator. When the linkage between signifier and signified (God) are strained or broken, our symbols float freely, blowing about like the balloon released from the hand of a child. The danger, so well understood by Jesus, was, and is, that spectacle will simply reference itself–that it will provide an escape, and float freely on the currents of social convention. Do the people simply want the rush of spectacle, or will the spectacle reorient them to the movements and emerging unveiling of the son of God?

When a miracle is experienced only as spectacle, it fails: The Red Sea will fill in again, leaving people to face new challenges, the food multiplied will be gone the next day, and the people healed will eventually die. Perhaps the best example is found in Jesus' first recorded miracle where he makes wine for those whose "hearts were already gladdened." If the spectacle of the wine fails to orient people to the wine maker, they will only be tired and empty the next day. If making wine is just about partying, its significance is rather limited. On the other hand, if those present at the wedding, and those who later read the account of the miracle can understand just how much "gladness of heart" is about the presence of the still-hidden messiah, and just how little it is about the spectacle of inebriated wedding guests, we begin to see why spectacle as an end in itself is rather empty. And, if we make the connection that this Jesus humbly making wine for a wedding between people whose names were not even recorded, is the same Jesus who stands at the center of the great wedding feast written about in Revelation 19, then we can begin to place spectacle in proper perspective.

C. S. Lewis provides a stirring example of the relationship between spectacle and the Word in the last of the Narnia chronicles, *The Last Battle*. In one of the final scenes we find Aslan running throughout his kingdom bringing renewal to everything he touches.[40] The talking animals of Narnia are enchanted, not only by the brightness and wonder of this renewed world, but by the lion who brings the wonder, the source of the spectacle.

Logocentrism

The idea of the *logos* lies at the heart of Western rationalism, and at the center of scripture. This concept and the tension surrounding it defines the postmodern struggle with the idea of truth. Christians are, of course, logocentric. We return to the Word, wrestle with the Word, pray that we may conform to the Word, and with regularity also resist the Word. In short, though we disagree about what it is, and how to approach it, Christians are people of the Word. Theologian Kathryn Tanner writes, "Continuing the argument is all by itself, moreover, a way of reaffirming a shared commitment to the importance of the materials over which one is arguing; commitment to them is deepened as the argument continues even if there is never any final agreement about their import."[41] Her point is that while believers disagree about many matters, they share common ground in their commitment to the centrality of the scriptures. This commitment reflects a shared belief in the existence of something meaningful, coherent, and enduring which exists "at the center of it all."

Earlier in this chapter, we explored the thought of Jacques Derrida, focusing on his efforts at deconstructing logocentrism. Derrida's work confronts us with the possibility of a frightening and destabilizing relativism. If there is nothing at the center of it all, if there is no logos, there is little basis for faith. And faith in faith is hardly something to build a life upon, let alone to be martyred for. It requires an object. However, despite the epistemological void left by Derrida, his critique of Western logocentrism can be helpful for the Christian.

Derrida, you will recall, is suspicious of society's dominant discourse and its constraining elements. He wants people to be free "writers"—free of all the intellectual ideas (what he calls "speech") which provide the basis for our understanding of the world. He thinks we delude ourselves in the search for a logos that doesn't exist–a search that has been enslaving and destructive. For Derrida, our logocentrism is a reflection of our power interests. In his view, we tend to believe in ways that support our self-interest, but which ultimately stifle human creativity and limit possibilities. His solution comes in the form of "decentering," a way of moving away from the socially constructed traditional center of the world with its focus on authorities, conventional meanings, and oppressive structures. Catherine Belsey (2002) provides a helpful explanation:

> Logocentrism puts meaning at the centre, imagines that the signified exists in some realm of pure consciousness and then finds its outward form in language....If there are no pure, free-standing signifieds, we look in vain, Derrida explains, for the transcendental signified, the one true meaning that holds all the others in place, the foundational truth that exists beyond question and provides the answer to all subsidiary problems. Metaphysical systems of belief, laying claim to the truth, all appeal to some transcendental signified. For Christianity this is God, for the Enlightenment reason, and for science the laws of nature. But if we take meaning to be the effect of language, not its cause, these foundations lose their transcendental status. This does not reduce belief to the level of fiction, but it does undermine its anchorage in a truth beyond question.[42]

To better understand Derrida's concern, it is helpful to look at hermeneutical approaches to interpreting scripture. At a very basic level, we often decide what a passage of scripture means by appealing to our best understanding of the writer's intentions. We try to place ourselves in, say, the Apostle Paul's shoes, and in his culture, in order to discern what the text "really means." Meaning begins with the author's intentions, is transmitted to some medium like papyrus, and then degrades as various people across time and cultures interpret it in ways never intended "by the author." From this perspective greater fidelity to the author's intention is seen as *truer* than cruder interpretations, and with this approach authorial intention is held as "truth." I've heard preachers say, "When I get to heaven I'm going to ask Paul what he meant by...". By contrast to this, a poststructuralist like Derrida would not privilege the author's intentions as the "truth," "reality," or only possibility of the text.

Writing, according to Derrida, continues to signify, even in the absence of the writer. For example, it is very common to hear Christians say something like "the Word really spoke to me." Such a person is saying is that through reading scripture, he or she perceived some truth–he came to see something more clearly. Now, the fact that this reader of scripture has no access to the Biblical writer, or even a knowledge of the language it was written in would not, for Derrida, detract from the meaning that has been found (or constructed). Writing continues to signify long after its authors are gone. On the one hand, this perspective allows for flexibility in interpretation–it allows us to apply scripture to our lives as they unfold; on the other hand, it raises questions of relativism popularized in the phrase "It's true for me."

Years from now, someone may read the chapter I am presently writing and find in it something of which I was unaware, never intended, or even opposed. Does my authority as writer negate the "truth" perceived by the reader? "Writing, therefore, demonstrates that sense may always be something that we make, that there may be no single true meaning, guaranteed by the word of the author, the *cogito* of consciousness, present to itself in thought, and uttered (outered, expressed) in the immediacy of unfallen speech." [43] In this way, Derrida deconstructs the logocentrism of Western thought with its linguistic emphasis on writing as "… no more than the transcription of oral exchange." [44]

How is Derrida of any help to the believer struggling to understand the scriptures as the Word of God and therefore "true?" He is helpful because his suspicion of logocentrism causes him to topple the idols of human understanding. Derrida, this great unbeliever, undoes our strong claims to have interpreted anything rightly. Theologian Kevin Vanhoozer explains that Derrida overthrows the "idol of the sign." He casts serious doubt on the fidelity between signifiers and signifieds–between signs and the objects they represent. In so doing he points out the conventionality of our interpretations. And, in a world of free-floating signifiers, especially a world which communicates through the amorphous medium of images, our interpretations can easily become simulacra. Derrida, for all his unbelief, helps us understand this, and in so doing encourages a sort of hermeneutic humility. He may also inadvertently push us away from human-based certainty and back into the realm of faith.

On the matter of where to lodge meaning in a text, Vanhoozer outlines two very different hermeneutical approaches. Both achieve essentially the same effect. "*Hermeneutical realism* is the position that believes meaning to be prior to and independent of the process of interpretation."[45] For the realist (or what Vanhoozer calls the *naïve* realist), "there is no gap between appearance and reality."[46] The non-realist, by contrast, does not hold that "human language and thoughts correspond to objective realities or stable meanings."[47] This position sees reality as a human construction. Proponents take their cue from Kant who:

> … exposed the lie of naïve realism by demonstrating that the 'world' is
> the product of human experience as *processed by conceptual categories*.
> The categories with which we think do not mirror the world but *mold* it;

> that is, they *impose distinctions on experience that may or may not be intrinsic to reality itself.* For Kant, we cannot know if certain features of the world are mind-independent or not, for human knowledge is limited to what we can experience, and experience is always already processed with categories imposed by the mind.[48]

While Kant held that the categories by which the mind processes experience are necessary, the non-realist holds that they are arbitrary. Consequently, there are no absolute, authoritative, ways of interpreting reality, only arbitrary and finite, incomplete perspectives on it. "For the hermeneutical non-realist, then, meaning is not 'there;' what one finds in a text depends on what aims, categories, and perspectives one brings to it."[49]

These two perspectives on interpretation, naïve hermeneutical realism and hermeneutical non-realism, oddly, produce similar outcomes: They both make interpretation redundant. For the former, no faith is required, only sight; for the latter, faith has no object and is thus without real value. Vanhoozer explains, "In the one case, all that is needed is observation and description; interpretation is not necessary. One either sees or does not see what is there. For the hermeneutical non-realist, on the other hand, interpretation is useless, for there is no 'reality,' no 'meaning' to get right."[50] These two perspectives reflect, in part, the two sociological traditions developed in chapter four of this work, *The American Tradition*. The first tradition, that of Comte and Durkheim, claims that society has a reality separate from the person. The second, that of Weber and the Chicago school, claims that it has no existence apart from the people who comprise it. And, as noted, neither tradition, and neither hermeneutic, is completely acceptable to the Christian. A brief citation illuminates this point:

> Since we are created by God, we are objects in the world he has created and governs by his divine will. In this sense, the reality of the world is prior to humans and must be understood if their actions are to be interpreted correctly. But since people are also made in the image of God and endowed with personality, they are different from the rest of creation. A person is subject as well as object and, in sinfulness, makes a world for himself or herself. There is a reality that belongs to that person alone, and to understand society, it is necessary to understand how social reality is constructed within it.

And so, we live caught in the tension between a world consisting of both seen and unseen. For the Christian it can only be navigated by faith in a Creator– who evidences Himself in the Logos–who animates and sustains the reality he created, and who alone gives meaning to life. This reality exists *apart* from us; it is there whether we are present to interpret it or not. It also lives *inside* of us, for example, in the indwelling of the Holy Spirit who brings meaning to our interpretive efforts. The human need for faith accentuates our finiteness in a world the reality of which is too much to grasp. As we live in a postmodern world which can overwhelm us, we do well to stand with Augustine who said, "I believe in order to understand,"[51] taking faith as our starting point, and believing that he who began a good work in us will see it through to completion.

Sometimes, out of fear of taking a wrong position, Christians can adopt overly concrete interpretations of scripture. The history of Christianity is littered with the remnants of passionately held positions that are embarrassing at best, and genocidal at worst. Sometimes our intentions are noble in so far as we aim to protect the integrity of the Word; frequently, however, they are ideological and function to protect power arrangements and other material interests. This struggle over interpretation, and even over what the scriptures are, is exacerbated in postmodern times as we seek to anchor ourselves in ground that seems to be constantly shifting. Sociologist Robert Wuthnow provides a helpful approach to living a life of faith in the midst of uncertainty and disequilibrium. He calls it "living the question."

> I have borrowed the much-used phrase "living the question" because it seem to me that Christianity does not so much supply the learned person with answers as it does raise questions. It has been said of Marxists that even apostates spend their lives struggling with the questions Marx addressed. The same can be said of Christianity. It leaves people with a set of questions they cannot escape, especially when these questions face them from their earliest years.[52]

Wuthnow goes on to explain how many of the narratives in scripture leave us not with an answer, but with a set of questions. For example, the parable of the Good Samaritan ends with a question, "Who then is my neighbor?" He says that the answer might be obvious in the context of the three options given in the parable, but the question goes on to animate Christian discussions in different contexts–in a variety of social worlds. Who is my neighbor in a global society? What does it mean to be neighborly in the digital age? And so on. Perhaps it is the character of the questions we ask, and the value we find in the shared materials (scripture) over which we argue. Perhaps living the question, and not forcing the answer, gives us traction on reality in a murky social world where truth is an especially rare commodity. For living the question is an act of faith, and faith is the only path to the real.

Identity

More than anything, the postmodern age leaves us with questions of identity. Who are we? It is ironic that at a time when we have such wealth, leisure time, educational infrastructure, and technology–all of which are tools that help with self-exploration–we are nevertheless haunted by such uncertainty when it comes to the question of identity. The boundless opportunities which confront us are both freeing and enslaving. The endless possibilities for who we are becoming tend to fill us with tension and ambivalence: Who am I, and what will become of me? We speak of finding ourselves, of being true to ourselves, and of having the courage to "be" ourselves. It seems that the more we try to anchor identity, the more it slips away and remains just beyond our grasp. In our effort to establish it we frequently adorn ourselves with signage from the mass culture, yet, at some level, we know that these things are just add-ons, that they merely disguise our fragmented selves.

The New Testament takes a counterintuitive approach to this problem of identity. Jesus says, "If you want to save your life, you must lose it." "If you want to be first (to have a positive social identity), you must be last." "If you wish to lead, you must serve." What we see in scripture is an inversion of the modern notion of status and status seeking. Jesus proclaims, "You must be born again," and this rebirth results in an *identity* that is "in Christ." Additionally, the scriptures proclaim that Jesus came to be poured out as a ransom for many. These images–pouring out, losing one's life, serving, and being born again–stand in stark contrast to the signs, simulated realities, and control offered by technology, by which we try to find ourselves. In contrast to this, the postmodern age, the age of signs, advocates completeness through consumption, actualization through accumulation of images. We are led to believe that to find ourselves, we need to fill ourselves.

Jesus offers a new way, described in the Mark 10:17 account of the rich young man who asked, "What must I do to inherit eternal life?" Jesus told him to give away all he owned. The man went away sad–the signs of social esteem with which he clothed himself were too central to his identity for him to seriously entertain this proposition. The connection to the postmodern condition is clear here. Anchoring our identities in signs that for a moment provide status, but function to point us away from God, enmeshes us with simulacra–and henceforth empty symbols that point back at empty lives. Perhaps such simulacra is what the author of Hebrews had in mind when he wrote, "Therefore, since we are surrounded by such a great cloud of witnesses, let us throw off everything that hinders and the sin that so easily entangles, and let us run with perseverance the race marked out for us. Let us fix our eyes on Jesus..."(Hebrews 12:1-2). The rich young man walked away from Jesus, fixing his eyes elsewhere, because he was entangled with the signs of wealth. Our signage is much more pervasive, sinister, and subtly ensnaring–and we also notice it less.

The other matter, relative to identity, concerns the breaking down of barriers between people. As we have seen, the postmodern age erodes the categories by which we structure identity. This creates a crisis, since we tend to define ourselves over against our out-groups. However, from this emerges the possibility for something very good–something echoed in scripture. The apostle Paul writes repeatedly of the need to break down identity barriers as they exist in the Church. His letters were written to both Jews and Gentiles. In fact, the people he greets in his letter to the Roman congregation have Greek, Latin, and Jewish names.[53]

In Galatians 3:28 Paul writes, "There is neither Jew nor Greek, slave nor free, male nor female, for you are all one in Christ Jesus." This passage has meaning on at least two different levels. First, Paul is addressing the need to remove spiritual divisions–all people are accepted by God on the basis of faith. Second, Paul is addressing the need to break down three critical *social* barriers–

racial (Jew nor Greek), cultural (slave nor free), and sexual (male nor female)–
for *all* are one in Christ Jesus. Being in Christ provides a new super-ordinate
category for identity that outshines all previous ones–especially social identities
based on out-group contrasts and the desire for elevated social position.

Conclusion

Postmodern social theory, though associated with relativism, and viewed
with suspicion by some Christians, provides a helpful perspective on a society
replete with unnoticed idols. Thinkers like Jacques Derrida call us to question
how easily we construct our own *truth* and hold it as absolute. Theorists like
Jean Baudrillard remind us of the importance of living in the *real*, and of the
dangers of giving ourselves over to a world of signs, simulations, and nothing-
ness. While postmodern social theory can invoke thoughts of despair, it can also
open us to new possibilities, a renewed faith, and a new vision for the ministry
of the Church.

Old Testament scholar Walter Brueggemann writes that "our context for
ministry is the *failure of the imagination of modernity*, in both its moral-
theological and its economic-political aspects."[54] While the toppling of modernism is unsettling to those for whom it brought power and position (those whose
identities it affirmed), the emerging paradigm of the postmodern era has the potential to reanimate our collective imagination–to set our sights on a new vision
of the kingdom of God and our place in it. Accordingly, Brueggemann calls for
a *counterimagination* of the world, "… a nervy offer of a world in and through a
radically different perspective."[55] He suggests three such modes of imagining:

1. *Imagine a self*, no longer the self of consumer advertising, no longer a self
    caught in endless efforts of self-security, but a self rooted in the inscruta-
    ble miracle of God's love, a self no longer consigned to the rat race, but
    one oriented to full communion with God–which is its true destiny and
    rightful home.[56]
2. *Imagine a world*, no longer a closed arena of limited resources and fixed
    patterns of domination, no longer caught in endless destructive power
    struggles, but able to recall that lyrical day of creation when the morning
    stars sang for joy, a world no longer bent on hostility, but under God's
    presence as a place where creatures "no longer hurt or destroy."[57]
3. *Imagine a community of faith*, no longer in exile, cast loose without mem-
    ory, no longer exposed without assurance.[58]

Seen in this light, the tension and uncertainty which we associate with
postmodernity may be the very things that will help us to turn away from identities rooted in the temporal world, to the infinitely more certain identity that rests
on the eternal Word. And, isn't faith, at least in part, a matter of imagination?
For as we walk through this world, we look to another, and we imagine how
things will be when Christ returns, we see him face-to-face, our signs and simulations are stripped away, and identity is renewed. Such imaginings can indeed
make for a better world here and now.

Chapter 13

Conclusion

To echo the opening statement of the preface, "Popular Christian social thought is, for the most part, shallow. Perhaps a better word would be simplistic." Having come this far, we should better understand what this statement means and how we might benefit from such an understanding.

Simplistic social thought occurs when one naively clings to either an exclusively objective or subjective view of sociology. Some follow the precept found in much traditional Christian thought, namely, that God's truth is objectively revealed in society and can be interpreted in only one way. These people argue that only one form of family is desirable and that form would be the nuclear family as it has been found in American society. They would also claim that the church is inviolate and continues today as God had mandated. Little room is allowed here for the interpretation of truth in the light of modern society with its problems and shifting needs.

Others reject this notion and suggest that all of social reality is subjective and completely open to individual interpretation. Absolute truths no longer exist for these people who constantly construct new realities as the basis of their conception of truth. They might claim, for example, that sex roles have no constancy as men and women interpret them to fit changing social and individual needs. They might also argue that, although the church's foundation was laid down by God, the superstructure is a human construction in need of constant evaluation and criticism. Truth, for these people, is largely relative and dependent on the definitions of reality needed at the time.

Neither of these views of reality, alone, adequately captures the social world as we experience it, either in life or in Scripture. Our study of social thought has shown that both objective and subjective forms of social reality may be found in society. And when we turn to Scripture, we find support for both forms of reality in the hidden threads found there. The conclusion is this: *social reality is a complex merger of both objective and subjective forms of truth that need to be kept in tension if they are to be understood correctly.* To ignore that tension or to misunderstand it produces the kind of superficial thinking so prevalent today.

Hidden Threads

In his book, *All Truth Is God's Truth,* Arthur Holmes describes a possible merger of objectivity and subjectivity. Although an idea may be "subjective," occurring within the mind, it becomes "objective" when applied to some universal quality. Holmes refers to this as *metaphysical objectivity.*[1] This is the kind of Objectivity found in early functionalism with its search for transcultural social principles. It is also the kind of objectivity we accept in believing that the gospel applies to all people,

We refer to a belief or idea that approaches objectivity in a passionate or concerned way as *epistemological subjectivity.* This kind of subjectivity we find in religious faith as it relates to that which it deems objective. Holmes claims that epistemological subjectivity and metaphysical objectivity are completely compatible.[2] Put more simply, *belief in something does not necessarily make it less real.* We can have deep concern in the belief that the gospel applies to all people.

Objectivity is separated from subjectivity when it refers to things that are verifiable only by empirical means, since such things rarely stir much passion in us. How can we have any commitment to a statistic that is acceptable at the .05 level of probability? We can't, because we don't clearly understand what it means. Thus, we approach the truth of this statistical claim in a detached and impersonal way—what Holmes calls *epistemological objectivity.* To merge metaphysical objectivity and epistemological subjectivity, then, requires some way of interpreting the meaning of some objective truth.

It helps to understand such questions of meaning as questions of concept.[3] These questions stress the meaning of facts in a particular context. Concepts are merely labels or symbols that provide an idea only when related to some contextually-defined concrete object. The term *fish,* for example, does not refer to only one kind of creature that lives in water. The concept of fish requires interpretation of various sea creatures to allow classification of those to be accepted as fish and those which will not. Commitment occurs when we accept a fish as different from other sea creatures and then label it as such.

Concepts, then, help us to distinguish between the level of objective fact and the level of subjective interpretation. We point to a fish (objective fact) and ask our friend if he believes (subjective interpretation) it is a fish (concept). Since words may have many different meanings, it is possible that the friend will disagree and see it as a flounder or a halibut. When the friend nods assent to the word *fish,* agreement is given to our concept and the meaning is shared. In this way, concepts link the objective and subjective levels of reality and give meaning to the truth about us.

Throughout the book, certain concepts have been referred to as *hidden threads.* They are threads in the sense that they tie together, conceptually, the objective truth God has provided in created social reality and the subjective interpretation of this reality offered by people in their attempts to reconstruct that reality in society. These threads provide some meaning of the truth that God intends for us to perceive in the world about us. Once we perceive the meaning of that concept as God intended and separate it from all the other possible meanings it might have, we become committed to that meaning and seek to apply it in the world.

But these threads are also hidden because the meanings are usually not readily apparent to us. Even reading Scripture with a trained theological eye, we might miss the meanings of these concepts for the world as we know it today. Since these concepts refer to social reality, they often benefit from sociological interpretations and the meanings they can provide. This fact should not surprise us. As a science, sociology may touch objective truth as laid down by God. Often it misinterprets this truth. On other occasions, sociology may interpret truth in Scripture as it would be interpreted by theology. On still other occasions, sociological interpretations may come closer to the mark than current theological interpretations. In any case, sociological and scriptural interpretations may approximate each other as they share some of the meaning of these hidden threads.

We might consider the *calling* as an example of a hidden thread as it was discussed earlier. Even though Weber understood the meaning of the calling to be "a task set by God," modern sociologists are more likely to accept the meaning of the *career* as the secularized form of the calling without a biblical basis for their understanding. They have lost the original meaning of the concept. Now the calling is merely an academic term, one that is treated objectively in its historic context. If there is to be any commitment to the term, it must be to the secularized meaning of the career.

By contrast, many modern Christians respect the biblical meaning *of* the calling but don't know how to interpret it in their daily lives. Indeed, theology fails to provide any such interpretation. Without a sociological understanding of the term to couple with biblical understanding, commitment to the ideal of the calling is lost. Consequently, Christians accept the secularized notion of the career as offered by modern culture and apply it in daily decision making. Thus, commitment to career replaces the priority originally given to the calling. This is not because biblical truth or even a proper understanding of it has been rejected. What is not understood is the principle of maintaining a tension between the calling and the career, a principle gained from the sociological views offered by Max Weber.

For another example of a hidden thread, we turn to the concept of idols as discussed in an earlier chapter. We understand that idols gain sacred meaning because they seem to provide answers for problems that would otherwise seem senseless. In a confused and disorganized world, idols offer a point of apparent stability for people, something to which they can show commitment. Consequently, idols become distorted when they provide answers different from those offered by the sacred. In short, they give a secularized interpretation of objective reality.

Interpreting the place of the sociologist in society, Robert Friedrichs focuses on the role of the prophet as one who "breaks icons" or false images.[4] With no concern for the prophet as a messenger of God, he sees a similarity between the social role of the sociologist and the prophet. Indeed, the sociologist, as prophet, does have the criticism of society as his or her primary function.[5] Rather than building new idols, the sociologist is one who tears down the old. Consequently, the sociologist is portrayed by Friedrichs as an Old Testament prophet in modern garb.

It should not seem strange, then, that sociologists may sometimes join with believers in the common cause of breaking idols. Indeed, they share a mutual concern for the abuse of drugs and alcohol. This is not to say they will always agree on the nature of today's idols. Nor will sociologists always understand idols as substitutes for the living God; they will usually see them as merely false images and nothing more. Nevertheless, the prophet, whether sociologist or believer, should manifest a commitment that prevents any position of neutrality. The prophet was always publicly engaged in "the choice of treating his fellow as an end in himself or as but a means to one's own ends."[6]

Friedrichs refers to the Hebraic analogue found in sociology.[7] He means by this that idols and prophets are concepts that had the same type of meaning in ancient Israel that they have in modern society. As the sociologist can learn from the Hebraic analogue, so the believer can be enriched by the meaning the sociologist brings to the concept. Each concept—*idol and prophet*—has an objective reality, which, when interpreted correctly by the believer and the sociologist, leads to a similar conclusion: prophets are to project "past behavior into the future, to *alter* that future."[8]

Modern social thought is rarely conceptual. Either we are concerned for values and think in broad, often ideological terms and social questions, or else we stress facts and narrow our thought to empirical data gathering. Consequently, we ignore the meanings of things that remain unquestioned and often unknown. Analyzing hidden threads requires a kind of conceptual thinking we seldom indulge in. First, the analysis of these concepts requires us to think about the meanings of words and what they refer to rather than taking these meanings for granted. Second, they point us to those meanings that sociology and Scripture have some common interest in and, indeed, may even agree upon. Finally, they require us to be self-conscious about those ideas or problems which, ordinarily, we rarely think about. In short, hidden threads are to be revealed and shared for the meaning they may have for us.

Conclusion

The contemporary sociologist Pierre Hegy offers this description of the forms of reality as we have been discussing them:

Language and cosmos are interrelated like the threads and images of a tapestry. Without threads there can be no design; without a design, there is no way to assemble the threads into a tapestry. Language and cosmos are coextensive, and together they constitute the tapestry of man's culture.[9]

Hegy goes on to say that language cannot be a faithful copy of reality because it is distorted by the multiple meanings it carries. As a result, language cannot perfectly describe the dialectical richness of reality. Any attempt at empirical fact finding will be limited, faulty, or both. To gain any understanding of such a dialectical world, one cannot step aside and try to analyze it objectively. We must be aware of our influence on the world, how we have unconsciously altered the design that is there, before we can hope to begin to understand it.

But Hegy reminds us that understanding begins at a more basic, fundamental level. The tapestry of culture has a design traced into it. We may understand that to be the objective truth that God has laid down for us to decipher, either with science or through his revelation. Our thought may employ the theories offered by science simply because they too seek to trace the designs that are in the world. We cannot arbitrarily reject certain theories because they are no longer faddish. Openness to all forms of social thought is needed if we are to understand the contributions they make to the interpretation of social reality;

Our attempts at interpretation, however, are always faulty. We fail to step aside and describe the world as a poor facsimile of the design that was intended. Our emotional involvement in the world blinds us to the corrupting influence we have had on it. In our criticism, we are unable to see how we contribute to the cause of the criticism. We become double-minded, and our language reflects that fact as we fail to accurately describe things as we experience them.

In one sense, then, good social thought means looking at the world from a distance. Berger's *ecstasy* offers a means by which we are able to face problems realistically and alone, if need be. There's a certain tension in attempting to understand objective truth in this way while saying "No" to the world and its claims on us. Only with such an action can we understand any meaning, any hope, transcending society.

It is also true, however, that we need to be involved in society if we are to understand our dialectical relationship with it. Berger's *praxis* offers the challenge to return to society fully aware that our actions will always fall short of expectations. We cannot be objective in our analysis of society unless we understand how we influence it in subjective ways. Good social science demands an awareness of our role as actors in society and not merely as observers.

Anyone who believes in a transcendent reality is in a unique position to understand and implement the expectations of this dialectical relationship. It is possible to be committed to praxis fully aware that as sinful beings in a sinful world our expectations will never be completely filled. Such an awareness demands that we place some distance between ourselves and society's illusions. Even when active in the world, we need some place to be apart, a fence with a knothole, perhaps, through which to observe the world constructively and with concern. A transcendent view of the world offers that place and that possibility.

Notes

Chapter 2: The Nature of Theory

1. These terms are used by Jacques Ellul to make the same distinction in his work. See, for example, *The Meaning of the City* (Grand Rapids: Wm. B. Eerdmans, 1970).
2. Thomas Kuhn, *The Structure of Scientific Revolution* (Chicago: University of Chicago Press, 1962).
3. See M. Scott Peck, *The People of the Lie* (New York: Simon & Schuster, 1983).

Chapter 3: The European Heritage

1. Quoted by Peter Gay, *The Enlightenment: An Interpretation*, vol. 2 (New York: Alfred A. Knopf, 1973), 167.
2. Ibid., 321.
3. Lewis Coser, *Masters of Sociological Thought* (New York: Harcourt Brace Jovanovich, 1977), 41.
4. Quoted in Isaiah Berlin, *Karl Marx: His Life and Environment* (New York: Oxford University Press, 1963), 81.
5. Quoted in George Ritzer, *Sociological Theory* (New York: Alfred A. Knopf, 1983), 17.
6. Ibid., 17-18.
7. Others before Marx, of course, also conceived of man's state of alienation. The difference in view largely depends on the definition of reality used. Calvin, for example, refers to the ungodly as "alienated from God." *The Institutes of the Christian Religion*, 2, 2, 16.
8. Quoted in Lewis Coser, *Masters of Sociological Thought*, 90.
9. Herbert Spencer, *The Study of Sociology* (Ann Arbor, Mich.: Univ. of of Mich. Press, 1961), 356.
10. Quoted in George Ritzer, *Sociological Theory*, 28.
11. A recent authoritative critique of Spencer's theory puts it in a more favorable light than it has enjoyed in the recent past. See Jonathan H. Turner, *Herbert Spencer: A Renewed Appreciation* (Beverly Hills: Sage Publications, 1985).
12. Emile Durkheim, *The Rules of Sociological Method* (Glencoe, IL: The Free Press, 1950), 1.
13. Emile Durkheim, *Division of Labor in Society* (Glencoe, IL: The Free Press, 1947), 169.
14. Max Weber, *The Protestant Ethic and the Spirit of Capitalism* (New York: Charles Scribner's Sons, 1930), 108.
15. Ibid., 194.
16. Ibid., 175.
17. Ibid., 194.

Chapter 4: The American Tradition

1. E. A. Ross, *Sin and Society* (New York: Harper & Row, 1973), 3.
2. Hinkle and Hinkle, *The Development of Modern Sociology* (New York: Doubleday & Co., 1954), vii.
3. Ibid., 3.
4. Quoted in Lewis Coser, *Masters of Sociological Thought*, 319.
5. Richard Hofstadter, Social *Darwinism in American Thought* (New York:

George Braziller, Inc., 1959), 10.
6. Edward Stevens, *Business Ethics* (Ramsey, N. J.: Paulist Press, 1979), 32.
7. Ibid.
8. Richard Hofstadter, *Social Darwinism in American Thought,* 29.
9. Benjamin Kidd, *Social Evolution* (New York: Macmillan & Co., 1895), viii.
10. William G. Sumner, *Folkways* (Boston: Ginn & Co., 1906), 2.
11. Hinkle and Hinkle, *The Development of Modern Sociology,* 8-9.
12. Ibid., 10.
13. Vidich and Lyman, *American Sociology: Worldly Rejections of Religion and their Directions* (New Haven, Conn.: Yale University Press, 1985), 1.
14. Ibid.
15. Charles Ellwood, *The Reconstruction of Religion: A Sociological View* (New York: Macmillan & Co., 1922), ix.
16. Ibid., viii.
17. Richard Hofstadter, *Social Darwinism in American Thought,* 105.
18. Charles Ellwood, *The Reconstruction of Religion,* 138.
19. Ibid., 123.
20. Ibid., viii.
21. Charles Howard, *The Rise of the Social Gospel in American Protestantism: 1865-1915* (New Haven, Conn.: Yale University Press, 1940), 164.
22. Ibid.
23. Ibid., 231.
24. Ibid., 232.
25. Vidich and Lyman, *American Sociology,* 180.
26. Much of the following section is based on the work of Roscoe C. Hinkle, "Antecedents of the Action Orientation in American Sociology before 1935," *American Sociological Review* (October 1963): 705-15.
27. Quoted in George Ritzer, *Sociological Theory,* 37.
28. Everett Stonequist, *The Marginal Man* (NY: Russell & Russell, Inc. 1961).
29. Robert Bierstedt, *American Sociological Theory* (New York: Academic Press, 1981), 491.
30. See Peter Berger and Stanley Pullberg, "Reification and the Sociological Critique of Consciousness," *History and Theory* 4 (1965): 196-211.

Chapter 5: Functionalism

1. Much of this section is based on the work of Turner and Maryanski, *Functionalism* (Menlo Park, Calif.: The Benjamin W. Cummings Publishing Co., 1979).
2. Ibid., 13.
3. Ibid., 43-44.
4. Kingsley Davis, *Human Society* (New York: The Macmillan Co., 1948), 401-4.
5. Robert Merton, *Social Theory and Social Structure* (Glencoe, IL: The Free Press, 1949), 71-81.
6. Ibid., 27-38.
7. Ibid., 61-68.
8. Ibid., 69-70.
9. Ibid., 133.
10. Ibid., 329-46.
11. Robert Bierstedt, *American Sociological Theory,* 441.
12. Parsons and Shils, *Toward a General Theory of Action* (New York: Harper & Row, 1951), 170.

13. George Ritzer, *Sociological Theory*, 194.
14. H. Richard Niebuhr, *Christ and Culture* (New York: Harper & Row, 1951), 32.
15. Ibid., 194.
16. Henry R. Van Til, *The Calvinistic Concept of Culture* (Grand Rapids: Baker Book House, 1959), 23.
17. Quoted in ibid., 37.
18. For an excellent discussion of these issues, see David Moberg, "Cultural Relativity and Christian Faith," *Journal of the American Scientific Affiliation* (June 1962): 34-48.
19. Walter Goldschmidt, *Exploring the Ways of Mankind* (New York: Holt, Rinehart and Winston, 1960), 535-44.
20. William Smalley, "Culture and Superculture" *Practical Anthropology* (May/June 1955): 60.
21. For a helpful discussion of these issues as they apply to politics, see Antho ny Campolo in DeSanto, Redekop, and Smith-Hinds, A *Reader in Sociology: Christian Perspectives* (Scottdale, Penn.: Herald Press, 1980), 491-503.
22. Robert Merton, *Social Theory and Social Structure*, 38-47.
23. C. Wright Mills, *The Sociological Imagination* (New York: Oxford University Press, 1959), chap. 3.

Chapter 6: Conflict Theory

1. Judson Landis, *Sociology: Concepts and Characteristics* 7th ed. (Belmont, CA: Wadsworth Publishing Company, 1989), 11.
2. Karl Marx, *Selected Writings in Sociology and Social Philosophy* (New York: McGraw-Hill, 1956), 4.
3. Ibid., 236.
4. Ibid., 240.
5. Ashley and Orenstein, *Sociological Theory: Classical Statements* (Boston: Allyn and Bacon, Inc., 1985), 243.
6. Kurt Wolff, ed., *The Sociology of Georg Simmel* (Glencoe, IL: The Free Press, 1950), 230.
7. Georg Simmel, *Conflict and the Web of Group-Affiliation* (Glencoe, IL: The Free Press, 1955), 13.
8. Ibid., 64.
9. Quoted in Ashley and Orenstein, *Sociological Theory*, 234. 10. Ibid., 246.
11. Ralf Dahrendorf, "Out of Utopia: Toward a Reorientation of Sociological Analysis," *American Journal of Sociology* (September 1958): 115-27.
12. See, for example, C. Wright Mills, *The Sociological Imagination*, chap. 5.
13. Ralf Dahrendorf, *Class and Conflict in Industrial Society* (Stanford, CA: Stanford University Press, 1959), 159.
14. Jonathan H. Turner, *The Structure of Sociological Theory* (Homewood, IL: The Dorsey Press, 1986), chap. 7.
15. See Pierre van den Berghe, "Dialectic and Functionalism: Toward a Theoretical Synthesis," *Amer. Sociological Review* (Oct. 1963): 695-705.
16. Lewis Coser, *The Functions of Social Conflict* (Glencoe, IL: The Free Press, 1956), 31.
17. Ibid., chap. 6.
18. Dennis H. Wrong, "The Oversocialized Conception of Man in Modern Society," *American Sociological Review* (April 1961): 183-93.
19. Ibid., 184.
20. Ibid., 185.

21. Quoted from a book review of Robert P. Ericksen, *Theologians Under Hitler* (New Haven, Conn.: Yale University Press, 1985), by Martin Marty in *Context* (1 July 1986).

22. John R. W. Stott, *Christian Counter Culture: The Message of the Sermon on the Mount* (Downers Grove, IL: InterVarsity Press, 1978), 15.

23. Theodore Roszak, *The Making of a Counter-Culture* (Garden City, .NJ.: Anchor Books, Doubleday, 1969).

24. J. Milton Yinger, "Contraculture and Subculture," *American Sociological Review* (October 1960): 625-35.

25. Ibid., 629. There is some irony in Yinger's observation that Parsons uses the term counter-culture to describe the feeling of ambivalence in groups that Yinger sees in contracultures.

26. Lecture by W. Stanford Reid, "Christianity as Counterculture," Regent College, Vancouver, B.C. (July 29,1971).

27. Jacques Ellul, *The Presence of the Kingdom* (New York: Seabury Press, 1967), chap. 2.

28. Ibid., 37.

29. Jacques Ellul, *Violence* (New York: Seabury Press, 1969), 24.

30. Ibid., 127.

31. Ibid., 68.

Chapter 7: Social Action Theory

1. Roscoe C. Hinkle, "Antecedents of the Action Orientation in American Sociology before 1935," *American Sociological Review*, 706-7.

2. Gerth and Mills, eds., *From Max Weber: Essays on Sociology* (New   York: Oxford University Press, 1946), 18-19.

3. Max Weber, *The Theory of Social and Economic Organization* (New York: Oxford University Press, 1947), 10.

4. Ibid., 12.

5. Max Weber, *The Protestant Ethic*, 175.

6. Ibid., 176.

7. Max Weber, *The Theory*, 98-9

8. Max Weber, *The Protestant Ethic*, 281.

9. In fairness to Weber, his description of the prophet as a charismatic   leader does not lean toward such an explanation. See, for example, Max Weber, *The Sociology of Religion* (London: Methuen & Co., Ltd., 1965), xxxiii—xxxv.

10. Hinkle and Hinkle, *The Development of Modern Sociology, 44-54*.

11. Talcott Parsons, *The Structure of Social Action* (Glencoe, IL.: The Free Press, 1949), 4.

12. Ibid., 718-19.

13. Ibid., 747.

14. Robert Merton, *Social Theory and Social Structure*, 330.

15. Gerth and Mills, eds., *From Max Weber*, 149.

16. Ibid., 155.

17. Talcott Parsons, *The Structure of Social Action*, 58.

18. Kingsley Davis, *Human Society*, 128-32.

19. Indeed, one social action theorist, Robert MacIver, claims that the Golden Rule is a universal, ethical principle in *On Community, Society, and Power* (Chicago: Univ. of Chicago Press, 1970), 302-7.

20. See Robert Bellah, et al., *Habits of the Heart: Individualism and Commitment in American Life* (New York: Harper & Row, 1985), especially

chap. 6.

21. This argument has been well developed in a Christian context by S. D. Gaede in his book, *Belonging* (Grand Rapids: Zondervan Publishing Co. 1985).
22. This section is based on Jacques Ellul's, *The Presence of the Kingdom*,Chap. 3.
23. Jacques Ellul, *The Presence of the Kingdom*, 63.
24. See, for example, William Whyte's *The Organization Man* (New York: Simon & Schuster, 1956).
25. Jacques Ellul, *The Presence of the Kingdom*, 70.
26. Ibid., 74-75.

Chapter 8: Exchange Theory

1. Marcel Mauss, *The Gift* (New York: W. W. Norton & Co., 1967), 63.
2. Ibid., 74.
3. Ibid., 75.
4. Ibid., 45.
5. Quoted from Crime *and Custom in Savage Society* by Bronislaw Malinowski, reprinted in Coser and Rosenberg, *Sociological Theory: A Book of Readings*, 4th ed. (New York: Macmillan Publishing Co., 1976), 59.
6. Described by Homans in his autobiographical sketch in George Ritzer, *Sociological Theory*, 366-67.
7. George Homans, *The Human Group* (New York: Harcourt, Brace & World, 1950), 454-57.
8. Ibid., 109 (italics mine).
9. Ibid., 82.
10. Ibid.
11. Gerth and Mills, eds., *From Max Weber*, 204.
12. Georg Simmel, *The Sociology of Georg Simmel* (Glencoe, IL: The FreePress, 1950), 293.
13. Jacques Ellul, *Money and Power* (Downers Grove, IL: InterVarsity Press 1984), 10.
14. Ibid., 11.
15. Ibid., 54.
16 Ibid., 84.
17. Ibid., 75-76.
18. C. Wright Mills, *The Power Elite* (New York: Oxford University Press, 1956), 3-4.
19. See David Moberg, "The Manipulation of Human Behavior," *Jour nal of the American Scientific Affiliation* (March 1970), pp. 14-17, for a good discussion of the general problem.
20. Pitirim A. Sorokin, *The Reconstruction of Humanity* (Boston: The Beacon Press, 1948), 58-59.
21. Herbert Schlossberg, *Idols for Destruction* (Nashville: Thomas Nel son, 1983), 53.

Chapter 9: Symbolic Interactionism

1. Leslie White, *The Science of Culture* (NY, Grove Press, 1949), 22.
2. Ibid., 25.
3. See Margaret Poloma, *Contemporary Sociological Theory* (New York: Macmillan Publishing Co., 1979), chap. 1.
4. George H. Mead, *On Social Psychology* (Chicago: Univ. of Chicago Press, 1956), 346.

5. This section draws from the work of Joel M. Charon.
6. Herbert Blumer, *Symbolic Interactionism: Perspective and Method* (Englewood Cliffs, N.J.: Prentice-Hall, 1969), 62.
7. Ibid., 70.
8. David Moberg, *Wholistic Christianity: An Appeal for a Dynamic, Balanced Faith* (Elgin, IL: Brethren Press, 1985), 74.
9. Ibid.
10. Christians and Van Hook, eds., *Jacques Ellul: Interpretive Essays* (Urbana, IL, University of Illinois Press, 1981), 292.
11. Herbert Blumer, *Symbolic Interactionism*, 109.
12. Ibid., 70.
13. Ibid., 109-10.
14. Joel M. Charon, *Symbolic Interactionism: An Introduction, an Interpretation, an Integration* (Englewood Cliffs, N.J.: Prentice-Hall, 1979), 152.
15. Herbert Blumer, *Symbolic Interactionism*, 109.
16. Christians and Van Hooks, eds., *Jacques Ellul*, 293.
17. Ibid.
18. Ibid., 298.
19. David Moberg, *Wholistic Christianity*, 6.
20. Os Guinness, *The Gravedigger Files* (Downers Grove, IL: InterVarsityPress, 1983), 34.
21. Jacques Ellul, *The Presence of the Kingdom*, 100.
22. Daniel J. Boorstin, *The Image: A Guide to Pseudo-Events in America* (New York: Harper & Row, 1961), 11.
23. Ibid., 239.
24. Jacques Ellul, *The Political Illusion* (New York: Alfred A. Knopf, 1967), 115.
25. Ibid., 188.
26. Gregory *Baum: Religion and Alienation: A Theological Reading of So ciology* (New York: Paulist Press, 1975), 238-63.
27. Ibid., 246-47.
28. Ibid., 249.
29. Ibid., 255.
30. J. A. Walter, *Sacred Cows: Exploring Contemporary Idolatry* (Grand Rapids: Zondervan Publishing Co., 1979), 16.
31. Herbert Schlossberg, *Idols for Destruction*, 6.
32. J. A. Walter, *Sacred Cows*, 43.
33. Ibid., 38.
34. Robert Bellah, et al., *Habits of the Heart*.
35. Ibid., 7.
36. Ibid., 6.

Chapter 10: Phenomenology & Ethnomethodology

1. Quoted from Edmund Husserl, *Phenomenology and the Crisis of Philosophy* (New York: Harper Torchbooks, 1965), 106-7.
2. Paul Filmer, et al., eds., *New Directions in Sociological Theory* (London: Collier-Macmillan, 1975), 124.
3. Ibid., 43-47.
4. This section is based on Mehan and Wood, *The Reality of Ethnomethodology* (New York: John Wiley & Sons, 1975), chap. 2.

5.   Quoted from Douglas Gasking, *Mathematics and the World*, in Anthony
Flew, *ed., Logic and Language* (New York: Doubleday & Co., 1955), 432; reprinted
in Mehan and Wood, *The Reality of Ethnomethodology*, 9.

6.   Ibid., 27-30.

7.   Ibid., 30.

8.   Ibid., 205.

9.   Ibid., 31.

10. Ibid., 37-38.

11. Ibid., 38-43.

12. Ibid., 70.

13. Noted by Merleau-Ponty, "What is Phenomenology?" in J. Kockelmans, ed.,
     Phenomenology (Garden City, N.Y.: Anchor Books, 1967), 365; reprinted in
     Paul Filmer, et al., eds., *New Directions in Sociological Theory, 129*.

14. Quoted from Merleau-Ponty, *The Primacy of Perception* (Chicago: North western
     University Press, 1964), 56; reprinted in Paul Filmer, et al., eds., *New Direc-
     tions in Sociological Theory, 128*.

Chapter 11: The Sociology of Knowledge

1.   Os Guinness, *The Gravedigger Files*, 38-39.

2.   Quoted from Robert Merton, *Social Theory and Social Structure*, 220.

3.   Quoted in ibid., 223.

4.   Karl Mannheim, *Ideology and Utopia: An Introduction to the Sociology of
     Knowledge* (New York: Harcourt, Brace & World, 1936), 279.

5.   Ibid., 280.

6.   Peter Berger and Thomas Luckman, *The Social Construction of Reality: A
     Treatise in the Sociology of Knowledge* (Garden City, N.Y.: Doubleday & Co.,
     1967), 18.

7.   Berger and Pullberg, "Reification and the Sociological Critique of Con-
     sciousness," 199.

8.   Ibid., 200.

9.   Ibid., 202.

10. P. Berger and H. Kellner, *Sociology Reinterpreted: An Essay on Method and
     Vocation* (Garden City, N.Y.: Anchor Press/ Doubleday, 1981), 72.

11. Berger and Pullberg, "Reification and the Sociological Critique of Con
     sciousness," 200.

12. Ibid. Several years later, Peter Berger reduced this four-step process to
     the three-step process that is used more often in the literature.

13. Ibid., 201.

14. Richard Perkins, *Looking Both Ways* (Grand Rapids: Baker Book House, 1987),
     158.

15. *Peter Berger, Invitation to Sociology: A Humanistic Perspective* (Garden City,
     N.Y.: Doubleday & Co., 1963), 136.

16. Ibid., 150.

17. Berger and Pullberg, "Reification and the Sociological Critique of Conscious-
     ness," 201—2.

18. Peter Berger, *Invitation to Sociology*, 54.

19. Peter Berger and Hansfried Kellner, *Marriage and the Construction of
     Reality: An Exercise in the Microsociology of Knowledge," *Diogenes* 16 1964).

20. Berger and Kellner, *Sociology Reinterpreted*, 107.

21. Ibid., 73.

22. Karl Mannheim, *Ideology and Utopia*, 272.
23. Ibid., 273.
24. Ibid., 282.
25. Berger and Kellner, *Sociology Reinterpreted*, 5 (italics mine).
26. Christians and Van Hook, eds., *Jacques Ellul*, 296.
27. Ibid., 304.
28. Jacques Ellul, "You Can't Act without Getting Your Hands Dirty," *Atlantic Monthly* (May 1968), 58.
29. Berger and Kellner, *Sociology Reinterpreted*, 4.
30. E. A. Ross, *Sin and Society* (New York: Harper & Row, 1973), xxxv-xxxvi.
31. Peter Berger, *The Precarious Vision* (Garden City, N.Y.: Doubleday & Co., 1961), 219-29.
32. Peter Berger, *The Noise of Solemn Assemblies* (Garden City, N.Y.: Doubleday & Co., 1961), 115.
33. Ibid., 116.
34. Jacques Ellul, *Perspectives on Our Age* (New York: Seabury Press, 1981), 8-9.
35. Jacques Ellul, *The Presence of the Kingdom, 18.*
36. Os Guinness, *The Gravedigger Files*, 112.
37. Jacques Ellul, *The Presence of the Kingdom*, 16.

Chapter 12: Postmodern Theories

1. Charles Lemert, *Postmodernism is Not What You Think* (Malden, MA: Blackwell Publishers, Inc., 1997), 3-4.
2. Gene Edward Veith, Jr., *Postmodern Times: A Christian Guide to Contemporary Thought and Culture* (Wheaton, IL: Crossway Books, 1994), 21.
3. Ibid., 21.
4. George Ritzer, *Modern Sociological Theory*, 5th Edition (Boston: McGraw-Hill, 2000), 454.
5. Ibid., 454.
6. William McNeill and Karen Feldman (eds.), *Continental Philosophy: An Anthology* (Malden, MA: Blackwell Publishing, 2005), 153.
7. Gila Hayim, *The Existential Sociology of Jean-Paul Sartre* (Amherst: University of Massachusetts Press, 1980), 5.
8. William McNeill and Karen Feldman (eds.), *Continental Philosophy: An Anthology*, 301.
9. Catherine Belsey, *Poststructuralism: A Very Short Introduction* (New York: Oxford University Press, 2002), xx.
10. George Ritzer, *Sociological Theory*, 594.
11. Scott Appelrouth and Laura D. Edles, *Sociological Theory in the Contemporary Era: Text and Readings* (Thousand Oaks, CA: Pine Forge Press, 2007), 383.
12. Ibid., 383.
13. Ibid., 384.
14. Ibid., 384.
15. Kevin J. Vanhoozer, *Is There a Meaning in This Text?* (Grand Rapids, MI: Zondervan Publishing House, 1998), 53.
16. George Ritzer, *Modern Sociological Theory*, 457.
17. Jacques Derrida, *Writing and Difference* (Chicago, IL: University of Chicago Press, 1978), 235.
18. Matthew S. Vos, "Excellence: The Emperor's New Clothes," *Phi Delta Kap-*

pan (June 2008): 776-777.

19. Peter Kivisto, *Social Theory: Roots and Branches* (Readings) (Los Angeles, CA: Roxbury Publishing Company, 2000), 382.

20. Kenneth Allan, *The Social Lens: An Invitation to Social and Sociological Theory* (Thousand Oaks, CA: Pine Forge Press, 2007), 543.

21. Ibid.

22. Douglas Kellner in George Ritzer (ed.) *The Blackwell Companion to Major Contemporary Social Theorists* (Chapter 12: Jean Baudrillard) (Malden, MA: Blackwell Publishing, Ltd., 2003), 313.

23. Ibid., 313.

24. George Ritzer, *The Globalization of Nothing* (Thousand Oaks, CA: Pine Forge Press, 2004).

25. George Ritzer, *The McDonaldization of Society* (5th edition) (Thousand Oaks, CA: Pine Forge Press, 2008).

26. Jean Baudrillard, *Simulacra and Simulation* (Ann Arbor, MI: The University of Michigan Press, 1994), 2.

27. George Ritzer, *Enchanting a Disenchanted World: Revolutionizing the Means of Consumption* (Thousand Oaks, CA: Pine Forge Press, 1999).

28. Ibid.

29. Ibid., 217.

30. For example, see D. Abrams and M. A. Hogg (eds.), *Social Identity and Social Cognition* (Malden, MA: Blackwell Publishers, 1999).

31. K. Allan, *The Social Lens: An Invitation to Social and Sociological Theory.*

32. Douglas Kellner in George Ritzer (ed.) *The Blackwell Companion to Major Contemporary Social Theorists*, 324.

33. Jacques Ellul, *The Humiliation of the Word* (Grand Rapids, MI: William B. Eerdmans Publishing Co., 1988), 10.

34. Ibid., 12.

35. Ibid., 27.

36. Ibid., 28.

37. Ibid., 30.

38. Ibid., 30.

39. John R. Donahue and Daniel J. Harrington, *The Gospel of Mark*, Sacra Pagina Series, Volume 2 (Collegeville, MN: The Liturgical Press, 2002).

40. C. S. Lewis, *The Last Battle* (New York: HarperCollins, 1994).

41. Kathryn Tanner, *Theories of Culture: A New Agenda for Theology* (Minneapolis, MN: Fortress Press, 1997), 175.

42. Catherine Belsey, *Poststructuralism: A Very Short Introduction*, 78.

43. Ibid., 78.

44. Ibid., 77.

45. Vanhoozer, *Is There a Meaning in This Text?*, 48.

46. Ibid., 48.

47. Ibid., 48.

48. Ibid., 49.

49. Ibid., 49.

50. Ibid., 49.

51. Ibid., 30.

52. Robert Wuthnow, "Living the Question: Evangelical Christianity and Critical Thought," *Cross Currents* (Summer 1990), 167.

53. Curtiss Paul DeYoung, Michael Emerson, George Yancey, and Karen Chai Kim, *United by Faith: The Multiracial Congregation as an Answer to the Problem of Race* (New York: Oxford University Press, 2003).

54. Walter Brueggemann, *Texts under Negotiation: The Bible and Postmodern Imagination* (Minneapolis, MN: Fortress Press, 1993), 19.

55. Ibid., 20.

56. Ibid., 49.

57. Ibid., 51.

58. Ibid., 52.

Chapter 13: Conclusion

1. Arthur Holmes, *All Truth is God's Truth* (Grand Rapids: Wm. B. Eerdmans Publishing Co., 1977), 6.

2. Ibid.

3. John Wilson, *Thinking with Concepts* (Cambridge: Cambridge University Press, 1963), 3.

4 R. W. Friedrichs, *A Sociology of Sociology* (N.Y.: The Free Press, 1970), 75.

5. Ibid.

6. Ibid., 66.

7. Ibid., 64.

8. Ibid., 65-66.

9. Pierre Hegy, "Transcendence and the Social Construction of Reality," Unpublished paper, n.d.: 29.

Index

28044186R00158

Made in the USA
Lexington, KY
10 January 2019